How to Read a Suit

Lydia Edwards

How to Read a Suit

A GUIDE TO CHANGING MEN'S FASHION
FROM THE 17TH TO THE 20TH CENTURY

BLOOMSBURY VISUAL ARTS

LONDON · NEW YORK · OXFORD · NEW DELHI · SYDNEY

BLOOMSBURY VISUAL ARTS
Bloomsbury Publishing Plc
50 Bedford Square, London, WC1B 3DP, UK
1385 Broadway, New York, NY 10018, USA
29 Earlsfort Terrace, Dublin 2, Ireland

BLOOMSBURY, BLOOMSBURY VISUAL ARTS and the Diana logo are
trademarks of Bloomsbury Publishing Plc

First published in Great Britain 2020
Reprinted 2020 (twice), 2021, 2022

ISBN: PB: 978-1-3500-7120-9
ePDF: 978-1-3500-7117-9
eBook: 978-1-3500-7118-6

Typeset by Lachina Creative, Inc.
Printed and bound in India

Dedication

For Holly (Bean).

Table of Contents

Acknowledgments

This book would not have come together half as happily as it did without the support of some wonderful people. My thanks first go to my editor, Frances Arnold, for her endless advice, encouragement, and belief in me. Yvonne Thouroude has also been wonderfully helpful and supportive and put up admirably with my stream of questions!

Dr. Karin Bohleke, of the Fashion Archives & Museum at Shippensburg University, has given her time and expertise with extraordinary generosity. Many of the beautiful nineteenth- and twentieth-century photographs in this book are from her personal collection and are reproduced here with generous permission. Along with Annika Neilson-Dowd, Karin made the selection and delivery of my Fashion Archives suits easy, stress-free, and lots of fun.

Many museums and historical societies have offered invaluable assistance, and I am grateful to several for their unrestricted access: in particular, the Rijksmuseum, Los Angeles County Museum of Art, the Metropolitan Museum of Art, the New York Public Library, Rhode Island School of Design Museum, and the National Gallery of Victoria. I also appreciate the individual advice and generosity of Allison Tolman from the Maryland Historical Society, Matt Jacobsen of oldmagazinarticles.com, and to the following for their permission to use treasured family photographs: Maureen and Leon Levy, Anna Hueppauff and the Tsoulis family, Brett Smyth, Daniela Kästing, Gary Wright, and Clare Simmonds.

As ever, love and thanks to my oldest friend Romanie Garcia-Lee for her professional advice as well as personal interest and support. Other dear friends who more than deserve a special mention are Louise Hughes, Nina Levy, Anna Hueppauff, and Tina Moss. I'd also like to thank my UniPrep 'family' at Edith Cowan University and Fleur Kingsland at WAAPA.

My parents, Chris and Julia, have encouraged and supported me throughout my life, and the writing of this book has been no exception. Extra thanks to my dad for such precise editing and proofreading!

Most of all, thanks to my husband Aaron, whose support, encouragement, and humour give me confidence in my writing and research.

Finally, my appreciation to everyone who read and enjoyed *How to Read a Dress*. I hope you find this new book interesting and informative.

LEFT
Atwater, A.J.
by C.M. Bell,
c.1873–1890,
Library of Congress,
Washington, D.C.

We have highlighted in bold throughout the text particular words and terms where we feel a definition would be useful and have put a definition in the Glossary at the back of the book (p. 190); these usually appear at the point at which they are first used. Use the Glossary to remind yourself of the terms as you read through the text.

Preface

Before the Suit

Long before the birth of the three-piece suit, notions of masculinity were deeply rooted in clothing. Of course, the idea of "measuring" historic masculinity is in the first place highly problematic, as Michael Antony puts it: "How can we possibly measure the masculinity of another age? We cannot measure the sperm counts or testosterone levels of the sixteenth century or the eighteenth."[1] Perhaps not, but as he continues, we can use art and literature to compare how the appearance and manners of men and women have changed over the centuries. Fashion is one of the most important indicators of how men constructed their own sense of what it meant to be "a man," and of how women perceived an "ideal" manly figure. Works of art (and sometimes, extant garments) give us the best chance we can hope for of uncovering more and creating a contemporary framework of understanding. This brief background will provide an outline of western European masculine clothing in the century and a half leading up to the birth of the modern three-piece suit. The aim is not to give a comprehensive overview, but to allow a comparative vision of how masculinity was sartorially constructed in the immediate preamble to the birth of the modern suit. It will also include four initial "analyses" of doublet, hose, and breeches in the late sixteenth and early seventeenth centuries.

On the face of it, men's fashions from the sixteenth and early seventeenth centuries seem far more complex and elaborate than the suit, particularly its nineteenth- to twenty-first-century incarnation. In *The Three-Piece Suit and Modern Masculinity: England, 1550–1850*, David Kuchta puts this down to the fact that, since the suit's inception in 1666, "male gentility has been associated with modesty and plainness in dress." In this way, Kuchta explains, the three-piece suit brought about "the fashioning of a new masculinity, a new ideology about the morality, politics, and economics of elite men's consumer practices, an ideology still present today."[2] One of the surest ways of recognizing and tracing this "new masculinity" is, of course, through clothes—the most obvious signifier of status and, as

Laura Gowing expresses it, a "public significance of sexuality" expressed through items such as the codpiece and padded hose.[3]

Our twenty-first century ideas of what constitutes "manliness" or "machismo" are so ingrained that it can be hard to step back and appreciate that what seems like a particularly "feminine" adornment would not have seemed so to a sixteenth or seventeenth-century viewer. Ideas around "effeminacy" were commonly linked to a man having excessive amounts of heterosexual intercourse, rather than as a sign that he was homosexual; frequently, ideas around what constituted "feminine" behavior were more closely linked to manners than to clothing. Only once men's clothes lost their fussiness in the eighteenth century—and women's became far more voluminous and adorned—was any male regression to excessive ornamentation received negatively. The importance of status—through, as it would later be termed by Thorstein Veblen, "conspicuous consumption"—cannot be underestimated in the sixteenth and seventeenth centuries.[4] Displaying yards of lace, ribbon, and costly fabrics was the most obvious way of indicating individual or familial wealth and power: a most masculine trait. Nevertheless, such fashions were, of course, not universally worn and never wholly approved of. For a brief period of time following the English Civil War, the quiet, plain dress of Puritans received greater attention and elements of it were adopted in fashion more broadly.

From the late medieval era until the mid-seventeenth century, breeches or "hose" and a **doublet** were considered appropriate dress for men. In the fourteenth and fifteenth centuries, they were often worn under a longer tunic or kirtle, but by the early sixteenth century they were regarded as a complete "suit" rather than merely underclothes. The phrase "a suit of clothes" was used long before what we now recognize as a "suit" came into being— meaning simply the wearing of several complete garments to cover the male body. In the sixteenth century they were known as a "suit of apparel" when the doublet and hose were made from the same fabric.[5] Like the three-piece suit that would be introduced the following century, this suggested a unifying principle, later perceived as—in Anne Hollander's words—an "abstract, tripartite envelope."[6]

Hose were initially made with legs and feet attached—essentially a pair of tights. Over time they split to form two sections known as "upper" and "nether" stocks or hose. The "upper" came to be known as "breeches" and were eventually cut fuller than the lower hose, either ending at the knee (the "Venetian" style) or hip (the "trunk" or "round hose," also known as "slops" when especially loose-fitting). For wealthy men, it was common for elaborate *panes* (vertical strips of material through which contrasting fabrics could be seen) to cover the hose. When the short variant was worn, thighs were covered with canions:

close-fitting extensions that finished above the knee and required stockings to cover the rest of the leg.

The doublet (so-called because it was made "double" with a lining) can be described as a fitted jacket worn over a linen shirt. Its original purpose was to support the hose as well as provide warmth, and the two were joined through lacing at the waist. The **shirt**'s function largely remained the same until the twentieth century, when standards of cleanliness rose and were more easily achieved. However, its aesthetics, and the amount put on display by the wearer, was subject to change. In this period, it kept the doublet clean by separating it from the skin, and the need for frequent laundering (and, if finances allowed, multiple shirts) made it an important part of the "domestic economy" of a household. It could, however, still feature extensive and elaborate "blackwork" embroidery on collar and cuffs, and doublets could be chosen that exposed more of the shirt beneath according to the wearer's preference. **Waistcoats** existed in the sixteenth century but were a minor garment, worn beneath the doublet and so rarely seen. A final layer was the tunic or **jerkin**, which could be described as the overcoat of the sixteenth century, the most visible garment. Because of this it was generally made of the best cloth the wearer could afford. From the elite to the layman, this garment elevated an outfit to "formal," and was required for most activities outside the home.

The layers and bulk of an elite man's clothing almost equaled that of women during the sixteenth century, making the "envelope" of the Tudor man one of power and dominance. Excessively broad shoulders led to a nipped-in waist from which flared the doublet's pleated skirts. Baggy hose finished above knee level and slim (ideally muscular) legs accentuated this top-heavy silhouette. Wide shoulders also served to diminish the head, an interesting construct at a time when Renaissance ideals relating to the worth and dignity of the human mind were being championed. In England, this shape was largely dictated by the whims of Henry VIII, who began to pad his clothing in an effort to hide a rapidly expanding waistline.

Courtiers followed suit, and in the spirit of padding and bolstering, two of fashion history's most notorious accessories developed. The first of these, the codpiece ("cod" meaning scrotum, and "piece" referring to the original flap of fabric), was introduced in the 1460s for reasons of modesty as the hemlines of men's tunics rose ever higher. At this point, it was nothing more than a fabric pouch attached to the hose with ties; by the middle of the sixteenth century, it was more a symbol of status and, it might be assumed, fertility. However, as Will Fisher has explained in his work surrounding gender in the Early Modern period,

ideas around virility and the codpiece may be "sexual rather than reproductive," at least in the case of Henry VIII—whose large codpieces were often alluded to in terms of his number of wives rather than the number of children he fathered.[7]

Other research has suggested less prurient reasons behind the adoption of bombastic codpieces. Grace Q. Vicary wrote in 1989 that the codpiece could have been developed as a protection against disease—most specifically, the 1494 syphilis epidemic. Its function was both to protect the clothing from medications that caused staining, and to make it difficult to distinguish who was suffering from the infection.[8] Whichever is correct, there can be little doubt that by the time the extravagant padding and external decoration of codpieces became fashionable, any original prophylactic purpose had been left far behind. Codpieces were shaped and decorated to fit with the ornamental bolstering of doublet, hose, and jerkin, and this was particularly evident in the 1560s and 70s, just before it finally fell from fashion. As the codpiece declined in size towards the middle of the century, the **peascod belly** rose to prominence. The peascod was a padded or bombasted point at the center front of the waist, sometimes stuffed with rags or sawdust to maintain its shape. It was cut to produce an over-hanging section of fabric that extended below the natural waistline, creating a peaked dip at the navel. This look became so fashionable that doublets were specially sculpted at the waistline to accommodate it, with the rest of the garment fitting close to the body to heighten its distinction. In its most extreme form the codpiece arched over at the tip, and the head of the peascod, as described, extended down beyond the natural waistline. Because of this, when worn at the same time, one almost seemed to be pointing down or up to meet the other. These doublets were teamed with jaw-height ruffs and capes worn over one shoulder. By the end of the century a man's shoulders were almost back at their natural width, leading into long, close-fitting sleeves ending in frilled cuffs. Beneath this the bulbous **trunk hose** continued to grow in volume until only the tip of the codpiece showed, resulting in an uneven silhouette of long, spindly legs and arms with portly torso; wide hips; and tall, stiff neck.

At the start of the seventeenth century, the male "suit" consisted of a doublet with sharply pointed waistline with long overlapping square tabs, shoulder wings, and, by 1620, a high standing collar. (Even though the codpiece had by now fallen from fashion, the pointed waistline was enough to still, in Susan Doran's words, "[draw] attention to a man's haunches and private parts."[9]) The waistline gradually rose until it was fairly high, creating a truncated torso that sat above a waistline sometimes bolstered with decorative ribbon loops. However, by the 1630s the most common and fashionable hose were long and straight, finishing past the knee where they were met by a pair of boots. This created a taller figure than seen in the previous century, as well as a far softer and more easy-wearing set of clothes.

LEFT
Doublet and breeches
worn by Gustavus
Adolphus of Sweden,
c.1620s, Royal
Armory, Stockholm

During the first half of the century there was some fluidity between male and female styles with the doublet or "jubon," for example, cut very similarly for both. Decorative ribbons and ties were placed in parallel positions on bodice and doublet, and the high waist with deep tabs was seen on the clothing of each. The softness of female skirts was mirrored in the line of men's breeches, with their gentle gathering at waist and knees (illustrated well in this surviving example from the Swedish Royal Armory). The 1630s saw a continuation of this looser fit, to such an extent that poet and cleric Robert Herrick wrote in 1648: "A sweet disorder in the dress/Kindles in clothes a wantonness."[10] In this context, "looseness" was equated with "wanton" behavior or outlook, a flaw that Herrick and others also attributed to the rapid changes in fashion (for men, seen particularly the length and width of breeches) at this time. The French influence of Charles I's wife, Henrietta Maria, was named by some as the cause of not only the speed of new fashions, but the perceived extravagance of them:

> Hence [from France] came your flashed doublets . . . and your halfe shirts, pickadillies . . . your long breeches, narrow towards the knees . . . the spangled Garters pendant to the Shoe, your perfumed perrukes or periwigs . . . a thousand such fooleries, unknowne to our many forefathers.[11]

To some extent this was to change after the execution of Charles I in 1649, though it would be inaccurate to assume that all men wore either the bright, extravagant clothing of royalist Cavaliers or the somber, modest dress of Puritans. The reality was probably somewhere between the two, with men borrowing aspects from each aesthetic but veering more towards the plainness favored by Cromwell's Protectorate. From the 1650s onwards, the looser silhouette seen in the last analysis of this preface continued—across Europe— to become more so. Dark colors were popular, but increasingly elaborate lace collars and ribbon loop ornamentation, sometimes brightly colored, were infiltrating the black. They adorned high-waisted doublets and skirt-like petticoat breeches, which are examined at the start of the first chapter and represent one of the most extreme male fashions in history. This was a supremely feminine garment that could hang as wide and loose as a woman's petticoat, and for this reason was heavily satirized. Its short lifespan was also due to practical concerns: breeches were usurped in the 1660s by the new and slim-fitting coat, which was too narrow to accommodate them. From then on men would, in the words of one "father to his son" (1701), "take Notice that Cloaths (sic) consists of Four Things, viz. First, Linnen, Secondly, Shoes and Stockings, Thirdly, Hat and Perriwig; and Fourthly, the Suit, or Coat Waistcoat and Breeches."[12] It would remain so for the next 100 years.

After Cornelis Anthonisz, Portrait of King Francis I of France,

1538–47, Rijksmuseum, Amsterdam

This early sixteenth-century print beautifully portrays the excessively broad shoulders and powerful stance of men's costume at the time of Henry VIII. Francis I ruled France from 1515 to 1547 and was known to be a fashionable and bold dresser. In his biographer Leonie Frieda's words, the King "never ceased to dazzle when it came to his appearance, wearing sumptuous clothes made of crimson velvet and embroidered with silver and gold, and surrounded by a retinue of men and horses clad in the same colors."[13] A similar color scheme can be seen in this representation, teamed with the most fashionable accessories of the period—most notably the codpiece, which had become prominent and indispensable by the 1530s.

The neckline and cuffs of a thigh-length white shirt can be seen at neck and wrist. This was the foundation garment worn by all men. For the elite, shirts would be made from linen fabrics such as cambric and lawn, both bright white or even transparent.[14]

The **gown** is lined with fur that turns back to form a collar and revers. It also edges the gown's hem and the sleeve slits, which are caught at intervals with gold or jeweled beads.

Voluminous gowns were worn open and finished at the knee, and it was their puffed sleeves that provided much of the sought-after width. These were a clear status symbol and were only worn by men in the highest ranks of society—and, in much simpler styles, by certain professions.[15]

Hanging sleeves were wide, long tubes with a central slit for the arm to pass through. They finished level with the gown's hem or, as here, just below it.

Pieter Cornelisz, *The Seven Acts of Mercy: Freeing the Prisoners* (detail), courtesy of the Getty's Open Content Program
This drawing shows a more modest version of Francis I's ensemble, worn by a middle-class, professional man. We can see a high-necked shirt, doublet, and gown with turned-back collar.

Black bonnets, sometimes referred to as caps, consisted of a stiff brim with soft crown. They could be decorated with feathers, as shown here, or jeweled hat badges that hinted at religious or intellectual interests of the wearer. These remained fashionable in various forms throughout the century and were referenced in *Hamlet* (1603): "Your bonnet to his right use: 'tis for the head."[16]

Doublets were close-fitting, waist-length, sleeved garments usually made with a low, square neck as seen here (this would rise after c.1540).[17] For the wealthy it was a perfect base on which to display elaborate ornamentation such as jewels, velvet, or gold trim and frequently, as seen on this example, slashings in the surface of the fabric. Sections of shirt fabric were sometimes pulled through to create small puffs. For lower-class men, doublets were purely practical garments worn for warmth, and to hold up the hose.

Pleated skirts would protrude either from the doublet (as seems to be the case here: the center front slit was a common feature on a skirted doublet) or a separate garment known as a **jerkin**, also contemporaneously as a coat or jacket (both terms appeared in Henry VIII's household accounts). This was a full skirt attached to a usually sleeveless body that was open from chest to waist, cut in a deep U or V shape.[18]

Short, full trunk hose were attached to the waist of the doublet with laces; these had graduated to hooks and eyelets by the 1570s.[19] Bands of fabric in a contrasting color form the outer layer, an effect known as **paned**.

Shoes during this period were flat with extremely broad, square toes. This was a practical shape in comparison to fashionable styles of the previous century, the very long-toed "piked" styles amongst them. For those wanting to display their leisured status, shoes could be decorated with slashing (seen here), stamping, openwork, and embroidery.[20]

Johannes Wierix, Unknown man with carnation,

1578, Rijksmuseum, Amsterdam

◆

This depiction of fashionable late sixteenth-century dress was made by accomplished engraver Johannes Wierix. Here we can see a detailed rendering of both the shape and surface decoration of garments, making Wierix a valuable reference for fashion historians. In terms of color, we can surmise that these garments would probably have been made in shades of red, blue, yellow, green, or black: the most difficult dyes to produce and therefore the most expensive and fashionable.[21] The figure, with a faintly mocking, perhaps self-satisfied expression, holds a carnation in his left hand: a symbol of conjugal felicity or marriage. These floral associations also relate to the exaggerated peascod belly of the doublet, which is discussed here and in the preface.

As is clear from this example, in the second half of the century men's ruffs generally sat higher at the back than at the front. From its humble origins as a slim ruffle appearing at the neck of a shirt, by this period the ruff had become larger and significantly more complex in construction. The one shown here is detachable and made with a center-front fastening. Closure would be in the form of ties, buttons and holes, hooks and eyes, or pins.

Soft hats with gathered crowns, such as this one, were especially common in France. The band would often be decorated with jewels, feathers or, as here, small bunches of flowers.

The peascod belly was a shaped, padded protuberance at the center front of the doublet. It is very evident on this example and was widely ridiculed in its time, described as "[a] monstrous big-bellied Doublet" by Philip Stubbes.[23] The peascod's shape was inspired, as the name suggests, by peapods, which were likened to male genitalia and suggested associations of virility and sexuality. It is also said to be suggestive of marriage and betrothal.

Sleeves were not usually sewn to the jerkin, but attached separately with ties. These were hidden from view by the shoulder tabs or wings: a similar design can be seen in this leather fencing doublet, c.1580, from the Metropolitan Museum of Art.

This sleeved jerkin, possibly made from slashed leather, is cut to mirror the doublet beneath (but usually not padded). It is worn open, revealing the widest point of the peascod. Towards the end of the century it also became fashionable for the doublet to be worn open or "unlaced"[24]: in contemporary parlance, "unbracéd." The term appears in Shakespeare several times, including *Julius Caesar* (which would usually be performed in contemporary fashionable dress):

Is Brutus sick; and is it physical
To walk unbracéd, and suck up the humours
Of the dank morning?[25]

By the 1570s, the codpiece had more or less disappeared from the court of Elizabeth I, and elsewhere by the end of the decade. The voluminous folds of this new style of breeches initially meant that the codpiece was simply hidden from view; as the breeches grew in popularity (as well as volume), it gradually fell from fashion entirely. These breeches would have fastened at center front with a tied or buttoned fly.[26]

Wide, rounded Venetian hose first became popular at around this date. They were pleated at the waist, with much of the fullness to the back and sides, sometimes achieved by "bombast" (padding made from horsehair or wool). They then tapered to fit snugly to the knee where they were, in Philip Stubbes's words, "tied finely with silken points, or some such like."[22] The fabric is gathered onto a narrow band (decorated with tabs) at the knee, and finished with a row of buttons and ornamental tassels at the side.

For the wealthy, silk stockings—knitted or cut on the bias to cling to the leg—were essential.

Wedding suit worn by Gustav II of Sweden,

1620, Royal Armory, Stockholm

◆

This wedding outfit of jerkin, doublet, and breeches belonged to Gustav II Adolf, who reigned as King of Sweden from 1611 to 1632.[27] He is remembered as one of the best-known Swedish monarchs, largely due to his success as a military leader, tactician, and strategist as well as the instigator of innovative domestic reforms. On November 26, 1620, he married Maria Eleonora of Brandenburg at Stockholm's Royal Castle. This wedding ensemble is a good example of the fashionable silhouette nearly fifty years before the three-piece suit was introduced. The three pieces of this outfit continue the lines of the sixteenth-century doublet and hose but show the developing softer silhouette of the early seventeenth century.

From the middle of the fifteenth century to around the date of this suit, jerkins continued to be popular outerwear.[28] They generally followed the same line as the doublet beneath, but with some extra additions such as the hanging sleeves seen here.

All the seams and edges are finished with gold galloon (a woven trim) to match the surface decoration.

Twelve overlapping tabs edge the deep, pointed waistline at front and back.

A design of carnations, roses and other floral emblems in gold thread and cord is arranged symmetrically across jerkin and breeches. The spaces between are adorned with single gold sequins.[29]

Breeches had by now replaced the shorter, rounder trunk hose—though there remains considerable volume in this pair. They were still attached to the doublet, usually with hooks and eyes or ties, as seen on the original violet-colored doublet beneath the jerkin.[30]

Small standing collars were fashionable for jerkins until around 1620, after which time they would usually be small, flat, and turned-down, or absent entirely.[31]

When a jerkin had hanging sleeves (and this was not obligatory) they were often detachable and fastened at the armhole beneath the shoulder wings.

Hook and eye fastenings are seen at the front and across one side of the chest.

The violet-colored doublet is just visible beneath the half-sleeves of this jerkin.

Doublet detail, c.1620, Royal Armory, Stockholm

Wedding outfit worn by Gustav II Adolf, alternate view, c.1620, Royal Armory, Stockholm

Hanging sleeves, originally a Spanish design, were suspended from the shoulders of both male and female garments, and featured horizontal or vertical slits through which the arm could be drawn. The V-shaped slits of this jerkin's sleeves can be seen here.

Wenceslaus Hollar, Standing man takes a bow,

1627–36, Rijksmuseum, Amsterdam

◆

Although Wenceslaus Hollar is well known as a valuable resource for fashion historians, his images depicting women's costume far outnumber those of men's. Therefore, this is a relatively rare specimen but one that shows his usual level of detail and exactitude. This engraving offers a profiled view of a fashionable man's doublet, breeches, and hat from the first half of the seventeenth century, presenting a far softer and looser line than the previous late Elizabethan example.

Ruffs remained popular in the Netherlands and Spain for the first half of the century, although the band—a type of collar that could be "standing" or "falling"—gradually replaced it entirely. This figure wears a falling band, a large, turned-down collar usually made from linen and trimmed with bobbin lace. As this illustration shows, the collars would often be as wide as the shoulders of the wearer.

It is just possible to make out bunches of ribbons, their ends trimmed with metal aglets. These were known as "ribbon points," placed along the waistline as decoration.

By the start of the 1630s, the waistlines of both men and women had risen significantly, particularly at the back. In the late 1620s and early 30s, men's waistlines often still featured a point at center front, but this would gradually straighten out over the next decade.

Deep, skirt-like tabs at the waist usually overlapped and encircled the wearer's hips.

Military influences were prominent in menswear of the 1630s and 40s. In this image, these are obviously discernible through the spurred riding boots. Spurs are held in place with distinctive "butterfly" spur-leathers, and the boots themselves topped by buckets.[32]

The sword is held by a sash shoulder-belt, another militaristic influence.

Hats with wide, round brims were very fashionable. They were often trimmed with a hat band and long plume.

The hang of these sleeves shows us that they are split to reveal the shirt beneath. The effect created would be similar to that seen in this portrait by Antony Van Dyck from the early 1630s.

Long, comparatively streamlined breeches were rarely padded by this date. The side of each leg is trimmed with a line of buttons, matching those on the doublet. A row of ribbon bows edge the bottoms.

Anthony van Dyck, *Robert Rich, Second Earl of Warwick*, c.1632–35, Metropolitan Museum of Art

Introduction

Why Suits?

It is always interesting to hear people talking about their clothing and what constitutes "normal" in their lifeworld. In the summer of 2017 I overheard three young to middle-aged men, sitting by a river overlooking a cityscape, discussing professional clothing choices. "You don't need to wear a suit anymore," said one. "Well, you'd at least wear the jacket," said another, "but with chinos or jeans." "You don't need to, but you just do," said the third. Three very different interpretations of what is considered "acceptable" in the twenty-first century still seemed to come down to what society deemed appropriate, rather than the individual.

We live in a world where contemporary ideals of fashion autonomy, of "anything goes" and a wish to break down sartorial boundaries are prevalent. However, the statements above reinforce that notion of the suit as a safe and familiar choice for men, one with which they can't go wrong. Such varied ideas illustrate an equally confused yet vibrant menswear scene in the second decade of the twenty-first century, a climate in which male confidence and anxiety seem to go hand in hand. While suits are still daily wear for many men, in increasing circumstances they no longer *have* to be, and men's relationship to this pivotal garment is therefore further complicated and compromised. In this book these themes will be retraced and re-examined across the centuries, charting a sartorial history that is inextricably linked to a social one.

"Fashion" is a complex term, easily misunderstood and easily trivialized. It refers to the clothing that covers our bodies but also, crucially, to the ways in which we consume and embody that clothing, and make it part of our identity. For the past four hundred years, men in western countries have used the three- or two-piece suit—jacket and trousers, often with a waistcoat—to express that identity, and as such it has become a universal symbol of masculinity. As a primarily western innovation, this book will focus on examples of suits from North America, Canada, Europe, Britain, and Australia, while acknowledging the fact that the suit has grown to encompass many elements of different cultures from across the world. As well as being worn in diverse countries, from the twentieth century onwards designers have imbued the suit with both subtle and overt cultural references, and this will be explored (particularly in reference to Japan) in the final chapter of this book.

Of course, the suit is not made up of just a jacket, waistcoat, and pair of trousers: fashion is crafted with the help of multiple elements. Shirts, collars, cuffs, neckties, cravats, hats, scarves, overcoats, and shoes combine to create what Anne Hollander described as "a certain fundamental esthetic superiority, a more advanced seriousness of visual form not suggested by the inventors of fashion for women in the past."[1] Nevertheless, it is the suit itself that shapes the body and most affects the posture of the wearer; accessories develop primarily to accentuate and complement that look. Therefore, the changes that took place in jacket, trousers, and waistcoat over the centuries will make up the primary focus of the analyses within this book. Shirts, overcoats, hats, ties, and the rest will be presented and discussed throughout each chapter introduction, and in individual analyses where appropriate, to demonstrate how the entire look and feel of a suit was achieved. They will also serve to aid the reader in the process of "detecting" these changes, but acting as an additional diagnostic tool to provide broader cultural and social relevance alongside the suit itself.

From the extraordinary beginnings of the modern three-piece suit to, arguably, the pinnacle of its development in the twenty-first century, the story of menswear is a tale every bit as surprising and scintillating as that of women's clothing. With a similar "base" for over two hundred years, it is the surface changes—some glaringly obvious, others subtler—that make the journey so intriguing. Slowly but surely social, political, and aesthetic influences have changed both the look and function of the suit over the last four hundred years. Unlike the dress, though, it remains a central (for some, a compulsory) part of the daily wardrobe.

Nonetheless, womenswear has enjoyed far more prominence in the discipline of fashion history than the clothing of men. It is easy to create a spectacle with an array of dresses, even when the garments are relatively plain. This is partly because, to the twenty-first century eye, attitudes and expectations of and towards women have changed so much that a corseted bodice and long, encumbering skirt evoke a kind of awe in the museum goer: the difficulty presents itself of trying to imagine what it would be like to wear such garments on a daily basis. Simultaneously, the glamour and luxury of wearing such dresses, of indulging in ultimate femininity, is an easily indulged fantasy for many museum-goers and period drama watchers.

The familiar uniform of trousers, shirt, waistcoat, and jacket present an altogether easier proposition for the modern viewer, even when confronted with high starched collars and detachable shirt fronts—obsolete and seemingly gratuitous items to contemporary eyes. "Familiarity" is probably the key word here. The fact that the basic cut of men's suits has remained largely the same since the nineteenth century (despite the huge social changes that have made male wardrobes, as a whole, far more diverse since then) perhaps makes it less ripe for the glamour and escapism inspired by corsets and crinolines. Nevertheless, the obvious splendor of elite clothing in the seventeenth and eighteenth centuries will be showcased in the first two chapters of this book, demonstrating that in the early years of the suit, frills, silks, satins, and lace were far from exclusively feminine. On the contrary, discernible luxury in clothing was a prime marker of what made a "man."

This book will begin with the three-piece suit's inception in the mid-seventeenth century. Since then it has been accepted that the suit is here to stay, although the twenty-first century man arguably has more choices in front of him than his ancestors. Tapping in to a recent swell of interest in the form of high-profile menswear exhibitions and influence of the "hipster" fashion and lifestyle movement, this book aids the reader in the skill and pleasure of recognizing both small and significant changes in the silhouette of the suit. Each chapter will analyze individual examples that illustrate particularly important or interesting shifts in fashion, and accompanying introductory text will add brief historic context and background.

Museums and historical societies across the world care for a staggering collection of suits, but these are not always as accessible as dresses and other female garments. Many (particularly the dark-colored nineteenth-century examples, which evolved far more slowly) are on display less frequently, so adequate photography can be difficult to come by. As skilled and beautiful as museum displays can be, suits are often shown to best advantage on a "real" body, where posture and the attitude of the wearer can convey so much in an otherwise somber ensemble. For this reason I have made use of selected portraits, photographs, and advertising material that illustrate certain styles particularly effectively.

This has also been useful when it comes to discussing more unusual suits—even ones that don't necessarily constitute generic ideas of what a suit "is," but which have a vital role to play in the story of the garment. It is also important not to lose sight of the clothing of those who could not afford silks and satins. One of the most intriguing aspects of the suit is its ability to transcend class boundaries: as examples in this book will demonstrate, by the end of the seventeenth century almost every man owned one, and wore it regularly – however ragged or behind the trends it may have been. Unlike wide hoop skirts or tight-laced corsets, a simple pair of breeches or trousers with a coat could be worn for both manual labor and clerical work, and while pre-nineteenth century depictions are not as frequent, they do exist thanks to early documenters such as Nicolas Bonnart, Wenceslaus Hollar, and Jacobus Johannes Lauwers. After the advent of photography in 1839, evidence of working and middle-class wear naturally becomes more regular and every effort has been made to analyze it here. This book is not only about clothing, but about the attitudes and aesthetics it inspired.

The Millennial Perspective

In June 2016, Radio 4's *You and Yours* consumer program ran a feature about the growth of menswear, focusing particularly on habits and influences of the millennial generation. A young man aged 20, from Manchester, agreed to be interviewed. "I'm wearing a white shirt, skinny jeans, a skinny fit blazer, and a dicky bow," he said. Sheepishly admitting that he spent more than he could afford on clothes, he followed up by admonishing that this was all right, since it was now "more acceptable to be interested in clothes." Rather than this being an overtly feminine trait, it is, he continued, more the mark of a "dapper" man in the twenty-first century and, in his view, more and more young men were now fitting this description (and proud of it).

Market analyst Mintel could confirm this interest from a statistical point of view, reporting to the program that menswear sales were flourishing, growing at twice the rate of women's in 2016. However, a spokesperson said, this was largely down to younger men and their enthusiasm for fashion. "Men are taking a greater interest in their appearance," she explained. "25- to 44-year-olds are more interested . . . in the latest styles, looking to buy more interesting and unique clothes."[2] This link between youth and "uniqueness" perhaps lies at the heart of a growing interest in the history of menswear, particularly suits. Ostensibly a pejorative term, "hipster" (originally used in the mid-twentieth century in reference to 1950s bebop aficionados) has come to be associated with vintage items: more specifically, a self-conscious appropriation of "the old" and a rejection of the mainstream, particularly when it comes to fashion.

Sustainability and slow fashion is undoubtedly a part of this, in a bid to live a more ethical life and to be more responsible as a consumer. However, the hipster's search for authenticity has perhaps placed him at the very heart of the mainstream. The vintage clothing, facial hair, and thick-rimmed spectacles that originally set him apart have become far more widely adopted, with young people taking different elements of "the look" and claiming it in individual ways. In an uncertain and unstable world, the appeal of nostalgia has never been greater and there may be something more to hipsters than a mere desire to appear original, of being cool by virtue of being demodé. Heike Jenss has suggested that this wish is intricately and intimately tied up with the complex concept of memory, that the interest in old clothes "as vintage, as recognisably old" shows a desire to recall "with distance," which she claims is needed in order to "give old clothes a new name" and to "evolve through passing a temporal . . . threshold: from passé to 'past' – from outmoded to ripe to be 'old-fashioned.'"[3] In essence, "vintage" is second-hand with an added mystique. Embraced by the hipster, it also seems to incorporate a perception that an association with the past, particularly the mid-twentieth century, is desirable and even enviable. To view the misery and trauma of the wartime years as glamorous presents multiple problems, however. It becomes, in essence, what writer and critic Owen Hatherley has called "austerity nostalgia," the tenets of which are most discernible in fashion.[4] For men (broadly speaking), tweeds, waistcoats, cardigans, trench coats, blazers, and slim-fit trousers evoke a broad date range of the 1930s to 1970s, and the twentieth-century examples in this book will no doubt draw comparisons to contemporary designers who have capitalized on the vintage resurgence.

Our concept of "vintage" is also, of course, highly influenced by television and film, particularly the ever-popular period drama. In recent years, series such as the immensely popular *Peaky Blinders*, chronicling the life and activities of a violent Birmingham-based gang in 1920s England, have reinforced the popularity and accessibility of historic styles for men. Gustav Temple, editor of tongue-in-cheek "journal for the modern gentleman" *The Chap*, believes that "men welcome any excuse to wear suits and dress smartly," but that many feel

LEFT
Fancy neckwear in the mid-nineteenth century, USA, private collection

they require "permission" in order to fully embrace it. The mix, in this television drama, of dapper upper class tailoring with more roughshod working-class turn of the century elements (flat caps, hobnail boots, and bell-bottom trousers) gives men who are "terrified of looking too smart, or too posh, or too stuffy . . . license to play with old fashioned clothes in a way that's more edgy."[5]

The idea of men (particularly, as Temple points out, young men) needing to channel the wardrobes of fictional characters to make suits acceptable is, possibly, at the heart of what "austerity nostalgia" and our loose definitions of "vintage" are about. The story of the three-piece suit, though, of course goes back much further than the early twentieth century world of *Peaky Blinders*, and it is the three-piece suit with which this book is chiefly concerned,

taking into account times when the fashionable ensemble was made up of two rather than three principal parts. When the style was born the new and revolutionary aspect was the waistcoat – it was this garment that was to change the course of menswear and firmly establish a uniform that was distinctly, unequivocally, male. The fact that this "base" has remained and flourished for more than three hundred years is testament to its staying power; the changes that have taken place within it confirm its versatility and transcendence.

The suit has also given rise to complexes around masculinity that still exist today, including confusion surrounding the "correct" way that men should show an interest in clothing, or even whether they should be permitted to show any interest at all. For some, the suit stands as a perfect excuse *not* to engage; for others, it is an ideal foundation on which to add vibrancy and even subversion. The examples in this book demonstrate these various attitudes, and each chapter provides basic historical introductions that alert the reader to key shifts in politics, society, and aesthetic values that prompted change.

The prime focus of this book is in the title: the challenge of learning how to "read" a suit. Because the stylistic changes in this garment's history are generally slower and less obvious, recognizing and dating suits presents a greater test than doing the same with dresses. Faced with two black tailcoats from the early years of the nineteenth century, where is a student supposed to start in attributing a date of 1815 to one, and 1830 to the other? The answers lie in possessing a keen eye that is fine-tuned to detail, a skill that is crucial for any student or professional working within fashion history. Modern designers need to be able to pinpoint key style shifts too, and to incorporate historical angles into their work that speak to contemporary moods and attitudes. I would argue that it is also important for any enthusiast wandering around a museum exhibit or watching a period drama and feeling curiosity about the accuracy of its costumes. To get a full and truthful sense of how men and women relate to each other over time, it is imperative that equal attention is paid to the clothing of both. Grayson Perry in his thesis on modern masculinity, *The Descent of Man*, puts forward some interesting suggestions about the way suits—and the wearing of them—are perceived in society. Firstly, they act as camouflage: specifically, according to Perry, a gray business suit. Its function is "not just to look smart, but to be invisible . . . The business suit is the uniform of those who do the looking, the appraising. It rebuffs comment by its sheer ubiquity."[6] In a sense the modern business suit is armor, worn by men so that they do not have to expose who they truly are. At the same time, Perry contends, men wear sharp suits not to attract women, but to "impress male rivals," to ensure that other men "understand his achievement."[7]

If both these suggestions are true, it only makes the narrative of the suit even more intriguing. If the suit is so drab and anonymous, why has it persisted for so long and how is it that it continues to be reinvented? If a man wears it purely to impress other men, doesn't that tell us something about the enormous power and potential of his "uniform"? The very fact that we unquestioningly accept the suit as a modern marker of man, but that questions like the ones above are still being asked, begs us to explore further.

Chapter 1
1666–1700

Thanks to diarist Samuel Pepys, the inception of the modern three-piece suit can be traced with certainty to a particular day: October 18, 1666. "This day the king begins to put on his vest," Pepys wrote, "being a long cassocke close to the body, and a coat over it, and the legs ruffed with black riband like a pigeon's leg. It is a very fine, handsome garment."[1] Being able to attribute an exact date to a fashionable innovation is incredibly rare, making the story of the suit an extraordinary one right from the very beginning. It gives license to start this book quite specifically at 1666, but it must be remembered that the development of the suit was not instant. As with most new styles, the suit took time to establish itself and to make the full leap from hose to breeches, and from doublet and cloak to vest and coat.

After the violent death of his father and years in French exile, Charles II's return to England and to the throne in 1660 was fraught with uncertainty. Those first years seem to have been a tense, careful period in which the King's advisers counselled him on the best ways to ensure both modesty and authority in his court. Sartorial considerations were at the heart of Charles's public image, and a suitable fashion statement could, adviser John Evelyn believed, put an end to swiftly changing fashions that had the potential to disrupt social and political equanimity.[2] The three-piece suit would present an image of a thrifty and grounded aristocracy: practical, serviceable, but still supremely tasteful and elegant. In short, the ideal portrayal of masculinity that would, the King hoped, inspire loyalty and trust in the people.

The Great Fire of London in September 1666 must also be cited as one of the reasons for this significant sartorial change. The devastating blaze was blamed by many on the French, one of the largest immigrant groups in the city.[3] The public called for a cessation of trade with France, along with a demand that nobody should dress in prevailing and perennially popular French fashions. Even the Archbishop of Canterbury, Rev. William Sancroft, hailed the fire as a warning from God against "French pride and vanity," and Charles's swift declaration that he would introduce "a fashion for clothes, which will never alter" was a powerful response.[4] Nonetheless, it must have been problematic for the half-French king, raised to admire French customs and fashions, and who owed his life to his safe exile in that country during the English Civil War and Commonwealth.

The initial result, however, was short lived and did indeed "alter," continuing in its original form only until the early 1670s. It comprised a vest, breeches and a tunic, worn with a lace collar or "falling band," a sash, and the customary sword. The vest (essentially an early waistcoat and initially known as a "petticoat") was collarless with short, loose sleeves,

falling softly to the knees or just below. It was held together by a sash or girdle, and could be made from a wide variety of fabrics, with optional trimmings and surface decoration. Orientalism is often cited as the main inspiration for the vest, although, as Christopher Breward has pointed out, it was only one of many influences.[5] John Evelyn claimed to have seen a similar garment worn in Italy by a Hungarian man, the satirist and poet Andrew Marvell believed it to be Turkish, author Randle Holme cited Russian inspiration, and John Evelyn famously referred to it as "Persian." The sheer number of different claims makes it unlikely that any iteration was accurate. Ironically, France has also been cited as an influence for the vest. Some have asserted that a very similar coat and vest was worn by Charles while he was in exile, and later, in the 1670s, Louis XIV introduced a comparable style.[6] Pepys indignantly pointed out that the French king "hath . . . caused all his footmen to be put into vests, and . . . the noblemen of France will do the like; which, if true, is the greatest indignity ever done by one prince to another."[7]

According to Pepys, Charles preferred a vest made from "plain velvet" in keeping with his initial determination to promote modest and rational dress. Above this was worn a tunic or "surcoat," a cloak-like coat that was worn open apart from one fastening at the throat. Accompanying breeches were known as "Spanish hose," trimmed with layers of ribbon loops in the manner of the existing petticoat variety. The Spanish style was cut with a high waist and long legs, closed by rosettes or bows below the knee, and often trimmed with buttons or braid. These were not a new design, having been worn earlier in the century from around 1630–45, but they had a brief life in court as a revived historical element of the new suit. There were obvious military influences to the whole ensemble, not least in the perceived need to create a uniformity of style that had, Breward explains, become "a potent agent of court and state control" in the French army, and henceforth across Europe.[8] This notion of "control" ties in to Pepys' assertion that the king's new clothes would "teach the nobility thrift," and the suit has subsequently made it more difficult to distinguish between different social classes.

Shirts were already in existence when the suit first appeared on the scene. When men's doublets shortened in around 1640, the shirt was exposed in the gap left between doublet and breeches (see illustration to the right). In addition, doublets were sometimes left open to further display an elaborate shirt front. This would change in the middle of the century when a fashion for long cravats developed; these fell straight from the neck down the center of the torso, thereby obscuring any view of the shirt beneath. In the main, however, this century was one that allowed and encouraged the open display of shirts, seeing them as both an erotic suggestion and as a necessary adornment.[9] An increasing emphasis on visible cuffs is explored throughout this chapter and follows through to the next, when cuffs are discussed as an intrinsic part of the eighteenth-century man's ensemble.

The opening example will discuss one of the first iterations of "the suit" (or in French, **justacorps**, as it would often be known) following the King's early court-based attempt. The bands of "black riband like a pigeon's leg" that adorned Charles's Spanish hose were a key element of one of the most extravagant, outrageous trends in fashion history: petticoat breeches, also known as Rhinegraves. Though short-lived, these illustrate the transitional period between doublet and hose and what we would start to recognize today as a three-piece suit. Petticoat breeches were also an important marker of the return, after a brief hiatus, to the splendor of pre-Civil War court attire. Shortly before the King's death in February 1685, John Evelyn, who had so supported Charles in his sartorial reforms and attempt at humility, expressed deep disappointment when he visited court to find "unexpressable luxury, & prophanesse, gaming and all dissolution, and as it were total forgetfulnesse of God."[10]

By the close of the 1680s, the suit's future was far more secure and some of the ornateness that Evelyn objected to—manifested perhaps most obviously in rows and rows of sumptuous ribbon trimmings—had dissipated. The recognizable coat of the eighteenth century with its vented skirts, long sleeves, button fastening and exterior pockets was starting to take shape, and the breeches now fit relatively closely to the leg, fastening just above or below the knee. The main difference in waistcoats was that they were usually sleeved in the late seventeenth century, a fashion that would have completely fallen from favor by the middle of the eighteenth. The 1690s reinforced what Breward describes as "the sober formality and rigid models" that typified a "heavy vertical emphasis of the coat and waistcoat [with] . . . the flat expanse of the torso."[11] By 1700, regular, everyday clothes consisted of a coat, waistcoat, and breeches. This was testament to the extraordinary journey of the suit since its birth in 1666, and its relatively swift transition away from, as the author of the 1701 *Father's Advice to his Son* put it, "ridiculous [. . .] Doublets and wide, full Breeches trimm'd with a Load of Ribbonds."[12] In less than fifty years that mode had come to seem outrageous, and no doubt some contemporaries felt that the current suit would also be a passing phase.

Historian Marieke de Winkel has pointed out that seventeenth-century dress sources are "unevenly distributed" throughout Europe. Certain countries hold a good selection of extant garments, but next to nothing in written evidence; others—like the Netherlands—enjoy a wealth of visual evidence in the form of painstakingly detailed paintings that offer broad social commentary. As de Winkel says, though, despite this disparity, when all are viewed together it becomes clear that "the sentiments regarding dress were very similar."[13] This is not surprising when we consider that the seventeenth century ushered in that most unifying and universal of garments, the three-piece suit. This chapter will utilize existing garments from England (one of the countries with the best inventory in this regard), and feature early fashion plates from France, which are amongst the best and most reliable originators of early fashion illustrations.

As Aileen Ribeiro rightly observes, depictions of clothing in art are often in danger of being perceived through "allegory and the fanciful or romantic impulse," particularly in the seventeenth century.[14] However, as mentioned in the Introduction, it is often necessary (and sometimes ideal) to consult works of art, particularly for an era when relatively few complete examples of clothing survive. This is especially crucial in order to get any understanding of lower-class clothing, and in this chapter the works of French artist Jean Dieu de Saint-Jean have been consulted to directly compare the clothing of an upper and lower-class man, highlighting clear differences but also some surprisingly close similarities. Saint-Jean made a significant contribution to the rise of fashion prints ("modes") in the 1670s and 80s, and had the support of the influential *Mercure Galant*, a gazette and literary magazine that covered a wide range of contemporary discussions—including fashion.[15] Any "fashion illustration" inevitably constructs an ideal, but Saint-Jean was particularly adept at focusing on clothing. With completely plain backgrounds in his original works, he gives little distraction from his figures, and his use of interesting and uncommon details allows the modern viewer to play fashion detective.[16] Nicolas Bonnart is the other engraver referred to several times; although his works (and those of his brother Henri) generally provide more of a narrative, they are also remarkably detailed and give a helpful overall picture of the manners and eccentricities of the era.

Nicolas Bonnart, Recueil des modes de la cour de France, "Le Financier,"

1678–93, Los Angeles County Museum of Art, Los Angeles, California

◆

Along with women's wheel farthingales at the end of the sixteenth century, petticoat **breeches** (also known as "Rhinegraves") remain, at their widest, one of the shortest-lived fashion trends in history. It is easy to understand why when we consider the impracticality and excess of the garment. It was also laid aside when the three-piece suit, or justacorps, really took told as the staple of men's fashion: it was simply not possible to wear such voluminous breeches underneath the new, slim-fitting coat. Although images of Charles II in early versions of the suit show him wearing petticoat breeches, many met the fashion with derision, believing it to be feminine in the extreme. Other people even felt it was a slightly sexless item, equally suitable for a man or woman: for example, J. Evelyn in *Tyrannus or The Mode* described their appearance as "a kind of Hermaphrodite and of neither sex."[17]

The dominant black of this ensemble marks out the wearer as a professional man; as the title of the engraving suggests, he works in finance. Nevertheless, the color scheme is the only somber aspect of this suit. From the head down he is decked out in lace, ribbons, bows, and multiple accessories, starting with his lavish wig. These became indispensable as the fashion for long hair increased.

This short doublet finishes at the natural waist, leaving a large expanse between it and the breeches, which sit at the hips. This space is filled by a billowing white linen shirt that is arranged to fall softly over the waistband.

He is holding what is probably a tall-crowned "sugar-loaf" hat or a "boater" style with shallower crown.

Row upon row of ribbon loops (sometimes known as "fancies")[18] decorate the waist and hem of the breeches. This would become less popular with the advent of closed "Spanish" breeches later in the decade.

Stockings of wool, silk, or linen are gartered at the knee. Between c.1665 and 1680 these garters often featured ribbon bunches or, as seen here, a gathered flounce of lace at each side. Larger, bell-shaped styles were known as **canions** and could reach to halfway down the calf.[19]

Shoes with red heels ("talons rouge" in France), were an essential component of court wear and, consequently, of the young, fashionable man's wardrobe. Popularized by Louis XIV, they can be seen in portraits across Europe, including England, Scotland, Germany, and Portugal.[20]

The financier wears a wide **falling band** around his neck—in essence, the first iteration of a tie. It has an inverted box pleat at center front, and is tied closed with tasseled strings, which can be seen hanging down beneath.[21]

Cloaks were now worn over both shoulders, and often arranged so that the ornate frilled cuffs of the shirt would be visible.

The breeches are too voluminous to be worn under the new, slim-fitting coat that was starting to become firmly established by the 1670s. An initial attempt by some, of pinning the coat hem up to make room, did not last long, and men continued to wear capes with their open breeches until the style completely fell out of favor in the 1680s.

The breeches shown in this ensemble give a good idea of what the style would have looked like when worn. The image below is an extant pair from Stockholm's Royal Armory, and shows the sheer volume of fabric that was needed to create the correct silhouette.

Looking at this surviving pair of petticoat breeches laid flat, and witnessing the amount of fabric used, it is easy to visualize Samuel Pepys' account in the 1660s of one man who "put both his legs through one of his Knees of his breeches, and went so all day."[22]

Wedding suit,

1673, Victoria & Albert Museum, London

◆

This two-piece suit (which would originally have included a waistcoat, possibly red) was worn by James, Duke of York, for his wedding to Mary of Modena on September 20, 1673. It is an excellent example of the now firmly established suit, and was subsequently owned and worn by Sir Edward Carteret, a courtier who was gifted the suit for his service.[23] Made from wool with silver embroidery and a vibrant red silk lining, it was (as of 1999) the most expensive garment in the V&A costume collection.[24] It represents the ceremony and luxury of a formal royal garment, as well as indicating some burgeoning fashionable trends. It also displays a nice rare touch: a seventeenth-century garter star still in its original position on the front left side of the coat.

This stylized floral design, incorporating embroidered renditions of honeysuckle and lilies, covers both coat and breeches and is non-repeating. As the Museum points out, this suggests that it was drawn freehand onto the fabric.[25] The silver and silver-gilt threads are couched to the surface, with further silver threads wrapped around strips of parchment to form petals. This results in a three-dimensional effect that highlights the level of detail and artistry involved.[26]

Long, elaborate lace cuffs were a prominent feature on the shirts of wealthy men.

Walking sticks, sometimes trimmed with ribbon bowknots, were in fashion during the 1670s and 80s. They would often be topped with gold, silver, or ivory heads.

When collarless coats came into fashion in the mid-1660s, **cravats** became popular and were constructed of a strip of fabric with lace-trimmed ends.[27] For wearers such as the Duke, this lace would—as seen here—comprise more than just the ends, and it is recorded that on the day of his coronation in 1685, James paid the huge sum of £36 for a new cravat made entirely of Venetian point lace.[28]

The coat hangs fairly straight from the shoulders: at this point, fashionable coats retained a similar shape to that of a 1660s doublet, with side seams in a natural position and the hem resting gently at hip level without a pronounced flare. Details like this demonstrate how slowly fashions actually change, and how many transitional stages exist.

The sleeves are three-quarter length with narrow, turned-back "hounds-ear" cuffs,[29] faced with the same bright coral silk that lines the coat. This provides a flash of color amidst the gold and silver of the embroidery.

Rows of tiny buttons, composed of silver-gilt thread over a wooden base, line the front of the coat and the narrow flaps of the two pockets.[30] Small and difficult to fasten, buttons on fashionable dress throughout the century were usually purely decorative.[31]

The coat hem does not yet quite reach the knee, as it would later in the decade. Waistcoats would do the same by about 1680.

These breeches have huge turned-up buttoned cuffs, indicative of the transitional style from doublet and full breeches to coat and closer-fitting breeches. A very similar technique, applied to slightly wider breeches, is seen in the engraving to the left.

Jan van Troyen, *Elegantly dressed gentleman at a doorstep*, c.1660, Rijksmuseum
Buckles were used on shoes from the late 1650s onwards, but wide ribbon bows and/or roses were also popular, seen on this example and in this c.1660 engraving.

Engravings by Nicolas Bonnart,

1678 and 1674, Los Angeles County Museum of Art, Los Angeles, California

◆

These two 1670s engravings provide a valuable comparison between clothing of the upper and lower classes. They both illustrate important fashionable trends of the era, executed very differently, and show how men of lesser means still prioritized the daily wearing of a "suit," even incorporating decorative trimming and accessories where possible. It also, crucially, demonstrates the extent to which class barriers were breaking down in the second half of the seventeenth century: as historian Elizabeth Ewing has put it, "the ordinary man counted for much more" and "the coat and waistcoat illustrated at least part of that social shift."[32] On the face of it, the coat and breeches shown in each example are not vastly different in terms of cut and fit. What makes the distinction is the quality of fabric and the manner in which they are worn—the trimmings and accessories—and in the way the wearer carries himself and relates to his clothing.

It was a fashionable "look" to be seen combing one's wig in public. This became so common (and affected) that a trend developed in 1660s and 70s theater, whereby a play's prologue solicited certain behaviors from the audience, usually those that suggested privilege and the misplaced sophistication of a spoiled upper class. Boyle's Mr. Anthony (1669) makes a special welcome to those who come to the theater purely to be seen "to comb a Perriwig, or to show gay Cloathes."[33]

A lavish and extravagant bunch of red ribbon loops forms the fashionable **shoulder knot**, with additional gold surface decoration. This red theme is continued all the way down the coat, with bright red lining on the cuffs and additional knots at the waist, thighs, hat, and gloves.

These wide, open breeches are relatively short, displaying much of the wearer's slim stockinged legs (from this date, stockings were usually buckled in place above the knee). Hip-length side vents in the coat help to make space for their mass of fabric.

Neither man wears a waistcoat; for the figure to the left, this was in order to show off an abundance of shirt frill; on the right, for reasons of practicality and economy. We can see that the seller's far more modest shirt is tucked into the waist of his deep red breeches.

Two horizontal pockets are set just above the coat hem. A tasseled handkerchief dangles from one—a fashionable accessory that was meant to be displayed rather than used.

The seller wears a plain, practical and untrimmed tricorne hat. He may be wearing his own hair or a modest wig.

One of the most notable aspects of this orange seller's suit is its pretensions to the details of fashion. A red bow adorns a plain neckline, in clear imitation of the other suit's cravat with wide, flat bow. Further down, the coat is loosely held together by another simple ribbon knot, emulating the layered ornamental bunch of ribbons on the left-hand coat.

Both figures display fairly voluminous shirt cuffs beneath their coat sleeves, but for the working man, these are untrimmed and finish with simple bands at the wrist.

Aside from a sleeker fit and closer shaping at the waist in the 1678 example, this lower-class coat corresponds to the long and slim silhouette of the era. While the richer man would probably have commissioned privately made suits, it is likely that the working man would have bought his coat and breeches from a peddler or "petty chapman," whose wares included a small selection of ready-to-wear clothing.[34] The image shows us that, consequently, a prime difference lay in fit: the coat would not be made-to-measure and would have been available in a limited range of sizes.

Both men wear shoes featuring a turned-over tongue known as a "Cupid's bow." The tip reveals a red lining, beautifully and subtly matching the red trimmings on both ensembles.

Jean Dieu de Saint-Jean, Recueil des modes de la cour de France, "Homme de qualité en habit d'hiuer,"

1683, Paris, France, Los Angeles County Museum of Art, Los Angeles, California

◆

This winter outfit, comprising coat, breeches, cloak, and seasonal accessories, is representative of the strong military influence that could be seen in men's clothes towards the end of the century. This mainly had its origins in France, which was involved in several conflicts during the second half of the century; as ever, French style found its way into the wardrobes of the British.

By the 1680s cravats were still made from lengths of lawn, often with lace-trimmed ends that fell over the chest. A stiffened bow, as seen here, sat under the chin.

It was becoming unusual to see cloaks worn as fashionable accessories after c.1680. Its use here, though, serves as a reminder that fashions rarely changed overnight, even amongst the wealthy, and personal preference could still prevail. As with the example shown here, when worn, a cloak would usually be full and knee-length with a flat, turned-down collar. A more popular option can be seen below in this illustration from the early 1680s: a gentleman wearing a **Brandenburg** overcoat, named as such when it was decorated with frogging.

Deep plumes cover the curved brim of this wide black hat.

The high, wide **collar** of the cloak is turned down in this portrayal, but in France it was commonly worn up around the wearer's neck and face. This was not just for practical reasons: in Parisian society, wearing the cloak collar so that it covered the lower half of the face was a signal that the man did not wish to be recognized. Going "incognito" helped to signal or suggest that the wearer was a person of some importance.[35]

In the 1680s and 90s, it became fashionable for gentlemen to carry a **muff** in cold weather: something since associated far more closely with female dress. They started out as wide fur-lined cuffs that would be attached to coat sleeves, gradually morphing to become a separate tubular appendage, hung around the neck by a ribbon. Although relatively popular, muffs when used by men were still a subject of caricature.[36]

An emerald green waistcoat is just visible at center front. It conforms to the fashion of the decade, being knee-length and featuring buttons from neck to hem.

By this point, swords were usually worn for show by civilians, as a fashionable accessory.

In this decade breeches were "closed": gathered into a band that was fastened at the knee. They were still full, especially in the seat and around the hips, cut so as to hang there without further support (except, sometimes, buckles or ties when required). Volume at the legs was sometimes caught up into cuffs, in the manner seen on the 1673 wedding suit earlier in this chapter.

Bonnart, 'Casaque d'hyuer à la Brandebourg', France, c.1675–86, Los Angeles County Museum of Art

Jacques Lepautre, Homme en habit despée (Man in a suit),

c.1680s, New York Public Library, New York, New York

◆

This print has an uncertain date attribution, but displays elements that allow us to estimate a timeframe of the 1680s. It was made by Jacques Lepautre, an artist specializing in producing images of theatrical figures in elaborate costumes. That attention to detail is evident in this portrayal of a fashionable young man, whose outfit depicts the changing shape of men's fashion at the end of the century, as well as some particularly interesting and short-lived accessory trends.

Coat collars were generally plain and undecorated in the 1680s, leading to an increased interest in elaborate neckwear. This combination of wide, flat bow and lace cravat reached peak popularity in the 1680s and is one of the factors that can help to attribute a date.

Relatively tight-fitting and plain sleeves help to draw attention to this longer, leaner profile.

From around this date until the end of the century we can start to observe a closer cut to the coat, with more emphasis on the waist and shaping on the underarm and center-back seams.[37]

Pockets are low-set, yet sit slightly higher than those in the previous examples. To be cut vertically or horizontally was equally popular, although vertical styles such as this were starting to lose favor from c.1680 onwards. Rows of small buttons and holes on either side draw attention to the lower portion of the coat. A similar extant example is shown below.

This wide-brimmed hat, probably made from felt, is cocked up slightly at the sides. It is decorated with ostrich plumes and bunches of ribbon loops.

These sleeves are very wide-cut, foreshadowing their shape in the following century. By the 1680s, cuffs were usually cut separately and attached to the sleeve.[38]

The sword is carried on a **baldric**, a wide belt worn over one shoulder. In the latter half of the century, these became broader, longer, and more lavish, as much (or more) a fashion accessory as a practical item.[39]

Sashes were a common decorative touch for fashionable men, alongside those worn by women to hold mantua gowns close to the body.

We cannot see the breeches in this image, but it's likely the gentleman would have worn the "closed" variety seen in the previous example.

Coat belonging to Karl XI of Sweden, c.1680s, Royal Armory, Stockholm

The shape and decoration of these shoes is typical for c.1680 onward. Broad, square toes are mirrored in the similarly shaped tongues that stand up high above the ankle. Buckles have by now replaced ribbon fastenings.[41]

At first glance, this close-fitting legwear looks like boots. It is, however, a pair of spatterdashes (also known as "leggings"), popular from the 1670s onwards. These would often be made from leather or other hardy material, and are so named because they "dashed away" spatters of mud when worn on horseback.[40]

Jacob Gole, Louis, Dauphin of France,

c.1680s–90s, Yale Center for British Art, Connecticut

◆

Louis of France (1661–1711), also known as Le Grand Dauphin, is depicted in this mezzotint. The work is undated, but various features suggest that it was made (or shows) fashions from the last two decades of the century, particularly the 1690s. He was said to be an influential figure in fashion, setting the trend in May 1678 for ribbons "à la dauphine," which featured green designs on a white background. In 1687 he popularized a gold braid known as "wolf's braid" because it was commonly worn by royal hunting attendants.[42] This ensemble shows similar attention to detail and various different types of trimming and accessories.

··

Bicorne and **tricorne** hats, like this one, were worn by men of status— particularly Royals—until the start of the nineteenth century. The dauphin is wearing the hat cocked into a triangle with its point at the center.[43]

The fronts of the coat, the sleeves and cuffs are all trimmed with narrow arches of braid, one side forming a base for buttons, and the other framing buttonholes. None are being used, however, and the coat is held together loosely by the wide sash.

A tiny snippet of waistcoat is just visible beneath the sword belt and voluminous cravat, reappearing again towards the hem.

It is not possible to view the pockets on this coat, since the front skirts are covered by the extravagantly fringed ends of the dauphin's sash. In a manner popular at the time, it has been draped and twisted around his hips with its ends artfully arranged to fall over the front of each thigh. Rounded ends mirror curved sections of braid that adorn the body, sleeves, and cuffs.

Fairly full breeches are worn to the knee. It seems as though "roll ups" or "rollers" may be worn: these were stockings pulled up over the ends of the breeches and laid down in a flat roll over the knees. Stockings would usually be made in the same color as the rest of the ensemble.[44]

The Dauphin wears a **Steinkirk**, a style of cravat that was first seen in London and Paris in the early 1690s. One story behind the development of this long, flowing neckwear was that it originated at the Battle of Steinkirk in Belgium in 1692, where French princes were suddenly called to action. In their haste, they tucked the end of their cravat into a coat buttonhole to hold it out of the way. This look was in keeping with the kind of relaxed elegance in vogue at the time, though it was often quite self-consciously and fastidiously arranged, as in this c.1700 portrait.[45]

Thomas Forster, *Portrait of a Man*, 1700, Metropolitan Museum of Art

Soft fringing on the sash is echoed across the suit: here, on the cuffs, as well as in the hat's lavish plumage.

A decorative **sword knot**, with bow and tasseled ends, hangs from the weapon's hilt.

By the final decade of the century, coats were slit at the sides and at center back, which allowed the sword to pass under the rear back skirt.

Chapter 2

1700–1799

J ust as there were a bewildering number of female dress styles in the eighteenth century, so was there also variety in men's clothing. On the face of it this might seem unlikely: after all, the common uniform for men of all stations in life was the three-piece suit. As we shall see, however, the male silhouette underwent great alterations between 1700 and 1799, achieved often by seemingly subtle changes in cut, embellishment, and in the manner of wearing this one "base" garment. This century was the first uninterrupted hundred-year span in which "the suit," as we know it today, was worn by all men. It became stable, self-confident, and self-reliant, despite the continuation of an age-old debate on the moral difficulties inherent in any interest in fashion.

Although good for the economy and in need of public interest to sustain it, many found it hard to reconcile goodness of character with pleasure in clothes. "And let all remember," wrote *The Whole Duty of Man* polemically in 1770, "that clothes are things which add no true worth to any; and therefore it is an intolerable vanity to spend any considerable part either of their thoughts, time, or wealth upon them, or to value themselves ever the more for them, or despise their poor brethren that want them."[1]

The eighteenth century can also be seen as the swansong of the pre-twentieth century male peacock, before he embarked on his long sleep during the 1800s. Yet, as Anne Hollander has observed, the dress and mannerisms of this period that may seem effeminate to a twenty-first century audience were, on the contrary, "so distinctively masculine at the time that no one saw any femininity whatsoever in the pear-like form that art and fashion suggested was a man's ideal shape."[2] This is an aspect worth remembering in regard to apparently outré styles across all centuries that may, to modern eyes at least, seem at odds with what "should" be deemed innately masculine or feminine.

It is also important to bear in mind throughout this chapter that the clothing of groups such as the "macaronis" and "incroyables" (both heavily satirized in their day) did not in their entirety represent the dress of "most men," but rather supplied an outline that was taken to extremes by some, selectively picked over by others, and merely observed (often at a very great distance) by most. The image of the fop was nevertheless deeply ingrained in public consciousness as a dangerous one, particularly in America, where strong and sturdy men were needed to help build a new society. The eighteenth century is often posited more than any other as one in which, as Gillian Perry has described it, both masculinity and femininity were "negotiated and redefined" throughout.[3] Given that the suit was less than fifty years old at the turn of the century, it seems plausible that the future of its status as "the" masculine garment was still being assessed, and therefore some degree of uncertainty was warranted.

France and England were by far the greatest sartorial authorities in the eighteenth century, and despite being at war more than once over the course of the era, they still took a keen interest in each other's fashions. From the luxury of court wear at Versailles to the earthy, textured country clothing of both poor and rich in the English countryside, French and British men found plenty to admire in each other's suits. The first years of the century saw the shape of the coat change quite significantly across Europe from the extremely wide-skirted silhouette of the 1720s and 30s to the quieter, leaner influence of aforementioned English country styles from the middle of the century onwards. This was represented by a more practical three-piece suit that would characterize the 1800s: still elegant, certainly, but in a far more restrained way by the last quarter of the century.

The French and American Revolutions both occurred during this period, and were of course a massive influence on the future of dress for men and women. This chapter will explore some specific garments directly affected by these events, including the outfit of a post-revolutionary Parisian "sans-culotte" and a suit worn by the first American president, George Washington. At the same time, it will not lose sight of how these events impacted ordinary people, discussing middle and working class garments wherever possible.

From the seventeenth century onwards there were options other than the suit, but a man generally needed to be in the privacy of his home to wear them. In the eighteenth century, however, this started to change. The banyan—a type of informal dressing gown—first appeared in the early seventeenth century, when it was commonly known as a nightgown or "Indian gown" due to its similarity to loose, straight robes popular abroad, as well as its frequent construction from imported fabrics. Banyans were first referred to as such from c.1630, the name derived from the Hindu term for a Pakistani trader.[4] They could either be cut along the lines of a kimono—in a "T" shape with no sleeve setting—or as a more fitted garment with shaped sleeves, a collar, and buttoned cuffs. The name stayed throughout the following century, when banyans could be worn in the streets, often as shortened variants—and even, occasionally, in professional situations, when they were often known as "morning gowns." For the wealthy these would sometimes be made from pure silk, and canny merchants capitalized on the trend, as novelist Oliver Goldsmith discovered later in the century when shopping for a "silk night cap":

> The mercer entertained me with the modern manner of some of the nobility receiving company in their morning gowns; Perhaps, Sir, adds he, you have a mind to see what kind of silk is universally worn . . . conscience is my way of dealing; you may buy a morning gown now, or you may stay till they become dearer and less fashionable, but it is not my business to advise. In short . . . he persuaded me to buy a morning gown also.[5]

Despite the variety and interest such garments provide, it is wise to exercise caution when referring to them as part of the history of men's everyday dress. They were not part of a conventional three-piece suit, though they could be worn with one, nor were they a part of every man's wardrobe. They were, however, frequently depicted in portraits of wealthy and modish men in the manner known as "fashionable undress." This informality paradoxically signaled the wearer's status and luxury of leisure time, and offered the perfect opportunity to showcase highly ornate and expensive silks. While these are useful in determining many facets of dress, society, and culture, they should be consulted carefully and cautiously when considering the evolution of eighteenth-century suits.

Posture is an important element to bear in mind, particularly in the seventeenth and eighteenth centuries, when men's calves were constantly on show beneath their breeches. Portraits and other imagery from the eighteenth century show men standing in almost balletic poses (it can be argued that the development of classical ballet at this time was partly influenced by contemporary pose, and the reliance placed upon dancing lessons to improve posture), with their feet apart and slightly turned out, and hands held outwards away from the body. All boys whose families could afford it would have had fencing and dancing lessons, which naturally affected the stance and carriage of the body—as well as being quietly suggestive of class. As Judith Chazin-Bennahum has described it, social dancing was "perhaps the perfect display of aristocratic sang-froid," and its movements would be observed and practiced by all social classes in a position to witness them.[6] Some groups and individuals, of course, preferred to self-consciously avoid fashionable tropes, as Voltaire observed in 1778, on meeting a Quaker:

> I never in my life saw a more noble or engaging aspect than his. He was dressed like those of his persuasion, in a plain coat, without plaits in the side, or buttons . . . He did not uncover himself when I appeared, and advanced towards me without once stooping his body; but there appeared more politeness in the open, humane air of his countenance, than in the custom of drawing one leg behind the other, and taking that from the head which is made to cover it.[7]

Nevertheless, for a general overview, such poses and gestures can be a useful additional consideration when studying eighteenth century fashion. This is because, to a large extent, they were dictated by the cut and construction of clothing. Wearing a wig, especially one of larger and more exaggerated proportions, imposed a slower, more controlled walk to ensure balance was kept. Long lace cuffs needed to be waved away before reaching for an ink bottle or picking up a glass of liquid. Later in the century, narrower coats pulled shoulders back and chests out, inevitably drawing the wearer up. In order to display clothes to their best advantage, and to accentuate the most fashionable features, various "stock" postures can be seen in contemporary imagery.

To the left, the sitter puts his hand on his hip to draw the coat away, showing a red lining and the deep frills of his shirt cuff. At the right, the gentleman rests his hand in an opening at the top of the waistcoat, a familiar pose that also serves to display the cuff and, in this instance, a clearer view of the decoration along the front opening. A side view also allows the viewer to see the coat starting to slope away at the front, and a slight remaining flare to the skirt. When sitting, men would take care to display rich linings in the skirts of their coat, and to arrange the skirts so that fabric would not be crushed.

With a focus on "the suit" specifically, this chapter does not go into great detail concerning outerwear, though examples are mentioned where appropriate. It is helpful to bear in mind that men generally had a number of coat styles throughout the century, and these were nearly always made from wool. The greatcoat is probably the best-known and most represented style of the 1700s. Though the name could be used for any kind of "top coat" or heavier garment worn over the suit, the greatcoat as derived from English country styles featured several eye-catching cape collars, which extended over the shoulders and usually finished at the elbow. So voluminous could these capes be that the coat was sometimes satirized or used as a prop for less than savory fictional characters wishing to disguise themselves. Samuel Richardson's highly unpleasant Mr. Lovelace in *Clarissa* (1748) requests a greatcoat as part of his scheme to abduct the protagonist: "What I want *you* to do for me, is to lend me a great coat . . . A great coat with a cape, if you have one. I must come upon her before she is aware."[8] Aside from this, capes and cloaks were still worn as a standalone garment—particularly in some parts of Europe—and, in most places, for evening wear and traveling.[9]

Shirts will demand a much greater focus than outerwear in this chapter, since during the first half of the eighteenth century they had become increasingly elaborate and were still used as a central focus point of the overall ensemble. Their prominent display, especially in the form of cuffs, was more than ever a pivotal signal of wealth, a clear indicator that the wearer did not have to work to earn his keep: he was never in a situation where his cuffs would get dirtied by mud or ink. Less obvious but equally important to bear in mind is a change in the way shirts were constructed—both physically and professionally. Before the middle of the century they were usually homemade by wives, sisters, daughters, or servants, as they were constructed simply from a combination of squares and rectangles of fabric. Aside from the care needed when fitting the neck opening, creating a man's shirt was a relatively simple exercise.[10] A closer fit in the second half of the century, coupled with new emerging standards of cleanliness, meant that the demand for high numbers of tailored shirts increased. Crucially, the shirt itself was often used instead of drawers, as it was generally long enough to be tucked and drawn between the legs to act as a kind of loincloth.

The end of the century was when, in psychologist Carl Flügel's words, the "Great Masculine Renunciation" began. As he described it in 1930, men "gave up their right to all the brighter, gayer, more elaborate, and more varied forms of ornamentation . . . Man abandoned his claim to be considered beautiful. He henceforth aimed at being only useful."[11] While this is a powerful and persuasive argument—given that silks and embroidery for men did indeed disappear—it fails to take into account the complex reality of menswear during this period, which was migrating into a different type of elegance. The next chapter will introduce the figure of the dandy, men who strove for perfection in both dress and manners in the opening years of the nineteenth century. This did not come out of nowhere: the French Revolution's "reign of terror" quite literally scared men out of their flamboyant and ostentatious suits, since betraying allegiances by wearing them could result in imprisonment or even death. At the same time, the influence of English "countrified" modes of dress was continuing to impress upon French society in a phenomenon known as "Anglomania." From around the middle of the eighteenth century a fascination for all things English had permeated France, inspired by its political system (particularly following the Glorious Revolution of 1688, which resulted in a constitutional monarchy) and the interest of thinkers like Voltaire, who had always admired the English way of life. Clothes popularized by the English gentry at their country estates, consisting of deep, earthy browns and greens and minimal ornamentation, spoke to the atmosphere in France. Of course, as Andrew Bolton is quick to emphasize in *Anglomania: Tradition and Transgression in British Fashion*, Anglomania is a construct; a fantasy based on a caricature of England rather than an empirical reality.[12] However, this does not make the influence of that construct any less pivotal or meaningful to those who embraced it.

Habit of a French man of quality in 1700,

1757–72, The New York Public Library, New York, New York

◆

This French fashion engraving depicts what first appears to be typical **justacorps** of the late seventeenth/early eighteenth century. However, several aspects of cut and style do not correspond to a typical suit of this era. Rather, the coat appears more like a closer, shorter version of the loose, wide-sleeved **Brandenburg** (c.1674–1700), which had military origins and came to be worn as an overcoat by men of fashion. Further inspection reveals that it is probably closer still to a bona fide military "surtout," worn as part of a civilian suit of clothes. The later date of this illustration is also an important factor to bear in mind, since hindsight can create inaccuracy: however, in this case the costume shown aligns to other contemporaneous depictions.

....

This is a **shoulder knot**, a decorative bunch of cord or ribbon loops worn on the right shoulder. Its presence helps to confidently confirm the date of 1700. After this time, they were worn almost exclusively by livery.[13]

The relatively unstructured sleeves and wide cuffs share similarities with the loose fit of an at-home morning gown or **banyan**. Many banyans were worn open or with a simple sash, but some extant sources also show a short row of button fastenings and braid at chest level. In its first incarnation it was made of a lightweight flannel fabric and was worn by British soldiers in eighteenth-century India.[14]

Banyan, India, c.1750, Los Angeles County Museum of Art

In common with most coats of the era, this one seems to be cut with a short back vent to the rear, enabling a sword to pass through. The skirts could sometimes be stiffened to enhance their shape, in the manner of traditional tailored coats.

There is a military feel to these red breeches, with similar shades and styles worn by Dutch and English regiments in the late seventeenth century.[15]

The small standing collar was not fashionable on men's daywear at this time, nor was it usually seen on the Brandenburg, which typically had a square-edged soft collar. It corresponds to an 1830s description of a Turkish "surtout": "loose, long . . . with stiff straight collars [and] waistcoats."[16] A passion for Turkish culture and design, including fashion, known as "Turquerie," was felt across Europe during the seventeenth and eighteenth centuries.

The term "surtout" can be confusing as it often seems to serve as an all-encompassing term (especially by the nineteenth century), signifying a general overcoat that was often made without a collar. In the seventeenth and eighteenth centuries it was sometimes referred to in that way, but also, frequently, as a coat made specifically for military officers. Because the example shown here is worn in place of a usual dress coat, and because it is almost identical to the figure in the sketch after Watteau's *Man in officer's dress*, c.1700–39, it seems likely that the man in question is a "gentleman officer," a military man from a "good" family who would have risen quickly through the ranks and wore part or all of his uniform to show his status and profession.

Louis Desplaces, *Man in officer's dress*, c.1700–39, Metropolitan Museum of Art

Coat and breeches,

c.1705–15, England, Victoria & Albert Museum, London

—◆—

This suit is highly representative of fashionable men's clothing at the turn of the eighteenth century, despite some alteration to the breeches in the 1850s—perhaps to enable them to be worn for fancy dress. Probably made for a very young man, given its small size, the suit was clearly also made for someone with a strong fashion sense and the money to achieve it, red being a popular shade at the start of the century.[17] The basic shape and cut of the coat is simple, with a front and back panel sewn together with straight side seams. These were stitched to just below the waist, allowing space for the sword, which would hang from a belt under the coat and protrude from the side and back vents.

....

There is no surviving waistcoat to this suit, but between 1705 and 1715 it would have been worn with one. A waistcoat was cut on very similar lines to the coat, possibly with sleeves, and would not have been visible beneath the hem of the coat.

The coat would have been fastened across the waist only, in order to show off a frilled shirt front. This also created a nipped-in silhouette, in keeping with the French name for a three-piece suit, justacorps (literally meaning "close to the body"), showing off the flared skirts to best advantage.

Pocket flaps had straight edges for the first ten years of the century.

One woman fought back at the censure given to female dress by writing to *The Spectator* in 1711, "We find you men secretly approve our practice, by imitating our pyramidical form. The skirt of your fashionable coats forms as large a circumference as our petticoats; as these are set out with whalebone, so are those with wire . . . We make a regular figure, but I defy your mathematics to give name to the form you appear in."[18]

The *neckcloth*, as it was known in the early years of the century, was a narrow strip of linen or lace, wound around the neck and loosely knotted so that the ends (sometimes with extra embellishment) were displayed.

Sleeves were loose-fitting, widening further towards the cuff. This was the fashionable cut until around 1710.[19]

The length of this coat is another indicator of the likely age of its wearer. In general, coats from this era were knee-length or just below. Its higher hem may have been requested in response to the needs of a young, highly active man. Its flared sides, however, achieved through full pleats (each 12 cm. deep) inserted into vents in the skirt, are very representative of the clothing of fashionable men of all ages.[20]

Breeches, 1710, Europe, Metropolitan Museum of Art
The breeches are composed from four pieces of fabric, cut low in front and high at the back, fastening at the rear and with a button pocket flap on either side of the front.[21] A similar arrangement is seen on this pair of silk breeches.

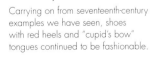

Carrying on from seventeenth-century examples we have seen, shoes with red heels and "cupid's bow" tongues continued to be fashionable.

Robe à la française, c.1745, Europe, Los Angeles County Museum of Art

Velvet suit,

c.1720–30, probably German, Los Angeles County Museum of Art, Los Angeles, California

◆

This ensemble's coat and breeches are both made from a deep plum-colored velvet and lined in a light green silk. During these initial decades of the eighteenth century, such color schemes were common and coats would often be seen in deep and elegant shades such as dove gray, forest green, plum, and dark midnight blue. The fact that the suit is made from velvet singles it out as "full" formal dress rather than "undress," and it would have been worn by the wealthiest of society. There is little surface decoration to this suit and no colored embroidery or trimming, but its striking silhouette provides ample interest and offers an excellent example of early eighteenth-century tailoring.

The undersides of these coat cuffs feature a long slit, leaving them open to display underlying sleeve ruffles. The technique is illustrated well in this image, which also shows the very deep side pleats and center vent on this style of coat.

"Das Tanzen" (detail), c.1720–40, New York Public Library
This image also offers an excellent view of a double row of buttonholes running along the length of the center back vent. This was a feature particularly aligned with the 1720s/30s aesthetic.

From c.1720–30, coats started to be made with a deep inverted pleat at either side of the center back vent, as seen here. This would become especially common between 1730 and 1760.[22]

These **boot cuffs** extend well above the elbow, making them a focal point of the entire coat. The wings curve deeply towards the rear and were initially attached to the sleeve with buttons.[24] Those seen here, however, are purely decorative.

It was fashionable for buttons and buttonholes to extend from neck to hem until c.1735. Covered buttons are often seen on coats from this era, although Acts of Parliament passed during the reigns of William III, Anne, and George I made it illegal for tailors to make clothes with any buttons other than those made from brass. This was largely in order to assist and protect the metal buttonmakers, based in Birmingham, who were rapidly losing business and who petitioned the King directly for assistance. An 1854 account of this bizarre law ends by exclaiming that "The judge who admitted the plea, the barrister who set it up, and the client who profited by it, were themselves all buttoned contrary to law!"[25]

Triple-pointed scalloped pocket flaps were fashionable from c.1710.

This waistcoat, made from **voided velvet**, would have been cut on very similar lines to the coat above. At this date it would usually feature sleeves, which would be made from a plain, cheaper fabric. As with the coat, the waistcoat features long buttonholes that are slit open just enough to allow the button to pass through.

It was around 1720 that pleats (up to as many as six at each side before 1720, and four thereafter) were inserted at either side of the center back opening. This allowed the skirts to hang more smoothly, and gave a better fit around the back and hips. It was from these that the skirt's characteristic fan shape originated.[23] They were stitched down at the base and topped with a decorative hip button (missing from this coat), which would often be covered with the same fabric as the rest of the coat.

The breeches are barely visible in this example, but what can be seen corresponds to the simplicity of this garment in the early eighteenth century. Generally cut to hang from the hips, they were wide and roomy at the top and made for comfort rather than close fit.

Wide stocking tops, a remnant of the late seventeenth century, were worn rolled at the start of the eighteenth but then became modest cuffs, fitting just above the knee, until the early 1740s.

Corded silk coat, waistcoat, and breeches,

c.1735, Britain, National Museum of Scotland, Edinburgh

◆

This mushroom-colored coat and breeches are displayed with a floral brocade waistcoat, the fabric of which is also used on the cuffs of the coat. This creates a synchronicity to the ensemble, with the soft yet effective color scheme allowing the sharp, dramatic silhouette of the 1730s to stand out.

Dress coats were still collarless throughout the 1730s, but now sit higher up at the throat, fitting flat around the neck.

Medium-sized, dome-shaped buttons made of metal adorn this coat. Unlike the previous example, laws regarding the use of cloth buttons have been adhered to.

It's easy to see why these boot cuffs were known as an **open sleeve**: the deep slit on the underside remains, and is even more pronounced on these exceptionally long cuffs, made from a different fabric to highlight their size and shape. They allow elaborate sleeve ruffles and full, gathered cuffs to be visible, a feature illustrated well in the print below.

Louis Pierre Boitard, *Man Standing*, 1737, Library of Congress
This 1737 engraving provides a good standing view of a similarly cut suit, with the wearer posing in a fashionable stance: one hand in the waistcoat opening, and one in the pocket.

This ornate brocaded waistcoat features a large exotic flower design, and matches the fabric used on the cuffs. Like the previous example, it would most likely have been made with long sleeves, and corresponds closely in shape to the engraving above.

"Das Tanzen" (detail), c.1720–40, New York Public Library

The legs of these breeches are fairly close-fitting, in stark contrast to the very wide sleeves above. This effect was commented on in an imagined dialogue from 1738, "Between a Gentleman and a Taylor":

"Are not the sleeves too wide?"
"No, Sir, they fit very well. They wear them very wide, and very long."
"The breeches are very narrow."
"That is the fashion. That suit becomes you mighty well."
". . . Bring your Bill."[26]

These breeches finish just below the knee, but are largely covered from view by the long skirts of the coat. This effect was lamented by *The Gentleman's Magazine* in 1736, which commented that "A handsome well-shap'd Leg, that never shews itself to such Advantage as under a Habit that reaches no lower than the Knee, is almost half conceal'd by the Length of the Coat."[27]

Frans van der Mijn, Portrait of Jan Pranger,

1742, Rijksmuseum, Amsterdam

◆

The attention to sartorial detail in this portrait is striking, offering us almost as comprehensive a view as a surviving suit would. The painting depicts Jan Pranger, director-general of the Dutch West India Company in West Africa from 1730 to 1734. The authority of his position is shown in this lavish ensemble, the waistcoat and coat cuffs of which are especially prominent. So important were waistcoats in the eighteenth century that even a wealthy and influential man would rely on them for effect and variety, sometimes owning very few sets of matching coats and breeches to wear alongside them.

Pranger's coat and breeches are made from velvet, a fashionable fabric and one especially popular for portraits (particularly when teamed with a brocade waistcoat, as seen here).

In the early-mid years of the century, it was very common for coat and cuff linings to be made in a contrasting color to the outer fabric.

High, scalloped pocket flaps had been seen on coats since the first decade of the century. It was usual for them to be worn unbuttoned, and holes would sometimes be shams.

Suit, c.1740, British, Metropolitan Museum of Art
Even though the coat was already sharply angled, with its skirts fanning out from heavily pleated side vents (see this photograph of a rear view of a similarly dated coat), until c.1750 waistcoats closely resembled the coat.[28] They fitted to the waist and often featured flared, stiffened skirts. With stiffening (using buckram or occasionally wire supports) on both coat and waistcoat, the silhouette became extreme.

Neckwear includes a **solitaire**, a black ribbon attached to the bag of a wig and passed around the front of the neck, to be fastened over the stock and lace ruffle of the shirt.[29]

Pranger wears a lavish waistcoat in gold brocade that matches the cuffs of his coat. The fabric displays the kind of exaggerated floral motifs that were so popular in the early eighteenth century, but which would become steadily smaller and smaller as the length of the waistcoat rose. By the middle of the century, most fashionable waistcoats finished at around hip level.

Gold domed buttons adorn the front of both coat and waistcoat; they sit just below each curved point on the pocket flaps. Each one is embossed with a floral design.

The fronts of the coat are starting, extremely gradually, to slope away from the waist down. This means that wearing the coat open from mid-level (sometimes entirely open or with only one or two buttons fastened) was becoming increasingly fashionable from the 1740s onwards.

A continuing style from the seventeenth century, rolled stockings were becoming rare by this date (see 1720–30 plum velvet suit).

Wool and silk suit,

1750–75, Britain, Metropolitan Museum of Art, New York, New York

◆

This suit, though bold and imposing in its crimson-and-gold color scheme, represents the growing trend for a more practical, "countrified," sporting appearance. A large part of this comes down to the fabric used: wool, rather than pure silk, allowed for freer movement and was also far more durable, giving greater longevity to the garment. There is also a distinct military feel to this ensemble with its red base, gold buttons, and feathered tricorne hat.

The collarless neck of an "informal" **frock coat** such as this one was usually finished with a half-inch thick band of self fabric, stopping a couple of inches from the edge.

Unlike "full" formal dress and court clothing of the era, the long buttonholes on this suit are fully functional, but only the top few were ever fastened. In common with the remainder of minimal surface decoration, these holes are edged and extended with a line of self-color embroidery. The same technique adorns the cuffs and scalloped pocket flaps, where the flat buttons are entirely decorative (and the buttonholes are shams).

By the date of this suit, shirts were far less extravagant, including fewer ruffles and lace trimmings. This portrait illustrates a good example of what the wearer of this ensemble probably wore beneath his coat and waistcoat (Metropolitan Museum of Art).

By the 1770s breeches had become far more close-fitting, leading to the common nickname of "smallclothes." The example shown here are particularly long for the era, reaching to just below the knees. They are finished with a row of four buttons and silk knee bands.

The tied white necktie or **cravat**, worn with dangling or tucked ends, was popularized by the **macaroni** in the 1770s, who generally tied it in a single or double bow. When worn with a suit of this type, it would usually be very plain and made from muslin.

From the 1770s onwards, buttons were again frequently made of metal, with gold a popular choice from c.1760. The criss-cross design of these buttons was known as basket, replicating the weave of a basket or interlacing cloth.

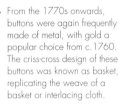

In line with the cut of the coat, the fronts of this waistcoat gently slope away toward the rear. Its buttons match those on the coat and breeches, and two scalloped pockets with sham buttonholes sit at either side of the opening—again mirroring those on the coat above.

A key indicator of 1770s coats is this significant curve at the front, beginning at mid torso and extending past the waist. This allowed an expansive view of the waistcoat and breeches beneath. This effect was enhanced by the increasing curvature of the coat's side seams, which pulled the sides in and narrowed the back.

White **stockings**, finishing at the knee, were usually made from cotton or silk, and could be plain or ribbed. Hand-knitted varieties were especially popular in the 1740s and 50s.[30]

Round-toed black shoes (sometimes known as slippers) are worn with this ensemble, slightly heeled and finishing with a rectangular silver buckle.

Gentleman's court suit,

c.1760s, Britain, Mint Museum, Charlotte, North Carolina

◆

The cut of this 1760s frock coat is not significantly different from others of the same date; what is notable is the use of this more casual style as part of a formal court suit. As court costume, the embroidery on coat and waistcoat is necessarily more elaborate, and the use of gold thread would make the ensemble glimmer in candlelight.

The great expense of producing purple fabrics—before the development of a synthetic dye in 1856—meant that for centuries, the color had been principally associated with the wealthy. In 1829 *The Magazine of Natural History* discussed the age-old process of extracting suitable dye from shellfish, commenting that the expense would "preclude it, we imagine, from answering the purpose of modern speculation, for one shell only affords a single drop." The amount of dye needed to color one pound of wool was, from Roman times to the nineteenth century, prohibitively expensive.[31]

The waistcoat is also single-breasted, fastening only to the waist but with a row of buttons from neck to hem.

Broad, turned-down collars like this one were often referred to as "capes," and were a main feature of the original working-class frock coat. Frocks for the working man were more loosely cut and often with a single rear vent, as seen in this contemporary caricature by Giovanni Battista Tiepolo. This image also gives a good impression of the back of the wide collar across the wearer's shoulders.

Giovanni Battista Tiepolo, *Caricature*, c.1760, Metropolitan Museum of Art

Robe à la française, c.1760-65, Los Angeles County Museum of Art

The curved, serpentine trimming on this coat and waistcoat mirror a fashionable decorative style also seen on women's dresses from mid-century onwards. This developed in response to a shift in aesthetic from baroque excess to the smaller motifs favored during the rococo.

These distinctive cuffs take inspiration from the popular "à la marinière" or mariner's cuff, which was derived from military uniforms (particularly those worn at sea, hence the name). It comprised a vent on the outside of the sleeve that was fastened with a flap and buttons, and often edged with braid. This 1785 portrait by Gilbert Stuart shows mariner's cuffs on the uniform of naval officer John Gell. The scalloped gold edging is typical, and its inspiration can be seen in the court coat under discussion.

Gilbert Stuart, *Captain John Gell*, 1785, Metropolitan Museum of Art

Wool and gilt metal suit,

c.1760, Britain, Metropolitan Museum of Art, New York, New York

◆

This striking blue and gold suit is a beautiful—and rare—example of menswear that has remained unaltered, not having undergone the retailoring that was often required to bring garments in line with new fashions.[32] Its simple wool fabric suggests a more relaxed English influence, and although the lavish metallic trimming is characteristic of French opulence, it is still far more restrained than the extensive floral embroidery that was popular in this period.[33]

The stock or cravat was popular from c.1760–90, and a useful replica is shown here. During this decade it would have been tied twice around the neck and finished with a flounce, hanging over the jacket and waistcoat.[34] The collarless style made this mode of display particularly suitable, but by the middle of the decade standing collars were becoming fashionable and neckwear less conspicuous: the ends were often tied into a discreet bow by 1770.

By 1760, waistcoats were usually around 6 to 8 inches shorter than the coat. By this date they were also frequently made without sleeves—but this suit's example shows an exception (below). As was common practice when making women's petticoats, the sections of the garment that would not be seen (in this case, the sleeves) are made from a plain, less expensive fabric.

It is unusual for precious-metal trim to survive intact, given the common practice of unpicking valuable trimmings to use on other garments. This exception is gold bullion braid sewn directly onto the wool base.[35]

Domed silver or gold buttons continued to be highly fashionable on coats and waistcoats.

Closed coat cuffs are adorned with the same metallic trim and gold buttons. Below them, extravagant lace cuffs give the impression of lengthening the arm, a style particularly associated with French fashions by the 1760s. Later in the decade, a British naval officer in France recommended that fellow travelers should, as a mark of respect and assimilation, consider dressing similarly while in the country.[36]

Skirts are still relatively full with a long center back vent at the rear. We can see a very slight slope of the coat front towards the back which, from this point on, would become ever more pronounced.

Stockings for daywear were still nearly always white and made from cotton or silk.

Gustav III's wedding suit "à la française,"

1766, Royal Armory, Stockholm

◆

Royal clothing has a complex role to play in the "reading" of historical styles. On one hand, the wealth and privilege of its owners usually guarantees the representation of highly fashionable garments. On the other, purely because of this fact, they are worlds away from the dress of ordinary men and women. However, they can also present unusual, even unique elements that warrant further investigation, such as this wedding suit worn by Gustav III of Sweden when he married Sofia Magdalena on November 4, 1766. It became a well-known, hugely admired garment, and when Christian VIII of Denmark married later that same year, he commissioned a strikingly similar wedding suit for himself from Paris.

This embroidered badge represents The Order of the Seraphim, allegedly founded in the thirteenth century and revived by King Frederick I in 1748. Its design comprises a Maltese cross with central shield flanked by four seraphim heads.[37]

The marriage of Louis Dauphin de France and Marie Thérése in 1745, Bibliothèque nationale de France

Prince Gustaf's envoy, Philip Creutz, took pains when organizing the commission of the Prince's wedding suit to discover exactly what was worn by the French Dauphin when he married in 1745. Sweden wanted to be seen as a modern European country, and emulating the elegance of French court fashions was a large part of building this identity. Since ceremonial clothing changed less speedily than "civilian," in any case, any similarity would not have seemed unusual to the crowds that flocked to see the bride and groom on November 4.[38]

Sumptuous embroidery of blue foil, gold thread, and sequins makes up a recurring design of sun rays shooting out from behind billowing clouds. This imagery symbolizes new and bright beginnings, of conquering darkness, and was an ancient motif used by Louis XIV—the "Sun King"—another French influence for the Swedish prince to embrace.

The use of colored metal foil, edged with silver braid, would have created a glistening, changeable blue sparkle in the candlelight. This was consistent with the way Gustav's court was presented during his reign: remembered as "glittering," "brilliant," and "cultured," he was described in 1841 as having been a "profligate though able monarch" until his assassination in 1792.[39]

As was common from the 1760s onward, these breeches finish just below the knee. They fasten with four embroidered buttons, and are ahead of their time in their use of embroidered knee bands, which did not become prevalent until the 1780s.

Despite this suit's few antique influences, particularly its relatively wide cuffs, Gustav still insisted that it should be made according to the latest fashions.[40] The coat's knee length, buttonholes finishing at the waist rather than hem, and curved fronts of coat and waistcoat are especially representative of developments in the second half of the eighteenth century.

Silk suit (habit à la française),

c.1775, France, National Gallery of Victoria, Melbourne

◂▸

From the nineteenth century onwards, soft pink—amongst most shades of the color—has been viewed in the West as the province of female fashion. Seen as an ultimate marker of femininity, it is therefore surprising to find that in the eighteenth century, pink was largely reserved for menswear. Elegant, refined, and accentuated with floral embroidery, this suit is a good example of the pinnacle of male fashion in France.

We can't see any neckwear in this image, but it's likely that under the standing collar (which, fashionable from the 1760s onwards, contributed to the long slender line of the suit), the wearer would have accessorized with a **solitaire** or plain folded handkerchief.

Despite the lavish ornamentation, men's suits at this time retained the sleek, slim, rather flat line that had started to take prominence in the second half of the century. As seen in the 1750–75 wool coat earlier in this chapter, this was achieved by moving the side seams further towards the center back of the coat, thereby pulling the wearer's shoulders up and back. Curved side edges to both coat and waistcoat accentuate this positioning.

Sleeves are long and slender, cut with a curve at the elbow. This is offset by a relatively wide cuff, which would almost entirely disappear in the remainder of the century.

Single-breasted waistcoats such as this one were normally fastened only at the waist, with buttons for decorative purposes at the neck and on the lower, curved section of the waistcoat. As became popular during this decade, the buttons are oversized and become a prime focal point of the ensemble.[42]

As well as being a color closely associated with men, by the middle of the century the wearing of pink was also a way of distinguishing the upper from the middle classes. Previously, only the wealthy could afford fabric made in bright, rich colors. However, with the advent of new synthetic dyes, the variety and availability of shades underwent a drastic shift. Consequently, the upper classes singled themselves out by popularizing halftones and pastels, such as the soft pink shown here.[41]

Claude Louis Desrais, *Bourgeois de Paris en habit Simple*, 1778, Rijksmuseum
This etching from 1778 shows a pale pink suit cut on similar lines to the one under discussion here. It depicts the same fashionable silhouette, but without the elaborate embroidery.

Knee breeches continued to be cut relatively full at the waist, tapering down the thighs to a close-fitting band just below the knee. It was usual for the outer seam to fasten with three or four matching covered buttons, as seen here.

Macaroni ensemble,

1770–80s, Los Angeles County Museum of Art, Los Angeles, California

—◆—

While it is important not to assume that every fashionable young man in 1770s Britain was a macaroni (in reality, their notoriety far exceeded their numbers), this moment in fashion did mark a significant point not only in men's clothing itself, but also in perceptions of masculinity. For some men the macaroni presented a threat to clearly defined gender boundaries, and this was expressed with clear antagonism in 1790: "I am shocked beyond expression when I have the misfortune to be in the presence of a mincing macaroni; a lisping thing in breeches, who, aping the effeminacy of females, swoons at the pricking of a pin; and is uncomfortable if a speck of dirt should pollute one of his sky-blue stockings by falling on it."[43] The figure of the macaroni also encouraged a dialogue in society to suggest that fashion could be "self-made," as it became clear that macaronis could hail from bourgeois as well as elite backgrounds. This suit is a good example of the bold, bright color combinations favored by these young men, as well as of the exaggerations that gave satirists such ready fodder. It is also unique in terms of museum display, as Los Angeles County Museum of Art curator Clarissa M. Esguerra explains: "No major museum had utilized collected costume objects to replicate the macaroni image on an exhibition mannequin [prior to *Reigning Men: Fashion in Menswear, 1715–2015*]."[44] As she points out, the image of the macaroni is more readily recognized through the above-mentioned caricatures, than through surviving garments themselves. The mannequin here therefore represents a carefully curated and researched ensemble that highlights the cosmopolitan nature of the macaroni aesthetic.

....

After Samuel Hieronymus Grimm, c.1773, Metropolitan Museum of Art

This satirical etching, dating from c.1773, depicts a young man arriving on a visit home from London. His father, a prosperous farmer, meets him with horror at his appearance and exclaims, "Well-a-day, Is this my Son Tom."

The tiny, entirely impractical hat sitting on top of the macaroni's wig was a common finishing touch.

Like young Tom in the cartoon, the wearer of this suit displays two watch **chateleines** (with seals, used to stamp the wax on a letter) hanging from the waist. More ornamental than practical, their purpose in this case would have been to demonstrate that the wearer owned not just one but two ornate watches, hidden in a fob pocket in the breeches.

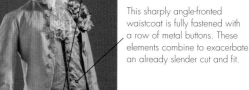

This sharply angle-fronted waistcoat is fully fastened with a row of metal buttons. These elements combine to exacerbate an already slender cut and fit.

The range of bright shades seen in this view correspond to fashionable colors from Spain, Italy and France, countries that favored brocaded and embroidered silks, spots, stripes and artificial dyes. The macaroni was notorious for mixing these influences together, with the colors here representing the fashionable pea green (especially sought after because it was a difficult shade to create, requiring double-dyeing) red, pink, and dark orange.[46]

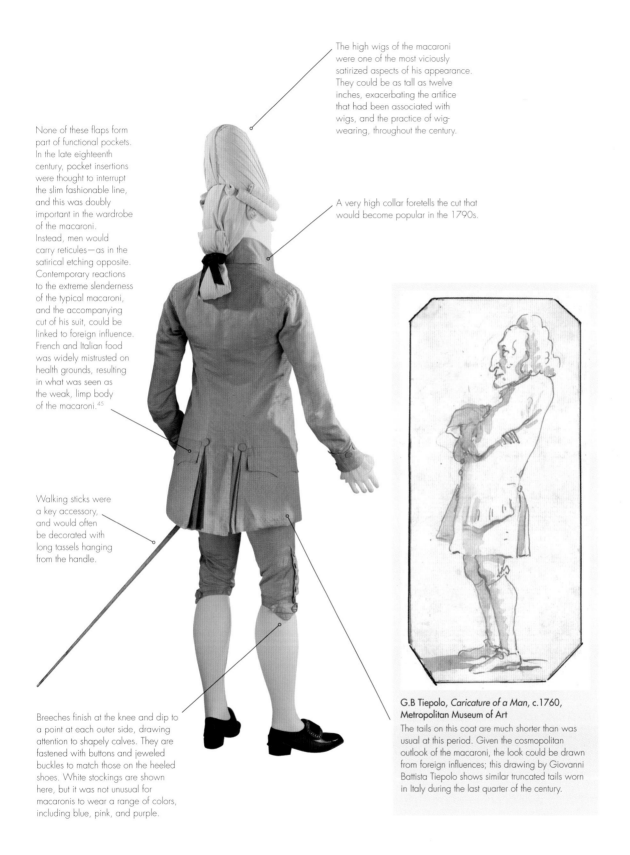

The high wigs of the macaroni were one of the most viciously satirized aspects of his appearance. They could be as tall as twelve inches, exacerbating the artifice that had been associated with wigs, and the practice of wig-wearing, throughout the century.

None of these flaps form part of functional pockets. In the late eighteenth century, pocket insertions were thought to interrupt the slim fashionable line, and this was doubly important in the wardrobe of the macaroni. Instead, men would carry reticules—as in the satirical etching opposite. Contemporary reactions to the extreme slenderness of the typical macaroni, and the accompanying cut of his suit, could be linked to foreign influence. French and Italian food was widely mistrusted on health grounds, resulting in what was seen as the weak, limp body of the macaroni.[45]

A very high collar foretells the cut that would become popular in the 1790s.

Walking sticks were a key accessory, and would often be decorated with long tassels hanging from the handle.

Breeches finish at the knee and dip to a point at each outer side, drawing attention to shapely calves. They are fastened with buttons and jeweled buckles to match those on the heeled shoes. White stockings are shown here, but it was not unusual for macaronis to wear a range of colors, including blue, pink, and purple.

G.B Tiepolo, *Caricature of a Man*, c.1760, Metropolitan Museum of Art
The tails on this coat are much shorter than was usual at this period. Given the cosmopolitan outlook of the macaroni, the look could be drawn from foreign influences; this drawing by Giovanni Battista Tiepolo shows similar truncated tails worn in Italy during the last quarter of the century.

Man's three-piece suit: Coat, waistcoat, and breeches,

c.1775–85, France, Philadelphia Museum of Art, Pennsylvania

◆

This three-piece suit could almost be regarded as an early business suit: it was purchased in Paris by American general Jonathan Williams, for use when he was away on business in Europe.[47] It is highly fashionable in its cut, construction, and embellishment, and showcases some detailed embroidery illustrating popular natural motifs. Although exquisite, the placement of these relatively narrow bands of embroidery—only on the front edges, cuffs, collar, and pockets—is indicative of the growing trend towards no embellishment at all.

The buttons on this coat are very large in comparison to those of the waistcoat. This was fashionable from c.1770s onwards, and partly explains the lack of buttonholes. The most popular material for these larger buttons was metal; here, the covered button offers the opportunity for further embroidery.

Golden sheaves of wheat make up the principal pattern of this embroidery. Wheat is rife with allegory, with Christian associations of abundance, renewal, rebirth, and self-sacrifice. All of these might be considered appropriate for a wealthy professional man seeking to make an impression in foreign circles.

Flowering vines are the other key decorative motif on this coat and waistcoat. The vine also has Biblical connotations, symbolizing peace and abundance.

The skirts of this single-breasted waistcoat are angled away at the waist, following the lines of the coat above. The garment is fully fastened, its embroidery perfectly displayed in symmetry with that of the coat.

The cut and construction of breeches did not change greatly during the second half of the century, with a continuing close fit.

The **bag wig** was worn mainly for full (formal) dress. The *queue* (a tied lock of hair hanging down the man's back) was encased in a small black bag, usually made from silk and stiffened with gum, and fastened with a drawstring. The string was concealed by a black bow.

A small standing collar, fitting quite closely to the neck, would soon be replaced by a much taller style in the later 1780s and 90s.

The coat's cuffs are the same width as the fairly tight-fitting sleeves. A very small section of shirt ruffle is visible, reaching to the wearer's knuckles.

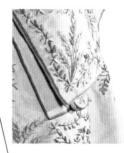

The pockets on this coat conform to the late 1770s or early/mid 1780s; after this time it was more fashionable to see plain pocket flaps with no decorative buttons beneath.

There are no buttonholes on this coat, decorative or functional. Since the fashion was to wear the coat open, holes were often dispensed with altogether.

Chain-stitch embroidery is used to form the wheat sheaves and surrounding vines. This ancient decorative technique involves the creation of a line of delicate loops, secured to a base fabric. The thread is drawn up from the underside to hold each loop in place, creating a chain-like pattern. The loops are not pulled tight, but remain loosely in place and are built up, one following another. The resulting effect can be feather-like and the stitch is sometimes referred to as "feathered chain." A detached variant, known as "lazy daisy," is still often used for floral embroidery.[48]

Frock coat,

c.1784–89, Netherlands, Rijksmuseum, Amsterdam

◆

This coat is a great illustration of a late eighteenth-century frock, a working-class style that was appropriated by the upper and middle classes. Like the next example, it is also a useful reminder of a situation so often encountered in fashion history: an incomplete suit. Further detective work is therefore required in order to understand how the full outfit might have been worn and accessorized. Luckily, in this rare instance, a portrait of the wearer in the same coat exists—valuable source material that allows us to view a single coat in a whole new light.

This very broad, turned-down collar extends almost to the edges of the shoulders. At the back, many collars of this date were made with a central point, as shown in this c.1790 example from the Metropolitan Museum of Art.

According to Rijksmuseum, the owner of the coat, Jacob Alewijn (seen below wearing it), dirtied the collar through years of wearing long, powdered hair in a ponytail. This necessitated removing a piece of the pointed section, and replacing it with glazed black material.[49]

The sleeves are relatively slim and do not finish in a substantial cuff, as they had done only a few years previously. A modest turned-back cuff is marked out by the placement of silver braid, and there are no decorative buttons or buttonholes.

The portrait on the right suggests that this coat was worn with a white or cream, lightly patterned silk waistcoat, cut with angled fronts. It may have looked similar to this Italian example from the Metropolitan Museum of Art, c.1780.

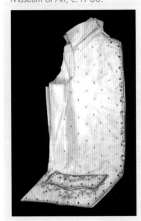

By the date of this example, the frock was acceptable everywhere except court. This was partly because its usual fabric—wool—reflected its less formal nature and humble origins. For a coat made from cloth rather than silk, it is perhaps not surprising that the applied decoration should be slight, but the deep moss green highlights these rows of silver thread embroidery, depicting a jewel-like cluster of leaves, tassels and feathered fronds.

There are only two buttons on this coat, and no corresponding holes: the fronts fasten below the neck with two sets of concealed hooks and eyes. The lack of fastenings makes complete sense, as the coat fronts slope away so sharply that they cannot meet below the chest.

Adriaen de Lelie, *Jacob Alewijn*, c.1780-90, Amsterdam Museum

By the 1780s, breeches were close-fitting and ended just below the knee. By the 1770s they were usually fastened at the leg with buckles or buttons, or occasionally, ties. In the above portrait Alewijn wears black breeches and white stockings, a combination that was most often seen from the 1780s onwards.

The coat skirts are slowly shrinking away to form narrow tails. This will become even more pronounced in the following decade.

Ribbed silk coat,

c.1780s, England, Shippensburg University Fashion Archives & Museum, Pennsylvania

◆

This soft blue coat with matching buttons is beautifully and plainly cut in the style of a riding coat, allowing us to witness some key tailoring techniques and some highly fashionable attributes. Like the previous example, it has no accompanying waistcoat or breeches, but would probably have been worn with garments in contrasting shades.

Narrow, sloping shoulders are particularly evident here, not being supported by any kind of padding, as they have been since. In historian Anne Hollander's words, this—coupled with an emphasis on stomach, hips, and thighs—gave men "a slightly squat and infantine" silhouette that is at odds with today's interpretation of the ideal "masculine" shape.[50]

Unlike the previous frock coat, which has only two buttons, those on this example cannot be missed. Very large buttons like this have become associated with the foppish macaroni (as examined earlier in this chapter), but they were a regular accessory for fashionable men of the period. As The Analytical Review put it in 1794, "In 1786, reigned the mania of buttons; they . . . wore them of an enormous size, as large as crown pieces."[51]

There is a single hook-and-eye closure behind the second button.

This collar sits quite high at the back, showing the beginnings of the "stand fall" cut of the following decade. As with the previous example, there is a slight dip at the center back.

Slightly curved side back seams remain as a consistent feature from the 1770s onwards. By the 1790s, they will almost meet at the center.

A center back vent (enabling the wearer to ride on horseback) is covered by a fabric overlap.

Buttons at the bottom of the side pleats allowed coat skirts to be caught up and held together, a useful feature for riding and other sporting activity. Here, one button is sewn to the bottom at each side, attaching the two coat pieces together.

As with most 1780s coats, pockets are placed at hip level. They have deep flaps with a row of buttons set just beneath. The image above shows a view of the pocket hole itself, cut in a convenient V-shape.

These cuffs are closed all the way around the wrist, though it was also common for frock coat cuffs to feature a slit at the back (an element still seen today). By the middle of the 1780s, it was less and less usual to see lace cuffs peeping beneath the coat sleeves.

These bottom sections are composed from smaller pieces of fabric, a procedure known contemporaneously as "piecing." This was a common economical device on male and female garments in the eighteenth century, used in areas of the coat that would not show.

Suit worn by George Washington,

c.1789, George Washington's Mount Vernon, Mount Vernon, Virginia

◆

This suit is part of the collection at Mount Vernon, the plantation house of the first President of the United States, George Washington. It was worn around the time of his first inaugural address on April 30, 1789; it is made of the same American-made brown broadcloth (a substantial woolen fabric) that had been rejected as "mean and coarse" by Secretary of War Henry Knox, but which became an important symbol of Washington's commitment to domestic manufacture. Its plainness also heralded his promotion of an elegant simplicity of dress, rejecting the elaboration and excess of the European courts. As he wrote in 1761, "I want neither lace nor embroidery. Plain clothes, with gold or silver buttons, if worn in genteel dress, are all that I desire."[52]

This high stand fall collar with its wide blunt-angled lapels adds breadth to the wearer's shoulders and torso.

By the 1780s coat sleeves were made with a curve at the elbow, so that when a man stood with arms slightly bent the sleeve would fall smoothly.

The only concession to surface decoration also had a function: these large metal "federal" buttons are emblazoned with the image of the American eagle and sewn close together down the front of the double-breasted coat. They were created especially for the inauguration suit, but finished only just in time for the ceremony. When he received the first examples, Washington wrote to Henry Knox that both they and the accompanying cloth "really do credit to the manufactures of this Country."[53] Many buttons with up to 22 designs were produced at the time of the inauguration, for the delegates in attendance but also as souvenirs for the crowd. Hand-stamped patterns ranged from the eagle to a sun accompanied with the words "The Majesty of the People" or "Long live the President." A similar style of button was used on men's hunting clothes across Europe and America.[54]

White silk stockings were worn with the brown breeches.

Anglomania, which hit France in the 1770s and 80s and promoted a "rural" simplicity and rationality in dress, strongly reflected America's revolutionary ideals. For Washington, the idea that men and women could eliminate class distinction through simpler clothing must have been invigorating, and is reflected through the plain color and restraint of this suit. Nonetheless, the close fit of the jacket and breeches does correspond to social indicators via fashion in the late eighteenth century. A tight fit was a clear indication that the wearer did not need loose clothes; did not need to labor in the fields. Instead, as befits a public figure, this suit ensured an elegant, upstanding posture and a dignified carriage.

Anon, *An Unknown Man, perhaps Charles Goring of Wiston* (detail), c.1765, Yale Center for British Art

Pockets are plain, with no ornamentation, including either real or sham buttonholes.

Research undertaken by textile scholar Linda Baumgarten has shown that Washington was a tall, slim man with long, thin arms and legs. This length would have been enhanced further by these knee-length coat skirts, which cover the hips and a significant fraction of thigh.[55]

Suit of a sans-culotte, France,

c.1790, Los Angeles County Museum of Art, Los Angeles, California

This 1790 suit of jacket, shirt, and trousers represents the clothing of a very specific, but important, group in French society. The sans-culotte (a phrase with layered meaning and context, but which can be literally translated as "without breeches") illustrates arguably the most radical phase of the French Revolution. Comprising members of the urban proletariat, the movement brought together angry and disillusioned men and women who established themselves as leaders of the common people, giving a voice to those who had been so disadvantaged under the Ancien Regime. As with so many political and revolutionary movements, clothing was hugely significant as an immediate indicator of a sans-culotte's partisan affiliations and background. The trousers are especially important here, although they do represent a hugely complex period in history, and it is prudent not to overplay their influence on men's fashion going forward. The introduction of trousers was gradual, and they were not accepted universally as fashionable daywear until the mid to late 1820s. Pantaloons, worn by some fashionable men of the period, were shaped, slinky, ankle-length garments that bore little relation to the easy and comfortable garb of the sans-culotte.

This detail of a 1792 caricature by James Gilray depicts an impoverished sans-culotte warming his (literally) breeches-bare legs by the fire (French Liberty, British Slavery, courtesy Metropolitan Museum of Art).

As Charles Dickens put it in 1860, "The Revolution tore the cravat from men's throats. How could men call loud enough for blood . . . with the windpipe shackled by muslin? The Sans-Culottes must have their throats free, for the exercise of their lungs; their enemies must have their throats free, also, for the convenience of La Guillotine."[56] Here, the sans-culotte wears a loosely tied linen scarf that could be easily removed, and hangs free without a waistcoat to retain its ends. Waistcoats were sometimes worn by revolutionary men, and were made to illustrate ideals rather than complement a suit. Like this 1789–94 example, also from the Los Angeles County Museum of Art, they were used as propaganda and were often made from homespun fabrics. The example opposite is highly significant in its details: the small caterpillar and butterflies embroidered onto the lapels, for example, are representative of the "flamboyance" of men in the 1780s. The butterfly's wings are being cut to symbolize an end to sartorial extravagance, with the left-hand caterpillar showing the resulting fashionable sacrifice. The text written across both pockets are familiar French sayings: on the right, "The habit does not make the monk," and to the left, "Shame upon him who thinks evil of it." Both relate to the English "Don't judge a book by its cover," whilst also reminding the viewer of the motto of the English Order of the Garter. Any reference to England was fashionable, recalling the continuing presence of Anglomania in French culture and taste.[57]

The origin of the **Phrygian cap**, also known as the "bonnet rouge" or "bonnet de laine," is debated. It was certainly inspired by Ancient Greek styles, which links in to the neoclassical rhetoric embraced by the sans-culottes, and is similar to variations of the working man's woolen cap.[58] It became a national patriotic symbol when the royal family were forced to wear one after the invasion of the Tuileries, and was often worn—as seen here—with a tricolor **cockade**.

This smock-like jacket was known as a **Carmagnole**, originating in the town of Carmagnola in Piedmont, Italy. Here, it had been part of peasant wear for generations and was successfully appropriated in France.[59] Cut short and full in the back, it would be made from wool or cloth and decorated only with buttons. A concession to fashion is seen in the wide revers.

These trousers close with a "fall-front," also a popular fastening for breeches in which a flap of fabric at the front is held in place by two buttons. The waistband was designed to be worn just above the natural waist.

Before the end of the eighteenth century, loose-fitting trousers often seem to have been regarded as a lower-class garment. Therefore they appear eminently suited to the uniform of a sans-culotte. However, according to historian Daniel Roche, this assumption poses a problem, since there are no records of the garment in inventories from the *journees* of the Revolution.[60] Moreover, we know that the majority of working-class men in Paris continued to wear breeches with stockings. Nevertheless, whatever their origin or correct placement in social history, they certainly were worn by this group and adopted as a symbol of militant idealism. The pair shown here are an especially useful example, with their colorful stripes, which served as a way of incorporating variety and interest without the ornate and luxurious embellishment of the aristocracy. The use of stripes, of course, also has its roots in the tricolor rosette and the French flag. On a purely practical level, stripes (both horizontal and vertical) were more achievable by the end of the century due to progress in the mechanization of thread and cloth production, and continued to be popular into the nineteenth century with the advent of another revolution: the Industrial.[61]

Vest, France, c.1789–1794, Los Angeles County Museum of Art

Silk coat and breeches,

1790s, France, Metropolitan Museum of Art, New York, New York

◆

This coat from the 1790s is shown with breeches and embroidered silk waistcoat. While not as high-waisted and exaggerated in cut as the 1795–1805 example, this **habit dégagé or anglaise** nonetheless provides a striking silhouette that is representative of the post-Revolutionary French male form. It is illustrative of styles worn by young men in particular, and we can clearly see the nineteenth-century tailcoat evolving from the cutaway styles of the eighteenth.

Waistcoats, as well as coats, were made with standing collars and revers from the 1780s onwards.

The striped pattern of this coat is a major indicator of its 1790s creation date. Its **passementerie** buttons, decorated in a criss-cross "basket weave" design, were worked in thread over a wooden base. They complement the fabric whilst subtly adding a point of difference.

These wide, rounded **lapels** are typical of the 1790s. As the decade progressed, the gap between the stand-fall collar and lapel grew ever wider.

A very prominent straight-cut waistline is visible in this tailcoat, and it sits relatively high so that much of the waistcoat and breeches are on view beneath.

By the 1790s, double-breasted coat fastenings were becoming ever more popular, helping to balance the very square cut of the waist.[62]

This single-breasted waistcoat features a "square-cut" or "Newmarket" waistline, accentuated by the rectangular plackets above. It is interesting to note that these have not been placed entirely level, suggesting either a homemade provenance or subsequent repair or replacement. At this date fashionable waistcoats were cut without skirts, and could be tightened to fit with one or several ties at the back. The plain ground with recurring embroidered floral and fruit motifs may seem simple at first glance, but a playful detail appears along the front edge. Its vertical green line of embroidery forms a vine from which sprout extra branches, curling in between the buttons and introducing more foliage to the design. The center of each corresponding button features an embroidered flower and stem with leaves.

This rear view shows how changes in cut achieved the fashionable slender line. Pockets are placed towards the very back of the hips; they were forced to migrate as the curve of the side back seams became more pronounced. It is interesting to note the marked difference between the cut of this coat and the previous 1780s frock.

Fashionable breeches were made to fit especially closely over the thighs, and were often cut high, well above the natural waistline.

Waistcoat, c.1790, Metropolitan Museum of Art

Jean Louis Darcis after Carle Vernet, Les Incroyables,

c.1796, Rijksmuseum, Amsterdam

◆

Following the revolutionary rags of the sans-culottes, young aristocratic men and women emerged out of the Reign of Terror into the Directoire, able once again to display fashionable excess, although in a somewhat different manner from pre-Revolutionary days. Along with their female counterparts the merveilleuses ("marvellous women"), these **incroyables** ("incredibles" or "unbelievables") donned exaggerated versions of English dress, harking back to the sartorial sentiments that had become popular just before the Revolution. The fashionable silhouette of the following two examples is clearly visible in the clothing of this pair, who—though they appear in a satirical drawing—are still a fair representation of what these outlandish Parisian "dandiacals," in the words of Robert Carlyle, wore.

....

Although incroyables were monarchists wishing to recall the lavishness of the Ancien Regime, their uniform of choice was intentionally crumpled and disheveled: "decadent" in its carelessness. This was accentuated through long, mullet-like hairstyles known as **hedgehogs** and extremely high, roughly knotted cravats. These were often made in green (see below) as an expression of royalist sympathies.[63]

This print became an overnight sensation in December 1796, and even incroyables themselves found its depiction of two foppish young men, one overtly scrutinizing the other, amusing. [63] This figure holds a quizzing glass up to his eye, an optical aid used as much for decoration as for vision. It is implied here that he is "quizzically"—and no doubt critically—inspecting the clothing choices of the other man.

The once common tricorne hat largely vanished in France after the Revolution, leaving the bicorne in its place.

Jewelry, particularly large earrings, pendants, and watches on chains, were a crucial part of the incroyable aesthetic. So well-known did this choice become that a group of Napoleon's soldiers even referenced it when they finally received some overdue pay: "They bought jewellery . . . everyone strutted around with . . . chains and ornaments, just as the fashion was in Paris at that time. We transformed ourselves into Incroyables!"[64]

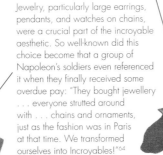

Coat, France, 1790, Los Angeles County Museum of Art

This figure's hat represents an early version of the nineteenth-century **stovepipe**.

Two waistcoats were sometimes worn by incroyables as a way of introducing further color and texture. Here, the floral lapels of the top waistcoat help to emphasize the exaggerated cut of the coat's beneath.

The coat worn by this figure (and in the image above) has a relatively high, narrow cutaway waistline. For both the incroyables in this print, huge spread-eagled collars appear even broader when paired with the coat's narrow waist.

As a move away from the wide, loose trousers of the sans-culottes, incroyables favored tight-fitting breeches with long loops of ribbons dangling from the knees. This evokes the frills and furbelows of the mid-seventeenth century—a return to more flamboyant masculine trends.

Bright colors, particularly shades of red and green, were popular for coats. Red was an especially pertinent anti-revolutionary signifier, often used to symbolize blood spilled on the guillotine.

Flat, open shoes with pointed toes, worn with white or colored stockings, were the most usual footwear.

Coat, waistcoat and breeches,

1790–95, France, Los Angeles County Museum of Art, Los Angeles, California

◆

The silk coat in this ensemble is highly representative of the unique, transformative style of the 1790s. It retains some of the flamboyant elements of the incroyable ensemble, but represents the shift away from such extremity and—as French émigrés returned from England—an emphasis on softer lines inspired by Anglomania. This coat, with its bold, sharp lines and exaggerated collar, perfectly echoes the changes taking place across Europe, as well as showing significant blending and borrowing between the masculine and feminine aesthetic.

The star of the show is this eye-catching striped silk coat, which carries on the straight lines of the 1770s and 80s. Its high collar is turned down at the back, covering the wearer's neck and almost reaching his jaw. Very broad triangular lapels extend just below the shoulders.

Large covered buttons add another focus point, also edging the cuffs.

Stripes remained popular, becoming the most fashionable patterning for menswear until c.1795.

Journal des Dames et des Modes, 5 January 1800, Rijksmuseum

This 1800 fashion plate conversely illustrates the masculine influence on female outerwear in the late eighteenth and early nineteenth century. Its high collar and wraparound fastening create a similar silhouette and emphasize the very high waistline.

A striking similarity to women's fashion can be seen in the very high cutaway waist. Mirroring the empire line, which sat just below the bust, this jacket allows a clear view of the patterned waistcoat beneath.

Journal des Luxus und der Moden, 1786-1826, Rijksmuseum

This fashion plate from c.1787 shows a gentleman wearing a striped coat with similarly wide revers and a tall (probably felt) hat, which illustrates the kind of headwear that would have been worn with the suit shown here. This slightly conical style would develop into the **top hat** in the following century.

A substantial section of this this single-breasted waistcoat is on view, making the coat's high waist even more eye-catching. It is made from plain weave silk with silk and metallic thread **passementerie** edging. The pocket flaps are trimmed to match.

The very long tails of this coat finish at knee length, and other examples from the period extend to the calf. This adds to the exaggerated aesthetic and, additionally, the indication of leisure that is posed by such impracticality. Legend has it that in Germany, by 1791, some fashionable coat-tails even reached the ground, and had to be held up by the wearer in the same way a woman held the skirt of her dress away from the road.[65]

Johannes Pieter de Frey after Jacobus Johannes Lauwers, Farmer with jug,

1770–1834, Rijksmuseum, Amsterdam

◆

This late eighteenth-century etching offers an important opportunity to assess the clothing of a lower-class working man, something relatively rare in fashion studies. Despite a more relaxed manner of wearing his clothes, and the lack of an accompanying coat, this ensemble is still clearly inspired by the fashionable silhouette and has adapted itself to the demands of manual labor. No precise date is attributed, but several elements allow us to estimate that the image was made around 1790–1800.

Working men and laborers may have started the day wearing a neckcloth or handkerchief to hold the shirt collar together. This etching depicts the realistic dishevelment that would come with the end of a long working day, and the relative freedom—and lack of propriety—of the countryside as opposed to the town.

Shirts of working men would typically be made from linen: light, breathable, yet durable.

Waistcoats were commonly made from wool or cotton, and the cut (if not the quality and decoration) of this single-breasted example is reminiscent of styles worn by the elite (right, silk waistcoat, c.1780, Metropolitan Museum of Art). However, many working men chose to wear a smock instead of a waistcoat and coat. This was a hip or thigh-length, shapeless garment with sleeves, worn over the shirt and breeches. It was hard-wearing and suitable for all kinds of manual work, being easy to move in and to repair. It also dispensed with the need for a waistcoat or jacket, offering the warmth and protection of both garments.

These breeches are looser and far less shapely than those worn by the elite. More of them can be seen in this image, however, than was usually visible beneath the longer waistcoats and coats of fashionable men. They probably fastened with whole or broad "falls," with the front flap extending from one side seam to the other. Consequently, the sides of the flap itself are hidden from view under the waistcoat, but we can see the buttoned center closure above. From around the seventeenth century, the breeches of all classes were usually lined, acting as a pair of drawers and adding warmth.[66]

Johannes Pieter de Frey, *Farmer with basket*, c.1770–1834, Rijksmuseum
This drawing by the same artist shows a farmer or laborer (quite possibly the same figure as seen here), fully dressed with a coat and neckerchief. The practical hip-length coat without tails is similar to the **Carmagnole** jacket favored by the sans-culottes of post-Revolutionary France, and by Italian workers for many years beforehand.

Breeches would be composed of leather, wool, or a thick cotton. This pair fasten with buckles, but the straps have been left hanging open.

White stockings would usually be made from cotton or worsted (yarn or thread spun from combed wool fibers). Buckled shoes or boots were the most common footwear.

Chapter 3
1800–1859

Any discussion of early nineteenth-century menswear will include reference to the dandy, also contemporaneously referred to as a "buck," "beau," and sometimes, more derogatorily, "fop." The figure of the dandy was distinct from the eighteenth-century "macaroni" that preceded him, but still rooted in similar principles of sartorial care and precision. He was, however, more than just a clotheshorse. His clothes represented a way of being, a state of mind—which, in the words of famous French dandy Barbey d'Aurevilly, was "made up of many shades . . . it is the direct result of the endless warfare between respectability and boredom."[1]

The very mention of "boredom" suggests a man with the time on his hands to devote to "dressing oneself with daring and elegance," as d'Aurevilly put it. This chapter will not delve too deeply into the psychology and approach of the dandy, since the actual number of men that can be classified as "dandies" was comparatively small and mostly belonged to a privileged elite. However, the phenomenon was hugely influential in shaping the impeccably cut, clean, ornament-free suits that would define nineteenth-century menswear, so a brief overview will be provided.

The dandy's uniform was essentially an immaculate version of late eighteenth-century riding dress, which all fashionable men across Europe, America, and Britain wore a variant of in the early 1800s. This consisted of the "morning" coat (so called because gentlemen would typically ride in the morning) and breeches, and is illustrated well in the last few examples of the previous chapter. The cut-back "swallowtails" of the coat gradually narrowed further to became the "tail" or "dress coat," a primary wardrobe staple until the introduction of the fuller-skirted frock coat in the 1820s.

Until the 1840s, dress coats and/or frock coats could be worn during the day, giving men some degree of choice. One of the most important and noticeable changes to menswear in this period, though, concerned legwear. Thanks in part to dandy George "Beau" Brummell, by 1820 the wearing of long trousers in place of breeches had become acceptable. Before this, tight-fitting pantaloons provided a stepping stone between knee-length breeches and ankle-length trousers, though they were far from suitable for every man. Their glove-like fit required the wearer to be gifted with shapely, ideally slightly muscular legs, and it was known for some men to resort to artificial calf padding to achieve this look. Longer, looser trousers had previously been associated with working class men, particularly sailors. They were adopted as a reactionary gesture by the sans-culottes in early 1790s France, but similar wider versions would not be seen in fashionable dress until around the 1830s–40s. During the period in question, the words "trousers" ("trowsers") and "pantaloons" could be used somewhat interchangeably, and both variants were long and slim-fitting.[2]

Coat and trousers
c.1830s, American,
Shippensburg Fashion
Archives and Museum,
Pennsylvania

For Brummell, the key to ultimate style lay in close fit and uninterrupted lines. Therefore, pocket flaps were moved to the very back of a coat to avoid breaking the silhouette, coats were shaped expertly to the body through the addition of darts, and layers of wool or buckram were sewn into the coat, across the shoulders and torso, to discreetly achieve the ideal outline. Multiple fittings were then carried out to ensure perfection, using the newly invented tape measure.[3] As a result, it was not just the clothes themselves that made an impact, but the manner in which they were worn, and the painstaking care Brummell took with every aspect of his wardrobe and appearance.

Many have observed therefore that for Brummell, the devil was in the detail. Rather than making a statement with brocade and embroidery, he famously experimented with— for example—tying a neckcloth in the perfect style, a fastidiousness that caused an originally satirical pamphlet entitled *Neckclothitania* (1818) to become a valued guide for aspiring dandies. Its preface summed up the dandy's goal in life: ". . . it must be a great *desideratum* to every gentleman, to persuade the *rest* of the world that he *is* one . . . he necessarily must accomplish it by his dress."[4] More broadly this suggested that men could—and should— define their respectability through clothing above all else. Part of this care was shown through cleanliness, another key aspect of Brummell's aesthetic, which was indeed crucial if the yards of linen around his neck were to retain their whiteness.

Legend has it that it could take up to ten hours for Brummell to dress in the morning, and this would sometimes happen in front of an audience who were keen to take notes on his technique. Such indulgence was subsequently described by Baudelaire as befitting a man who "is rich and idle, and . . . has no other occupation than the perpetual pursuit of happiness . . . whose solitary vice is elegance."[5] However, Brummell's background was a relatively modest one. Born in 1778 to a middle-class family, his rise into the inner circles of the Prince Regent was of his own making. This success made it possible for other non-aristocratic men to dress with as much confidence and elegance as the upper classes, something that would not have been possible with the hugely ornate fashionable dress of the eighteenth century. Nonetheless, Brummell died in poverty in 1840, by which time the rise of ready-to-wear clothing (see the following chapter) had set the death knell for the dandy's prime metier: his ability to "conceive" his outfit, as Roland Barthes expressed it, "exactly like a modern artist might conceive a composition using available materials . . . it was normally impossible for a dandy to *purchase* his clothes."[6]

As time went on, the cult of the dandy across Europe became linked with various social groups and codes of behavior, the "ruffians" (loud, flamboyant eccentrics) and "exquisites" (ascetics and perfectionists) amongst them. It is unrealistic to expect that Brummell's vision would have been carried on verbatim to future generations of men, and the legacy he left was more broadly about elegance without excess, of cut and fit above all else. In his own words,

RIGHT
Louis-Léopold
Boilly, *Portrait of a
Gentleman*, c.1800,
Los Angeles County
Museum of Art

"If John Bull turns to look at you in the street, you are not properly dressed." As John Harvey has described it, Brummell left a "prototype for the plain, smart, dark outfit that all Victorian England was presently to wear, with a still more sober and sombre demeanor."[7]

However, although this was acknowledged by some, by the end of the century early dandies seem to have been viewed with even more suspicion and unease than they had been at the beginning. In 1898 William Connor Sydney wrote that "In 1819 the dress of the Bond Street dandy was partly male and partly female, for his pantaloons being gathered into his waistband presented the appearance of a petticoat under the waistcoat, while the coat itself was made full before, tight in the waist, and with very wide gathers about the hips."[8] To twenty-first century eyes, and as dress historians acknowledge, men's clothing of the early nineteenth century left very little to the imagination. As Anne Hollander expressed it, a "suave idealization of plain country gear . . . emphasizes the body under the clothes."[9] This meant raised waistlines and long legs encased in light-colored, close-fitting breeches or pantaloons that emphasized every manly feature.

By the end of the century suits had undergone substantial change, but the dandy's uniform of coat, waistcoat, and trousers had become firmly entrenched. Nevertheless, a new emphasis on sport and physicality now arguably dominated notions of masculinity, and contributed a very different and rather defensive and threatened construct of manliness.

As this portrait shows, the Regency period—though comparatively more somber than the silks and satins of the eighteenth century—can in many respects be considered the swansong of color before a distinct change of tone in the Victorian era. The sitter is wearing an aubergine-colored coat over a floral waistcoat dotted with crimson flowers; a rich, warm palette that shows a careful pairing of color and pattern. Despite this, and although the philosophy of dandyism encouraged men to carefully consider each element of their appearance, not everyone felt it was appropriate. Writing to her sister Cassandra in January 1796, Jane Austen said of Tom Lefroy, with whom she had a brief flirtation: "He has but *one* fault, which time will, I trust, entirely remove—it is that his morning coat is a great deal too light."[10]

This chapter will illustrate the slow changes in cut and fit that led from the high-waisted, puff-sleeved, pigeon-breast of the early nineteenth century dandy to the long, lean, smooth-shouldered outline of the 1850s. For men in the first half of the century, however, fashionable shifts must have seemed interminably slow in comparison to that of women. *The Sydney Gazette and New South Wales Advertiser* summed this up well in 1831 when it wrote forlornly:

> The only alteration in the fashion since last month is as follows: – The waist is a trifle shorter, and the hip buttons nearer together; the lapels not so pointed, and rather larger at top; the collar is a degree longer, and shows a part of the quilting behind.[11]

Observed as a fluid timeline, however, these changes are far more discernible and should help the reader to navigate through museum collections, works of art, and film and television interpretations of the era.

Many contemporary images, including fashion plates, show men with only the trousers of their suits visible beneath long and voluminous **topcoats**, making an understanding of the coats' type and variety useful in any "reading" of the suit. The previous chapter introduced the **greatcoat**, and until 1840 other options consisted of long, collared cloaks or long coats cut very similarly to the frock (including the **mackintosh** waterproof coat, patented by Charles Mackintosh in 1823).

BELOW
Fashion plates,
Costume Parisien,
1825 and 1823,
Rijksmuseum

From the 1840s onwards, two styles in particular were to dominate men's outerwear until the twentieth century; in fact, they are still in existence today. The **Chesterfield**'s namesake was the Sixth Earl of Chesterfield, a fashionable socialite and politician. This coat, like the lounge suit that was soon to follow, had no horizontal seam around the waist and a plain back. The only shaping came from discreet darts and side seams, and it could be either single or double breasted. These factors combined to make it a comfortable, versatile, and immensely popular garment. A variant known as the "sac" overcoat was even looser with no shaping at all—though even in contemporary writings, the two terms are sometimes used interchangeably.

RIGHT
Chesterfield
overcoat, W.C. Bell,
c.1860–70, USA,
private collection

The **Ulster** was another favorite, an import from Ireland in the late 1860s. Unlike the Chesterfield, it could be made with either a half or full belt, and could be worn with or without a detachable shoulder cape.[12] If a man liked this latter feature, he could also opt for the "Inverness" topcoat, which, as the name suggests, originated in Scotland, and was usually made from tweed or plaid cloth. It was also long, full and belted, and always featured a collar and elbow-length cape. Extra flexibility was given in the option to have the Inverness made with or without sleeves; as a voluminous cape or as a coat.

Of course, all these styles were suitable for travel, and the number of available designs increased after the advent of the railway in the 1830s. From the 1840s onwards we can see numerous newspaper articles promoting the benefits of specialized "railway coats" (sometimes this term referred to overcoats in general) and the flexibility and comfort of the Inverness meant that it was frequently cited favorably, even after it had fallen from fashion. In 1867 *The West End Gentleman's Gazette* said that it was "not fashionable but is a permanent favorite as a kind of wrap or over garment for railway travelling. There is no garment which surpasses it for this and similar purposes, so that it will always be in use."[13] Such garments went on to influence styles such as the Carrick and, later, the "duster," which was specifically designed for motorcar driving.

Velvet three-piece suit,

c.1800, Europe, Los Angeles County Museum of Art, Los Angeles, California

◆

This exquisitely embroidered suit carries a date of c.1800, by which time the combination of frock coat, breeches, and stockings (known as "full dress") was firmly out of fashion except for court wear and other highly formal occasions. The ascension of Napoleon in France brought about a resurgence in previously defunct court fashions, and as a result it is possible to see highly ornate, painstakingly symmetrical designs that are perfectly mimicked between coat and waistcoat. This is a good illustration of the style's continuation in one very particular corner of society, and of several techniques that were popular for such garments throughout the century.

Until around 1800, "full dress" for men generally kept up with the changing pace of fashion, mirroring the popular silhouette of the decade but imbuing it with luxurious and highly skilled embroidery, applied to the best quality fabrics.[14] By the turn of the nineteenth century, however, this began to change, perhaps in an attempt to differentiate court dress from the increasingly plain fashions of ordinary men and women. The 1790s examples at the end of the previous chapter, with their double-breasted fastening and high, wide revers, illustrate what was now accepted wear for most men. The antiquated cut of this coat, with curved fronts and wide cuffs, is a clear indication that it was intended for the most formal occasions only.

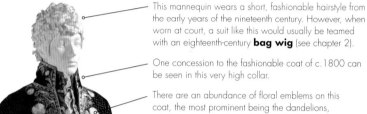

The ground of this coat, waistcoat, and breeches is composed of **voided velvet** (sometimes referred to as cut or "burn-out," though that technique is slightly different), which is made by removing sections of the pile to create a pattern.[15] This laborious technique could be seen throughout the century on the clothing of the elite.

This mannequin wears a short, fashionable hairstyle from the early years of the nineteenth century. However, when worn at court, a suit like this would usually be teamed with an eighteenth-century **bag wig** (see chapter 2).

One concession to the fashionable coat of c.1800 can be seen in this very high collar.

There are an abundance of floral emblems on this coat, the most prominent being the dandelions, which are given a three-dimensional effect through the application of padding (probably vellum or parchment) under the embroidery (a technique known in the eighteenth century as "guipure").[16] This creates raised sections in the satin stitches, mimicking the puffed layers of a dandelion head.

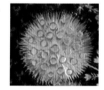

Ironically for such a lavish suit, dandelions were well known in the eighteenth century as "l'or du parre" (gold of the poor), acknowledging the fact that they were plentiful and a common addition to the soup pots of the very poor.[17] Other specimens shown include forget-me-nots, lupins, and daisies.

This 1790–1810 **bicorne**, made from beaver and silk, represents a hat frequently worn with full formal dress. The style had military origins, popularized by Napoleon, and by the early nineteenth century had begun to eclipse the popularity of the **tricorne** amongst military officers and diplomats (Metropolitan Museum of Art).

Académie et salle de danse,

c.1800-09, Paris, New York Public Library, New York, New York

This c.1800–09 image depicts four dancing figures, and the male characters nicely represent the early nineteenth-century silhouette with their frilled shirts and cravats, knee breeches, and heeled pumps. Their coats are unusual and valuable examples of the male **spencer**, a tailless style that had a very short masculine lifespan before being adopted, in a shorter form, by women.

The waistcoat was usually square cut at this date, matching the waistline of the coat above it. Very early in the century an underwaistcoat was sometimes also worn, largely for warmth, and was usually sleeved. It would not be visible.

This 1800 French fashion plate shows an early female version of the spencer, cut with a masculine-inspired collar and lapels, private collection.

This tailless, skirt-less coat would probably have been known contemporaneously as a spencer. The jackets worn by pupils at Eton can also be referred to under this name, as can military officers' mess jackets. There are several tales attributed to its invention, none of which have been decisively proved. The first is that George John Spencer, the 2nd Earl of Spencer, tore the tails from his riding coat after a fall. He continued on the ride, sporting his "new look," which was said to have become a fashion staple almost overnight (not to the surprise of Spencer, who apparently claimed that he could make "any style popular"). Two other versions involve his coat tails being singed off in a fire and cut off for a bet.[18] Whichever is true, the style became one of the most recognizable parts of the early nineteenth-century female wardrobe and, as we see here, initially enjoyed some popularity with men. The absence of tails and the long, slim sleeves must have made it a comparatively free garment, suitable for sports and riding. This image, dating from 1800–09, shows young men in a dancing class wearing a very similar style of coat, slightly higher at the back than the front and with long, slim sleeves.

In the final years of the eighteenth century, it was fashionable for wealthy American and European men to wear low-heeled pumps with rounded toes. By the turn of the century, low-cut slippers were popular.

Around 1800 the shift from knee breeches to trousers gradually started to take place, although breeches were still worn as daywear until c.1830.[19] They were commonly made of a lighter color than the rest of the suit, as seen here.

Journal des dames et des modes, c.1797–1839, Rijksmuseum

Shirts were often made from muslin, with stiffened three or two-tier frilled fronts. This served to exacerbate the fashionably overflowing "pigeon breast" effect of the torso. A very similar arrangement is seen in this *Costume Parisien* fashion plate from 1803 (detail).

Sir Thomas Lawrence, Lord Granville Leveson-Gower, later first Earl Granville,

1804–09, Yale Center for British Art, New Haven, Connecticut

This imposing aristocratic portrait depicts a dandified young lord, dressed in the height of Regency fashion. The sitter was a British Whig party statesman and a diplomat, and widely regarded as one of the handsomest men of the age.[20] The cut and fit of garments, and the way they clung to the body, was key to a **dandy**'s aesthetic, and as with women's wear, neoclassical statues were emulated for men. Both Granville's pose and his clothing correspond to what Anne Hollander described as the Romantic-Neoclassic idealization, which "emphasizes the body under the clothes," cleverly depicted by contemporary artists who managed to portray "the male classical figure unified by clothes instead of nudity."[21]

The sitter wears a bright white neckcloth with the ends tucked into a waistcoat, the standing collar of which it is just possible to see.

During the first half of the century it was common to find a contrasting lining of fur or velvet on the collar (see right), but here the entire coat seems to be both lined and trimmed with thick fur, probably beaver. As well as the fashion for top hats made from felted beaver-fur wool, unfelted pelts were used extensively to trim garments in the early 1800s, and were considered extremely valuable.[22] Wearing such a lavishly trimmed coat would certainly be evidence of Granville's standing.

Anthonie Willem Hendrik Nolthenius de Man, *Man with top hat*, 1828, Rijksmuseum

The head-to-toe use of black here is as much an artistic trick as a fashionable choice; clothing Granville in one dark shade maximizes the flattering effect of his already slender figure. At this point in the history of men's fashion, a rainbow of colors could still be worn—but Lawrence's portrait forecasts the all-pervading use of black into the remainder of the nineteenth century, while at the same time depicting it as the epitome of elegance, taste, and the luxury of choice.

These black breeches with their ribbon ties correspond most closely to styles worn as full or "half dress." The term half dress could be applied to clothing worn at social gatherings such as private parties or the theater. Worn with black stockings and the high-waisted coat, they lengthen his legs and add to the long, lean, languorous image.

These pumps, with their slightly pointed toes and soft ribbon fastenings, also correspond to correct modes of half dress.

Wool broadcloth coat and pantaloons,

c.1805–10, National Society of the Daughters of the American Revolution, Washington D.C.

◆

The "drab" wool used to make this coat incorporates multiple shades of gray, creating a greenish hue. Broadcloth was a closely woven and labor intensive fabric, involving production on a large loom (so as to create a cloth that was more than twice the usual width) and, later in the process, felted to thicken the material.[23] This made it a top quality, durable winter fabric that was in high demand by those that could afford it. It could also be a strongly patriotic gesture of support if the fabric was woven in the United States, since efforts were being made to establish a national textile industry.

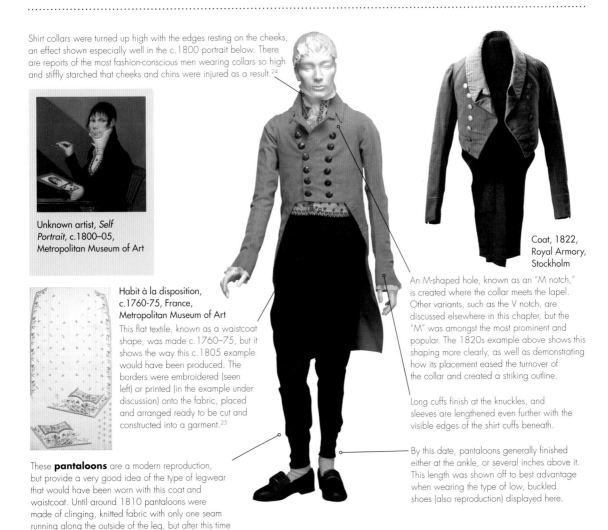

Shirt collars were turned up high with the edges resting on the cheeks, an effect shown especially well in the c.1800 portrait below. There are reports of the most fashion-conscious men wearing collars so high and stiffly starched that cheeks and chins were injured as a result.[24]

Unknown artist, *Self Portrait*, c.1800–05, Metropolitan Museum of Art

Habit à la disposition, c.1760-75, France, Metropolitan Museum of Art

This flat textile, known as a waistcoat shape, was made c.1760–75, but it shows the way this c.1805 example would have been produced. The borders were embroidered (seen left) or printed (in the example under discussion) onto the fabric, placed and arranged ready to be cut and constructed into a garment.[25]

These **pantaloons** are a modern reproduction, but provide a very good idea of the type of legwear that would have been worn with this coat and waistcoat. Until around 1810 pantaloons were made of clinging, knitted fabric with only one seam running along the outside of the leg, but after this time they would be seamed on the inner leg as well.[26]

Coat, 1822, Royal Armory, Stockholm

An M-shaped hole, known as an "M notch," is created where the collar meets the lapel. Other variants, such as the V notch, are discussed elsewhere in this chapter, but the "M" was amongst the most prominent and popular. The 1820s example above shows this shaping more clearly, as well as demonstrating how its placement eased the turnover of the collar and created a striking outline.

Long cuffs finish at the knuckles, and sleeves are lengthened even further with the visible edges of the shirt cuffs beneath.

By this date, pantaloons generally finished either at the ankle, or several inches above it. This length was shown off to best advantage when wearing the type of low, buckled shoes (also reproduction) displayed here.

Jacket and trousers,

1820s, National Museum, Copenhagen

◆

This blue and white striped cotton jacket, displayed with buff yellow nankin trousers, offers a shape very representative of the 1820s. Its light color scheme, however, presents a different image to the one commonly seen throughout the early nineteenth century; black or dark-colored coat with lighter trousers or pantaloons. Given the neoclassical model of dress for both sexes and the widespread popularity of white for women, it is surprising that light-colored clothing for men is not more regularly seen in this period.

These sleeves, slightly gathered at the shoulders, present a developing trend for men in the 1820s. Subsequent suits in this chapter show coats with far greater puff—and often padding—at the shoulders, mirroring the fashionable line in women's bodices.

By the 1820s it was usual for most double-breasted coats to include an extra band of fabric along the inner front edges to support the buttons and buttonholes. This was known as a button-stand.[27]

Nankin (or nankeen) was a sturdy cotton fabric imported from Nanking in China. It was very fashionable in the early years of the nineteenth century, particularly for use in loose summer trousers such as those shown here. Imitations were produced but were, as a commercial dictionary described it in 1810, "inferior . . .and can scarcely undergo three washings without being altered."[28] However, it was not difficult to obtain the imported fabric, and indeed, at times supply outstripped demand. Head clerk of the East India Company, William Simons, reported in 1820 that "London is at this time entirely overstocked with China raw silk and nankeens; they cannot be sold at all; there are 800,000 pieces of nankeen cloths at this time in the Company's warehouse."[29]

The suit would have been worn with a white shirt and white cravat. Darker colors would not become fashionable until the following decades.

Pockets are still set very close together at the back of the coat, creating the appearance of a small waist and accentuating broad shoulders above.

Unlike previous examples in this chapter, these trousers are more obviously derived from a working man's wardrobe: long, loose and practical.

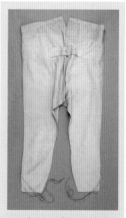

Pantaloons, Italy, 1820s, Metropolitan Museum of Art
Trousers of this style would have been tightened to fit with a metal buckle or buttoned strap (seen above) located at the back of the waistband. They are baggy at the rear but are flat fronted, and more or less cut straight all the way down the leg.

Lord Thomas Busby, Scavenger,

c.1820, The New York Public Library, New York, New York

◆

Not surprisingly, very few extant pieces of working men's clothing survive from the nineteenth century and before. It is crucial, however, to document and discuss their wardrobes as far as is possible. A large proportion of the population of Britain, where this engraving was produced, would have worn such clothes and their study can tell us so much not only about the lives of its wearers, but the development and influences of dress more broadly. This image depicts a "scavenger," employed by local governments to clean city streets. This dirty, backbreaking work resulted in disheveled clothes but, as this image shows us, there were recognizably fashionable elements that could be seen on male suits in all levels of society.

....

In essence, there are very few differences between this working-class man's coat and that of his wealthier counterpart: as we can see from the image below, both even sport similar gilt buttons placed at either side of the center back vent.

Hats were worn by all classes. This battered example is similar to the "John Bull" top hat, identifiable by its shallow crown and curved brim.

Busby, "Rabbit-man", 1820, The New York Public Library

Ensemble, c.1820, American, Metropolitan Museum of Art

Accessories would commonly have included some kind of necktie or handkerchief around the neck, worn more for warmth than for fashion.

The tails of this working man's coat are rough and truncated, suggesting that they were probably cut back to make manual work easier.

Trousers were largely associated with the lower classes at the start of the nineteenth century, worn mostly by sailors for protection and ease of movement on deck. From the late eighteenth century, men like this scavenger would have worn cotton breeches with a linen shirt, smock, cotton waistcoat, and woolen jacket.[30] Stockings would normally have been worn with the breeches, and we can see them bunched around the wearer's ankles in this example. Trousers became fashionable day wear by about 1810, but it was not until the mid-late 1820s that ankle-length styles became standard for most working men—as seen in this image above by the same artist.

Tailcoat, pantaloons, and waistcoat,

c.1825–30, Los Angeles County Museum of Art, Los Angeles, California

◆

This suit provides a perfect illustration of the dandified Regency gentleman, with high collar, padded and gathered shoulders, nipped-in waist, and slim, sculpted legs. Every part of the ensemble is expertly crafted to portray elegance, composure, and taste. In the 1820s the dandy was associated with elegance above all else, but by 1830 perceptions were starting to shift, partly thanks to Balzac's essay, *Traité de la vie élégante*, which was published that year. In it, he put forward the idea that dandyism was a "heresy of the elegant life," a dandy nothing but "boudoir furniture, an extremely ingenious mannequin."[31]

During the 1820s and 30s coat collars were wide and tall, often stiffened with buckram to hold their shape.

These sleeves, known as "gigot" ("leg of mutton") are gathered at the shoulder to create a small puff at the head, leading into an elongated sleeve that bunches up the arm to increase volume. Combined with the tall collar, this contributes to a broadness and emphasis of the top of the torso: we can see the V-shaped silhouette emerging, which is still associated with ideals of masculinity in fashion. At the same time, the exaggeratedly high "fall" collar, coupled with gathered sleeves, high waistline, and frothy shirt frills, bears similarities to the fashionable female silhouette. The effect is noticeable in this 1824 fashion plate.

Plate from Costumes Parisiens, private collection

These silk crepe **pantaloons** are almost skin-tight, closely emulating the alabaster smoothness of classical statues. Unless a man had a perfect physique, however, this choice of legwear was not necessarily the most flattering, and during the first twenty years of the century some men resorted to padding to achieve the desired muscular silhouette. Along with the much-lampooned practice of male corsetry, this caricature from 1819 depicts a fashionable young man with cushions of padding tied to his thighs.

Anon, *Laceing [sic] a Dandy*, January 26, 1819, Metropolitan Museum of Art

Stocks were shaped bands made from horsehair or buckram and covered with silk, satin, or velvet. They were fashionable after about 1822, popularized by George IV. It has been suggested that the King's influence in neckwear stemmed from his interest in military uniforms, which traditionally featured stocks as part of their full dress.[32] This example is covered in a light buff pleated silk, finished with a starched and pleated bow.

The smooth line of this coat is partly achieved by a lack of pockets at the front of the garment. At the back, two rectangular flaps appear on either side of the vent (most likely sham or blind), but a new innovation is also found: concealed pockets in the skirt lining.[33] Not large and not hugely practical, they are a prime example of fashion over utility.

When fastened, these close-set vertical rows of buttons heighten the illusion of a small waist. This is also aided by internal padding at chest level, which, along with the shirt ruffles, contributes to the "pigeon-breasted" effect.

The pantaloons in this example display the fashionable "fall front" fastening very clearly. The technique simply involved cutting a flap, typically around 5 to 8 inches wide, across the front of the breeches or pantaloons.[34] This would be fastened to the waistband or underlying fabric with buttons. A similar technique was sometimes seen on women's bodices (particularly in the earlier part of the century) known as a "fall" or "bib" front and on skirts as an "apron front."

Linen trousers, 1830s, USA, Shippensburg University Fashion Archives & Museum, Pennsylvania

Tartan suit,

1830, National Museums Scotland, Edinburgh

◆

This striking suit illustrates contemporary trends in cut and design, but its bold tartan adds an important regional element. It presents another dimension for the Scottish man in history: not a kilt ensemble, and not a dark tailcoat with lighter trousers, as was fashionable elsewhere—but something that skillfully and colorfully combines the two. In doing so, this suit makes a vibrant national statement and gives an insight to the life and clothes of style-conscious men living far from London. It also, importantly, illustrates the revival of tartan in Scotland at around this time, part of the "Highlandism" that saw tartan and tartanry resume a status it had not enjoyed since the 1746 Disarming Act. This law prohibited its use in an attempt to avoid political tensions after the Jacobite Risings, removing the right to wear national dress or tartan, or to view it as a "national symbol" of Scotland. Although the Act was repealed in 1782, it would take another thirty years before interest was stoked by neo-Romantic and Gothic sensibility and aesthetic. [35]

The waistcoat worn with this suit features a standing collar, which was starting to fall from fashion by about 1830.

So far in this chapter we have seen coat lapels made with M and V notches; this example shows a square notch with horizontal groove. Such details are less obvious amidst the busyness of the fabric, but have been no less expertly rendered.

Metal buttons were popularized by Beau Brummell's ubiquitous dark blue coat with brass buttons, and remained relatively plain and undecorated until the 1820s. They can be a useful way of dating a garment, and those used on this coat and waistcoat are beautiful examples of the gilt buttons (brass covered with a wash of gold) that were first manufactured around 1790. [36] They featured hand-chased or machine-molded decoration by the date of this suit. They were made by Hammond Turner and Dickinson of Birmingham, established in the eighteenth century and known as Hammond Turner and Sons by the 1820s. [37]

The cloth is cut diagonally; not, as *The Highland Light Infantry Chronicle* put it in 1906, "as now with the stripes running up and down." [38] The design is matched with lengths of fringe at each side seam, a common decorative touch.

When thinking of traditional Scottish dress, the kilt is probably the main garment that springs to mind. However, trousers or trews date back as far as the sixteenth century as a practical alternative to the kilt in winter months. Tartan trews were famously worn by the Rothsay and Caithness Fencibles regiment, a controversial choice but one that their Colonel strongly endorsed, and to whom this poem is attributed:

> Let others brag of philibeg,
> Of kilt, and belted plaid
> Whilst we the ancient trews will wear,
> In which our fathers bled. [39]

Sleeve gathers are not as voluminous here as on the previous example, but there is still a noticeable accentuation at the shoulders.

Man's Hunting Jacket, Scotland, 1825–1830, Los Angeles County Museum of Art

This tartan coat is a tail coat, and the example above is a riding jacket made for fox hunting. The tail coat originated from earlier riding styles, but developed to feature a straight horizontal cut across the waist. This coat is cut with similarly curved fronts, suggesting a garment that combined active as well as formal wear.

The distinctive tartan of this suit is the Royal Stuart (or Stewart) variant, one of the best-known and worn by the Scots Guards and members of the Royal Family; King George V. reputedly referred to it as "my personal tartan." [40]

Ensemble of silk tailcoat and waistcoat, natural linen trousers and black silk stock,

c.1833, Metropolitan Museum of Art, New York, New York

By the 1830s men's dress coats were frequently made in black, but, as one newspaper stated in September 1831, they could also be made in "blue or dark green" and remain fashionable and respectable.[41] This deep sapphire coat, accentuated with highly fashionable black velvet collar, is paired with high-waisted "Cossack" trousers. These were a brief but interesting trend that gave men broad hips and slim lower legs. Despite this new emphasis, the only change in construction was, *The Art of Cutting Breeches* wrote in 1833, that trousers were "fulled, or pleated on, all across the fronts; being cut 4 or 6 inches extra on each side." Aside from this, they were "formed the same way as any other Trowsers [sic]," making them both a fashionable and accessible option.[42]

The shirt is accessorized with a stiff black silk stock, fastened with hooks or buckles at the back of the neck. The example shown here is reminiscent of the "Joinville" style, a flat bow with the ends tucked away.[43]

The body and tails of this coat are cut separately. This allowed for a longer, tighter fit around the torso, drawing the eye to a small waist and close-fitting sleeve cuffs.

Fashion plate, c.1830s, private collection

These flax trousers are a good example of the **Cossack** style that was fashionable from c.1814 to 1850 (and known simply as "pleated trousers" by the date of this suit). Derived from uniforms of the Russian cavalry and from an English visit by the Czar in 1814, this style was a significant change from the plain-fronted trousers that prevailed.[44] Fabric is gathered into pleats at the waist to create fullness at the hips, but then tapers off significantly towards the ankles.[45] The volume created by the pleats produced a fullness akin to that of women's skirts, and was frequently satirized in the press.

On the back waistband are two braces' buttons, a common addition by the early 1830s.

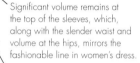

This detail shows a quilted section from inside the front of the coat. It gave the wearer the desired padding and shape to accentuate or mimic a toned, masculine figure. Coats were sometimes padded in other areas too, depending on the individual needs of the wearer. As one fashion column suggested in 1830: "If the person be small about the hips the skirts should be wadded."[46]

Significant volume remains at the top of the sleeves, which, along with the slender waist and volume at the hips, mirrors the fashionable line in women's dress.

This single-breasted waistcoat is cut to waist level, with a slightly discernible point at center front. After c.1825 this would become more marked.[47]

Like men's drawers (underwear) in the 1830s and 40s, pantaloon legs usually featured eyelets for tape ties, which, as *The Workwoman's Guide* (1840) explained, "draws them to the proper sizes" according to the wearer's shape and preference.[48]

Silk dress, c.1831–35, Metropolitan Museum of Art

These buttoned straps were sometimes known as "anchor" straps, so called because they anchored the trouser legs to the foot, fastening under the boot or shoe. The rather dramatic arch is there to ensure the fabric is held taut without creasing. There were difficulties involved with wearing such straps, however, including that of hygiene and mobility. The press was quick to offer remedies but also to highlight sartorial absurdities of this technique. *The South Australian Register* quoted a young boy in 1845:

"Pa, why do you wear straps?"
"To keep my trowsers down, John."
"Pa, why do you wear braces?"
"To keep my trowsers up, John."
"Well, pa, that is funny."[49]

Tail coat, trousers, and waistcoat,

1840, England; 1845, Scotland; Los Angeles County Museum of Art, Los Angeles, California

◆

As will be shown in the next example, by the 1840s frock coats were rapidly gaining popularity for all kinds of daywear. Tail coats or cutaways were still worn, however, and those shown here are a good example of the details that characterize the style during this decade.

Both these examples show medium-sized bow ties in white and cream. By the end of the decade, darker colors would be more fashionable.

The sleeves are cut in what would sometimes have been termed "easy": fluidly following the natural line of the arm down to the wrist.

To achieve the snug fit of this coat (ideally, the front two waist buttons should not meet), a new development was made in the late 1830s. It involved inserting an extra panel from below the armhole to the waist seam, a piece known as a **sidebody**.[50]

These trousers show a slightly wider, looser fit, which emerged around the middle of the decade. Front fly closures with buttons were common by 1840.

A tailor's guide from 1848 describes the construction of a dress coat, corresponding closely to the designs seen here. The author describes the collar in some detail, highlighting the importance of the lapels being "necessarily long, because of the length of the waist . . . and should be broad and square at the top to correspond with the front of the collar, and they ought to lie over down almost to the lowest button-hole."[51] Subsequent generations would look back on this style as ridiculous—in 1872 *The West End Gazette* commented that 1830s and 40s coats' collars were of an "interminable length" and the garment itself "very heavy"—as well as costly to produce: "For making a coat in 1840 . . . the wages were 21s. per week, but the work being so heavy it was found that men could not earn the wages paid."[52] Comments like this, made in reference to tailoring strikes, are important reminders of the social cost of fashion over the course of history.

This distinctive collar gives the impression of fabric rolling high at the back of the neck, and "standing away" as it continues around to the front. Known as a "horse's collar," it represents a notable development in the cut and design of 1840s dress coats. The smooth shape is probably achieved by pad stitching on the bias-cut under-collar: sewing (in effect, quilting) a stiff hair canvas lining to the outer fabric (similar finishes are achieved in contemporary tailoring by using fusable interfacing).[53]

Man's Vest, England, c.1845, Los Angeles County Museum of Art

This velvet waistcoat would have provided warmth at a time when it was fashionable for the coat to be left open. Its central point, nipped-in waist, and padded chest contribute to the ideal male silhouette. The collar is cut in a style known as a "roll": rolled over in a curve and without the interruption of a notch. Bright, flamboyant patterning complements the rest of the suit and adds a flash of color to the outfit, with buttons covered in self fabric (which, by 1850, were starting to exceed the popularity of metal, glass, and jeweled buttons).[54]

Both pairs of shoes represent a dominant style in the mid-years of the century: very low heels with a low tie fastening. Patent leather, introduced in the 1790s for footwear, was very popular for men's formal day shoes.[55]

Man's shoes, c.1848, Metropolitan Museum of Art

Frock coat ensemble,

1840, United Kingdom, Powerhouse Museum, Sydney

◆

Until the end of the century, the long-waisted, short-skirted frock coat was the main form of "formal" urban day wear. It was usually made in black, though dark blue was also popular and is shown in this example. The outfit corresponds to a description of "walking dress" in an Australian newspaper from November 1840, which describes a "frock coat, double-breasted . . . sleeves tight and waist rather long; the skirts fit tight round the person."[56]

Black cravats, particularly those made from silk, were replacing white muslin by the early 1840s. The example here is knotted and may have been held in place with a pin. The shirt collar is still worn high and not yet turned down over the cravat.

Simple horizontal stripes adorn this waistcoat. It is double-breasted with wide notched lapels, a particularly common choice for morning wear. Sometimes, lapels would be held back and fastened in place with a separate button at the corners. Until about 1845, waistcoats could be tightened and shaped to the body by tape ties at the back—as in this British example from the Metropolitan Museum of Art.

Frock coats were usually double breasted and nearly always worn open, as seen here. The coat is long-waisted, and skirts finish just above the knee. By the middle of the decade, they had extended to below the knee.

Until around the middle of the decade, trousers were cut narrow on the lower leg, and still often held close to the ankle by an instep strap.

Throughout the 1820s and later, "tall" hats often had noticeably curved crowns at the top, along with a curved brim. Though those features are very slightly in evidence here, they would disappear entirely as the decade progressed, leaving a flat edge to the crown.

Fashion plate, c.1840s, private collection
The coat's skirts are level all around, as illustrated in this fashion plate from 1843. The gentleman facing us in this image wears a similar waistcoat to that in the ensemble shown, made from a light cloth with a large "shawl" collar. This fashion plate also demonstrates the popularity of wearing trousers in a different shade to the coat and waistcoat, seen in the soft gray example on this page.

Sleeves are close-fitting and of a similar width all the way down the arm. As the decade progressed, sleeve cuffs would lengthen to cover the wrist.

"Small" or "whole" fall fastenings (using a central flap and two or more buttons) were common up to the early 1840s when, as seen already in this chapter, the fly front closure was becoming increasingly popular.[57]

Black wool ensemble and cotton and linen checked suit,

c.1850 and c.1845, Museum at the Fashion Institute of Technology, New York, New York

◆

This pair of suits, from 1850 and 1845 respectively, provide a good illustration of the ways in which men could inject some color and texture into their wardrobe. They show two common styles, the **tail coat** and the **frock coat**, that were worn daily during this period. After the padded shoulders and generally rounder, softer feel of the early nineteenth century, both illustrate a far straighter and sleeker silhouette.

With lower shirt collars came the demand for a lower and narrower necktie (a term used, along with cravat, to describe many kinds of neckwear in the middle of the century). The bow knot, as seen here, was amongst the most popular, and could be purchased loose or ready-tied. Black silk was a fashionable choice, but preferences varied across America and Europe, and in some locations a necktie's color could denote social class or political affiliations.[58]

This black tail coat would have been common day wear for the urban man until around 1855. We can tell that this is a day rather than an evening variant, as the waist is cut straight across just above the hips, and the tails are square rather than rounded. This longer body required extra seams to shape and fit the coat under the arms and around the waist, making it a more complex piece of tailoring than previous higher-waisted styles.

It was usual for coats to be left open at the front, partly so that the colorful waistcoat beneath could be appreciated. Sometimes, coats were purposefully cut so that the fronts would not meet and fasten. Tartan designs were made popular first by Sir Walter Scott and, by the time of this waistcoat's production, by Queen Victoria's part-time residence at Balmoral Castle in Scotland.[59] Tartan and check was also fashionable in women's and children's wear, and the fabric of a waistcoat would often match popular dress styles of the era (as this 1860 example shows).

Checks and plaids first made an appearance in fashionable wear around 1845–50, and would remain in style for much of the century. This frock coat, waistcoat, and trousers all utilize the same pattern, in a manner known as a **ditto**.

A single chest pocket is placed on the left-hand side. Two others would often be placed at the hips or, as here, concealed in the pleats of the skirt.

Back view of a similar frock coat, c.1845, from the collection of the Los Angeles County Museum of Art.

Before 1850 it was common for waistcoats to be cut straight across, and to match the coat in length and in the cut and style of lapels.

By the 1840s, frock coat skirts were cut relatively full and flared, and usually finished at thigh level. The image above of a similar coat, c.1845, shows a back view of the long waist and short skirt.

Child's ensemble, c.1860, Metropolitan Museum of Art

Trousers like these, in a checked design and/or light fawn color, were also a popular choice when worn without a matching coat and waistcoat (or even, as in this 1847 fashion plate, with a waistcoat and coat of a contrasting pattern or color).

Fashion plate, 'Paris Modes', Germany, c.1840s, private collection

Frock coat and trousers,

c.1852, Northern Ireland, Los Angeles County Museum of Art, Los Angeles, California
◆

The frock coat in this ensemble is similar in shape to that seen in the previous example. However, certain details set it apart as a significantly different look, especially its use of black, a somber choice that would become so representative of menswear in the mid-late nineteenth century. This example is also a good illustration of the most popular accessories for men in this period: top hat, walking cane, and watch fob.

Similar to the previous examples, this suit's necktie is fastened in a broad, flat bow. This was probably the most common method of tying, along with another variant: the very slim shoe-tie, which could also be tied in a bow or with a simple knot that fell into loose ends. Both options are illustrated in these contemporary photograph details, which also demonstrate that black was by no means the only color choice available. Like waistcoats, neckties offered a chance to add some vibrancy to a suit.

Men wearing shoe-ties, c.1850s–70s, USA, private collection

This waistcoat, dating to 1846, features a blue and white interlocking pattern similar to the kind of stylized, bordered fronds seen in seventeenth-century embroidery and blackwork.

Panel of blackwork, linen and silk thread, c.1580–1620, Metropolitan Museum of Art.

It features a shawl collar (popular since the 1820s) and finishes at waist level, just covering the trouser waistband.

Sleeves are relatively broad, attached to a higher armhole than in the previous decade.

Frock coats were now starting to replace the tail or dress coat (seen in the previous example) as the usual daily wear for men. Contemporary newspapers and magazines extoled its various advantages, which included practical as well as aesthetic—as the *Sydney Morning Herald* pointed out in 1851, "The frock is better . . . than the evening or dress coat; as when buttoned up it protects that valuable part of a man, the chest, and also is a complete garment."[60] The photograph below, of a similar date, shows this effect, private collection.

By 1850, trousers were no longer made with an understrap. They finished at the ankle or just below and were cut in a fairly straight, tubular line. Sometimes—as seen here—there could be a slight widening towards the ankles.

"L'Elégant," *Journal des Tailleurs,*

October 1, 1854, Anonymous, Rijksmuseum, Amsterdam

—

By the mid nineteenth-century, fashion plates had become increasingly detailed depictions of not just clothing, but fashionable society. Though idealized, they nonetheless provide useful information regarding the aspirations of middle and upper class men and women (aspirations being a key word, since nineteenth-century plates were made to forecast fashion, not to document current trends). Often they depict different styles worn in realistic scenarios, and this detail from an 1854 plate shows three gentlemen in a domestic setting. The central figure, holding a calling card, is presumably being visited by the other two, who wear evening dress and fashionable daywear. He wears smoking attire, which, though a leisurely outfit worn in the privacy of the home, still corresponds to the basic premise of a suit: coat, trousers, and shirt worn with a necktie.

This short smoking jacket from the 1860s (Metropolitan Museum of Art) is very similar in cut and trimming to the one shown on the central figure.

A pork pie cap with tassel was a common accessory to the smoking jacket. As shown in the later smoking "suit" example in this book, Turkish and vaguely "middle eastern" inspired styles were incredibly popular for smoking and private home wear. Turkish tobacco and smoking practices were influential and widely discussed in men's publications of the day.

This overcoat closely matches the description of a similar fur-lined example held by the Victoria & Albert Museum. With a date attribution of 1850–90, it covers the same period and is described as being "fully lined with wolf-skin . . . fastened with olivets . . . and rows of frogging made from a heavy black braid." The coat shown here does not seem as excessive in its use of fur (according to the museum, 32 pelts were used to line their coat), but corresponds to the fashion for Russian-style, fur-trimmed evening topcoats.[64] The photograph to the right shows a longer coat with very similar fur collar and frogged fastenings, illustrating the range of variants available.

Photograph, c.1860-70, USA, private collection

Judging by its waisted fit and moderately full skirts, this seems to be a frock overcoat, cut along the same lines but longer than an ordinary frock. *The Habits of Good Society* (1859) declared that "The frock-coat, or black cut-away, with a white waistcoat in summer, is the best dress for making calls in."[61]

The tailcoat or "dress" coat would have been worn for evening and formal occasions. Until c.1860, it was fashionable and acceptable to find evening coats made in a variety of colors other than black; most commonly, dark blue, brown, or green. A short, square-cut waist or cut-in helps to identify this as a fashionable style c.1850–70.[62]

Single-breasted, white waistcoats with long lapels were usual for formal evening wear.

Fly-front fastenings had almost completely replaced fall-front trouser closures by the 1850s. *The Gentleman's Book of Etiquette and Manual of Politeness* of 1860 commented, "all" evening trousers should be made from "black cloth" only.[63]

Trousers are close-fitting and taper toward the ankle, held in place by a strap under the shoe. These instep straps were becoming less and less popular (or necessary) after c.1850.

Both men and women could wear colored, decorative slippers in the privacy of the home.

USA, private collection

During the decade, trousers could be patterned in a bewildering variety of designs. These sport a thin, zig-zag stripe and a band of contrasting color along the side seam. Some designs could be outlandish as Punch remarked in 1854: "Those stupid stripes down your trowsers, what do they mean? Must you be marked all over like a giraffe? Need you be scored about with broad gashes like a leg of pork?"[65] This last example probably refers to "Exhibition" checks, which were thick and bold and coincided with the Crystal Palace "great exhibition" of 1851. The trend existed in a more modest way into the 1860s and 70s, as seen in the checked stripe of the trousers in the photograph to the left.[66]

Chapter 4
1860–1899

While it is unrealistic to imagine that all men everywhere only wore black, the acceptable color palette was certainly more limited at this point than it had been for the first half of the century. The rising professional middle classes seemed to embrace a centuries-old association with black for certain professions, which perhaps made this an inevitable choice for the evolving and expanding world of work in the nineteenth century. As John Harvey observes, however, it was also during this period that a proper discourse opened up around the notion that this may not be a positive or healthy thing.[1]

Nonetheless, this fifty-year span was responsible for a pivotal shift in the male wardrobe by forming the basis for modern leisure wear. This developed in the 1860s with the so-called lounge or "sack" suit (as it was known in America), a looser and lighter-colored move away from the rigid, uniform, black-and-white world of professional and formal suits. Simultaneously, the growing market for ready-to-wear clothing made such options available for middle and even lower-class customers.

However, it would take time before the matching three-piece lounge suit was completely accepted as urban daytime wear, and the word "gradual" is a crucial one to bear in mind when studying nineteenth-century menswear, as overall, nothing happened quickly. In the words of an 1867 article from *The Queen*, "Men's fashions are, perhaps, not quite so conspicuous in their variations as are those of women; but the changes, like the gradual upheaval of certain portions of the earth's surface, though slow, are sure."[2] Such slow pace can make this period an especially difficult one to date, so examples have been chosen that highlight not only large and significant changes, but those less discernible details that often need to be relied upon to form a comprehensive overview.

Commercial and industrial developments in the second half of the nineteenth century had a direct influence on the way people valued their clothes. As Philippe Perrot pointed out in his seminal *Fashioning the Bourgeoise* (1981), the second-hand clothing trade, made up of "frippers," "old-clothes merchants," and "wardrobe dealers" began to decline from the 1860s onwards as affordable ready-to-wear options became more and more accessible and affordable.[3] In urban areas at least (provincial towns and villages remained reliant on reusing and recycling clothes), second-hand clothing started to become associated with poverty and the fear of disease. Henry Mayhew's 1861 description of an old man in a cheap lodging-house illustrates the typical clothing of London's very poor:

> His clothes were black and shiny at every fold with grease, and his coarse shirt was so brown with long wearing, that it was only with close inspection you could see that it had once been a checked one; on his feet he had a pair of lady's side-laced boots, the toes of which had been cut off so that he might get them on . . . To this day the figure of the man haunts me.[4]

RIGHT
A poor family in their
Sunday best, mid
nineteenth-century.
Note the multiple
patches on the
man's knees, USA,
private collection.

The Times reported in 1865 that suits intended for re-sale had to be "tutored and transformed" by "clobbers," "revivers," and "translators," the last of whom had the job of converting one garment into another: "the skirts of a cast-off coat, being the least worn part, make capital waistcoats and tunics for children . . . It is a touching sight to see the class of persons who frequent the markets, and turn over the seedy black garments that are doing their best to put on a good appearance."[5] For those more fortunate, ready-to-wear suits were convenient, attractive, and something of a novelty. For the rich, garment purchasing pre-ready-to-wear required great expense and patience; for the poor, the question was not so much one of purchasing, but of mending and re-mending until clothes fell apart.[6]

Fashion etiquette for both men and women was strict and exacting, but men especially were faced with conflicting advice. A British manual from 1860 suggested that gentlemen should "follow fashion as far as is necessary to avoid eccentricity or oddity in your costume,

but avoid the extreme of the prevailing *mode*."[7] The author of an American guide from the same year wrote: "I unhesitatingly counsel you to dress *in the fashion*." In addition, men were advised that there were "shades of being 'dressed;' and a man is called 'little dressed,' 'well dressed,' and 'much dressed,' not according to the quantity but the quality of his coverings."[8] Cecil B. Hartley's well-known *Book of Etiquette and Manual of Politeness* (1860) explained that to be "little dressed" meant to wear unfashionable clothes, "having no pretensions to elegance, artistic beauty, or ornament," or to wear "lounging clothes on occasions which demand some amount of precision." To be "much dressed" was to be "in the extreme of the fashion, with . . . a touch of extravagance and gaiety in your colors." Hartley continues to explain that wearing bright colors—even a pair of yellow gloves—and "brand new clothes" on a regular basis equated to "bad dressing." To be well-dressed, then, was to achieve a happy medium between the two, and to attain the elusive "good taste," which, Hartley cautioned, was rare.[9]

In addition, many magazines and etiquette guides espoused the aesthetic benefits of black. In 1863 *The American Gentleman's Guide to Politeness and Fashion* remarked that "It is a very high compliment to any man to tell him that black becomes him, and it is probably owing to this property that black is chosen."[10] However, it was crucial for men to remain fashionable without betraying any interest in the subject. Women's bright colors gave them license to talk and read about dress (in place of work) incessantly, and indeed this was often expected. For men, it could be difficult to obtain clear and concise information regarding what was in fashion, or knowledge surrounding the best choices to make. Clearly, sartorial regulations for men were just as complex as those for women, and perhaps more so given their inconsistency and ambiguity.

Nevertheless, in April 1867 one San Francisco newspaper declared that although men, "owing to the great duties and responsibilities which devolve upon them," had little time for fashions and "the frivolities of life," many of them actually still wished to obtain "fashion intelligence." The reporter tried without success to buy printed periodicals that went into the same level of detail as their feminine counterparts, and so "decided to visit some of the fashionable establishments of the city where they keep gentleman's clothing . . . to see what there was to be learned there about fashion." What he found was that staff were generally enthusiastic and knowledgeable, able to advise about all aspects of clothing, from hats to shoes, and this enabled him to sum up just some of his findings on April's most fashionable and accessible offerings:

> A gentleman having golden hair, pretty blue eyes, and delicate features, would look perfectly charming in a suit of purple, with the Bismarck sack, or the New York business coat, or the Nabob . . . A gentleman with dark hair and eyes, and delicate features, dressed in a black and white Scotch plaid walking-sack . . . and wearing a light drab Croquet, would be made up exquisitely.[11]

RIGHT
A good illustration
of a mid-nineteenth
century morning coat,
which would eventually
come to replace
the frock, Glasgow,
private collection.

This article was found amongst others of a similar tone, and reaffirms several things: first, men were not disinterested in fashion in the late nineteenth century—"fashions are followed," one article put it, "just as slavishly as those of women"—and this was not the reason they so persistently wore black.[12] Secondly, sartorial expertise for men was available, if slightly covert. Thirdly, and perhaps most importantly, on many occasions the burgeoning ready-to-wear industry and department store greatly assisted men in their fashion choices, offering knowledgeable advice and service.

Although the "department store," classified as a single shop split into separate departments, has been in existence since the early eighteenth century, the store as we understand it today—a large enterprise bringing multiple buyers and products together— was more formally established in the 1850s and 60s. During the timespan of this chapter, stores such as Brooks Brothers and Bergdorf Goodman (both in New York), Marshall Field's in Chicago, Simpson's in Canada, Liberty's and Selfridge's of London, and Australia's David Jones were all created. Described by one historian as "a bourgeois celebration"[13] that was a visible symbol of a changing world, the department store's accessibility and sociability changed the way people shopped and, therefore, the way they selected their clothes. Whether a man was choosing his own clothing or his wife or mother was shopping for him, the availability of suits, outerwear, and accessories all in one place enabled him to create individual looks more easily. At the very least, it allowed him to create variations on a theme.

Some rather innovative styles were championed in the 1870s, amongst them the "angle-fronted" morning coat, an example of which is discussed in this chapter. It was also known as the "University" style because of its popularity with students, and while not worn by the majority of men, it illustrates the sometimes complex and surprising ideas that did develop in nineteenth century menswear. It was also an important player in the development of sports and leisure wear, serving as inspiration for the later blazer, and sometimes worn for sporting activities. An edition of *The West End Gazette of Gentleman's Fashions* described the coat in June 1870 as "the most novel style of coat which has been introduced this season. The peculiarity of this style consists of it being double-breasted and forming an angle in front . . . One disadvantage . . . is that it requires to be buttoned, otherwise there is a superabundance of material in front."[14] Because of this, the article continues, it would probably not be "generally adopted this summer; still it supplies what some customers require, a novelty in style." The introduction of a coat that was complicated in cut, requiring great skill and exactitude on the part of the tailor, inevitably made it a somewhat elite garment. Nonetheless, it helps to demonstrate that innovation in menswear had certainly not stalled since the eighteenth century.

An apparently simpler example of this can be seen in 1871 with first full button-front shirt for men, registered by British shirtmakers Brown, Davis & Co.[15] Known as "The Figurative Shirt," this revolutionary design made great strides in achieving a close and comfortable fit. By the 1890s men's clothing in general had become more tailored and fitted, seen in the two neat business suits of this chapter. Jackets were normally worn fully buttoned and typically made in black or gray cotton, wool, or flannel. Men's fondness for very high, starched white collars in the final years of the century led to the phrase "white collar worker," used initially to describe those who worked non-manual jobs. During the twentieth century it expanded to denote anyone who was employed in an office or other administrative role. By the end of the nineteenth century the white collar (and, frequently, cuffs) was therefore an important distinction, working with the three-piece suit to identify a professional and "respectable" man. The impracticality of clean white collar and cuffs obviously made them eminently unsuitable for manual labor, and this was the key reason that working-class men commonly chose shirts made in blues, greens, and browns.

Because of this emphasis on collars and cuffs, much analysis relating to shirts in this chapter will focus on those elements, as well as the shirt fronts associated with evening wear. Showing too much of the rest of the shirt was, by the middle of the century, considered improper for daywear: so, in most of the analyses in this chapter, it cannot be seen as part of the ensemble. However, a lack of visibility did not of course mean that shirts had ceased to be important in a man's wardrobe. More and more styles were commercially available by the 1860s, and tailors were keen to draft new patterns and innovations that made the fashionable close-fitting shirt more comfortable and easier to produce.[16] Some wives still preferred to make their husband's shirts, however, and a letter sent in to an Australian newspaper in 1874 comically depicts the challenges involved with this approach:

> My wife . . . concluded that she would make all my shirts, as bought shirts were not reliable . . . she made me a dozen shirts which were a little over two inches wide round the neck. I saw the shadow of disappointment cloud the radiant countenance of my wife, and . . . I told her it didn't matter; I preferred wide shirts . . . A second set of shirts wore out, before I had noticed what was going on, a third was made. Of the same size. So were the fifth, sixth . . . Is my case hopeless?[17]

The letter ends with this plea after even shop-bought shirts, purchased in desperation, failed to provide the appropriate fit. "I haven't been down to the shop yet," the writer finishes, "I can't trust my feelings, which you may understand after reading my experience." This demonstrates the care and thought invested by men in their shirts; as a foundation garment they were pivotal to the way a man felt in the rest of his clothes.

The closing years of the century also saw a (very) faint squeak of radicalism and reform in menswear, partly fueled by a broader anxiety surrounding the fin-de-siècle ("end of century"). The aesthetic and dress reform movements did not only concern women: small numbers of men, too, began to campaign for a different sartorial future, and the fashions of history were often cited as attractive influences. Oscar Wilde was one of the best-known and most prolific advocates for the cause, and he experimented with various historically inspired garments to ascertain their suitability. Viewing the second quarter of the seventeenth century as the time when English dress was "both useful and beautiful," he declared that the slitted sides of seventeenth-century jackets or doublets "exemplified what are always the true principles of dress . . . freedom and adaptability to circumstances."[18]

The idea of flexibility and of being able to use clothing as protection as well as display were at the forefront of his ambition. However, as with the female rational dress movement,

LEFT
Napoleon Sarony,
Oscar Wilde in
aesthetic dress,
1882, Metropolitan
Museum of Art

only a very small number of men seriously considered Wilde's propositions. It would not be until the late 1920s that the first official attempt was established in the form of the British Men's Dress Reform Party, which advocated particularly to banish the collar and tie. They also aimed to increase the variety on offer for men, although by the end of the 1920s some significant steps had already been made.

This chapter will address a broad spectrum of clothing in an attempt to display the very real, and frequently very noticeable, changes in menswear during this fifty-year period. It will pave the way for a discussion of the early twentieth century, a time when—after a brief Edwardian hiatus—the war would put an abrupt halt to all that felt stable about fashion, consigning the nineteenth century to the dim and distant past. As Fleur Forsyte observes to her father Soames in *The Forsyte Saga*, "I'm glad you don't consider yourself a Victorian; I don't like them. They wore too many clothes."[19]

Suit (sack jacket, waistcoat and trousers),

1865–70, Britain, Metropolitan Museum of Art, New York, New York

◆

This square-cut coat hung loosely from the shoulders and offered a markedly different option to the pervasive frock coat. Initially adopted for informal leisure wear, the **sack suit** (or "sac") became acceptable professional and city attire, and by the end of the 1860s most men would have owned one. It was common for trousers to be made in a contrasting fabric; however, each component of this three-piece suit is made from the same buff wool with silk binding, making it a "ditto suit" or a "set of dittoes," as seen in the previous chapter.

Wide lapels are an indicator of late 1860s/ early 1870s coats and jackets. Those seen here, in contrast to the narrower cut of the earlier style below, suggest that the suit was made closer to 1870 than 1865.

Sack coats were usually single-breasted and, as was common for the 1860s, this example features three buttons and buttonholes. It was fashionable for only the top button to be fastened.

The left breast pocket is slanted to allow easy access for the right hand.

We can just about see a watch chain, tucked through the top buttonhole of the waistcoat and draped across the chest. This was usually the only accessory a man would wear, as too much jewelry was considered a mark of bad taste.

There is no waist seam, allowing the coat to hang straight down from the shoulders without breaking up the torso.[20]

The coat's hem is only hip length, but could extend as far as the fingertips. By the end of the decade, however, it would be made no longer than the example here.

Cecil B. Hartley's claim that "light clothes are generally placed above dark ones" here extends to gloves. This tan leather pair would have been considered, in Hartley's words, "more esteemed than dark ones." However, no gloves were preferable to ones that appeared old and worn. Despite the almost bewildering set of rules regarding when to wear gloves and how to wear or hold them, he finished by recommending that "There is nothing to be ashamed of in bare hands, if they are clean."[21]

These trousers are relatively loose fitting at the hips, but taper towards the ankles. Their close fit from the knees downwards is another indicator that the suit was made towards the end of the 1865–70 date range.

Summer sack suit, c.1860s, USA, private collection

This summer sack coat is very long, suggesting a date of the early 1860s, but embodying similar features such as a very high-buttoning neck, loose fit, and braiding in a contrasting shade. The bottom front edges of this coat are curved, while in the Metropolitan Museum example, the corners are straight. Both cuts were popular throughout the decade.

Le Musée des Tailleurs illustré,

1869, Nr. 7 : Journal donnant les Modes de Paris, Rijksmuseum, Amsterdam, on loan from the M.A. Ghering-van Ierlant Collection

◆

This Parisian fashion magazine, founded in 1860, illustrated a wide range of fashionable styles for men and women, with input from professional tailors. It aimed to give the reader information regarding "civil, military and religious clothes" and is representative of a new phase in fashion illustration. As Breward has noted, by the 1870s fashion plates did not merely provide "propaganda," but sought to "underpin, massage and reflect the modern experience of the reader."[22] The consumption of clothes is therefore celebrated in journals such as this, and *Le Musée des Tailleurs illustré*'s engravings showed groupings of men, women, and children in different scenarios, including department stores and fashionable salons.

Light gray top hats became fashionable in the late 1860s, worn (along with brown) for daywear, with black starting to be reserved for the evening.

Both figures wear **morning coats**, identifiable by their waist seams and slightly sloping fronts. The example to the left reveals a very small section of the bottom of the waistcoat when fastened, and is a precursor to the more exaggerated cut of the so-called University coat. In August 1868, the *Gazette of Fashion* described a similar coat as "single-breasted . . . there are four holes and buttons at front, a narrow top to the lapel, and the end of the collar small and much sloped off. The waist not long, and the general appearance of the back, quiet and medium as to style. The skirt is short, and cut well forward on the leg. Full sleeve, with a narrow round cuff."[23] Elsewhere the volume describes the popularity of "double rows of stitching" on the cuffs, also seen here.

This figure wears a "bollinger" or "hemispherical" felt hat, introduced in the late 1850s and originally worn by cab drivers. Similar in shape to a bowler, it has a narrow brim and, not unlike a pith helmet, a round knob in the center top.[26]

From the 1840s onwards, an extra buttonhole in the lapel was sometimes specifically made to hold a flower. Usually, though, the top buttonhole was reserved for the purpose, sometimes made with extra reinforcement.[27]

From the late 1850s it became fashionable to wear a morning coat as part of a 'ditto' suit, with each piece made from the same fabric. Here, the waistcoat does not match, but the checked tweed fabric of the coat and trousers indicate a more informal style.

The shirts shown here indicate the large range of collar styles available during the 1860s. By the end of the decade the turned-down variety, seen on the figure to the right, appeared frequently. The image below, probably taken in the 1870s, shows a man wearing this style with bow tie similarly tucked underneath (New York Public Library).

These long trousers were termed "French bottoms," with trouser hems extending over the foot (described helpfully by a tailor in 1847 as being "hollowed over the front, and cut down from the heel on the under side").[24] According to the *West-End Gazette of Gentleman's Fashions* in June 1872, French-bottom trousers were by then out of fashion in London, but "we hear that in many of the large provincial towns they are still in general demand."[25] As with many fashions, the trend no doubt remained popular for far longer than fashion plates might suggest: in another edition of the *Gazette* from September 1873, for example, the correct method for cutting them was still being discussed. A rather exaggerated style can be seen in this photograph taken in Cleveland, Ohio, c.1860–70, private collection.

In both these pairs of trousers we can see varying degree of tightness down the leg; at the start of the decade it was still fashionable for trousers to be cut relatively full at the seat and thighs. From c.1865 on, the style seen here (sometimes fitting even more closely to the leg) was fashionable.

Wedding suit,

1869, North Carolina Museum of History, Raleigh, North Carolina

◆

By the 1860s the tail coat, which had loomed so large in men's fashion since the eighteenth century, was relegated to evening wear or weddings. The suit shown here bears the hallmarks of "full" dress, meaning that the wedding it was worn for almost certainly took place in the evening. An American journal from the late 1850s advised that, should the wedding take place in the evening, "a very elegant costume is a dark claret dress-coat, white ribbed-silk, or moiré antique waistcoat, black trowsers, silk stockings, and shoes." For a morning ceremony, the groom should consider: "a deep-brown frock-coat; waistcoat of black cashmere, with a small violet-colored palm-leaf figure; neck-tie of silk . . . trowsers of delicate drab, or stone-color; gloves of primrose, or slate-colored kid."[28] The substantial difference in these descriptions shows how important the sombre tone of evening dress was, and the example shown adheres even more stringently to the confines of full dress—which, as another etiquette guide declared, should consist of "A black coat and trowsers . . . the white or black vest is equally proper."[29] Given this similarity, both evening and wedding styles will be discussed here, since this suit would probably have doubled as evening dress after the wedding.

By the 1860s the cravat had become a narrow strip of white material, tied in a very wide, flat bow.

The collar is relatively low, with the fronts turned over to form wings: obligatory for evening wear.

Long lapels give a slim, streamlined effect.

Evening coats were not usually buttoned, revealing much of the white or cream waistcoat beneath. Waistcoats were normally single-breasted for evening wear and made from plain or figured silk (the latter seen here). Patterns would almost always be white-on-white.

Left: waistcoat detail, NCMH. Right: miser's purse, 1840–60, Metropolitan Museum of Art.

These covered buttons on each side of the coat fronts are purely decorative.

It was not only collars that were detachable during this period: dress shirt cuffs could also be bought and laundered separately to increase their longevity. It was usual for cuffs to show around an inch below the coat sleeve. They would often be fastened with decorative cufflinks.

The silk waistcoat features the motif of a hand holding a miser's purse. In use since the eighteenth century, these became especially popular in the nineteenth, and were carried by both men and women. Made from a long, usually knitted tube with tasseled ends, they had a slit in the center into which coins could be dropped, with two metal rings sliding across to close. This allowed the user to designate different denominations to different ends, making it easy to select the right amount. At the same time it was not a speedy process to retrieve the money, leading to the association of "miser."[30] In this design, coins are seen dripping out of each end, perhaps a symbol of the groom's wealth or as a play on the more usual marriage symbol of a cornucopia, a horn-shaped receptacle containing an abundance of produce and, therefore, wealth.

Evening pumps, rather than enclosed shoes, continued to be popular for evening wear.

Shirt ruffles had vanished by the 1860s after many years of prominence in evening wear. They were replaced by plain, starched fronts or "dickeys," originally known as a detachable bosom. These helped to avoid wrinkles and maintain a pristine smoothness, with the only decoration provided by frilled or pleated edges (seen in the example above) and/or, as here, decorative studs.[31]

Linen evening shirt, c.1860, Metropolitan Museum of Art, New York

Wool twill suit,

c.1860–70, Los Angeles County Museum of Art, Los Angeles, California

◆

Now known universally as a "lounge suit," this style has progressed from, but still retains features of, the earlier sack. It also shows a good example of the patterned fabrics that became popular during the 1860s, sometimes used only on waistcoats but sometimes, as seen here, on the entire suit. This example has been given a timeframe of ten years, but we can date it fairly closely to the end of the 1860s by focusing on a few key features.

Plaid or **tartan** fabrics became incredibly popular for suits and individual items of menswear in the 1860s and 70s. This pattern corresponds to Scottish designs such as the "Black Watch," but those specifically from the Scottish Borders were equally popular. In 1872 the *West End Gazette* remarked that "a great many shepherd's plaid trousers . . . are now worn . . . we observed more . . . on well-dressed gentlemen than we have seen for some years." This was a denser design of small light and dark checks, typically made from untreated sheep's wool.[32]

This small flapped pocket above the right-hand side, around half the width of the one below, was known as a **ticket pocket**. Originally used for storing small change, it became useful for—as its name suggests—storing train tickets when railway travel boomed.

Unlike earlier lounge jackets of the 1850s and 60s, this later example retains a waist seam and vent, meaning that it creates a closer, more structured fit, but still gives an impression of leisure and easy wearing. This effect is particularly heightened when combined with the soft, turned-down collar and tie seen here.

It was common for only the top button of these single-breasted jackets to be fastened, allowing a view of the (usually matching) waistcoat and watch chain beneath. This image, taken a little later in the period, shows a lounge jacket being worn in the same way.

Cabinet photo, c.1870s, private collection

The suit is accessorized here with a silk top hat, but it was more common to wear soft woolen felted bowlers with lounge and "transitional" lounge styles.

The curved cutaway edges to the front of the jacket are very distinctive of the 1860s and 70s. Towards and into the 1900s, it was fashionable for a straight front to be featured.

These trousers fit fairly closely to the leg. A pressed crease along both the front and back of the trouser leg was common.

"University" morning jacket ensemble,

c.1873–75, England, Victoria & Albert Museum, London

◆

This version of the morning coat was also known as an "angle fronted" jacket due to its obtuse angled fronts, which are cut away towards the hips in a similar manner to the "traditional" morning coat seen in the following example. Worn for sport and leisure as well as more formal occasions, this style is a precursor to the **blazer**, which would become fashionable for recreational wear in the 1890s. The University style enjoyed considerable popularity, described by the *Gentleman's Magazine of Fashion* in 1871 as "the leading garment of the day."[33]

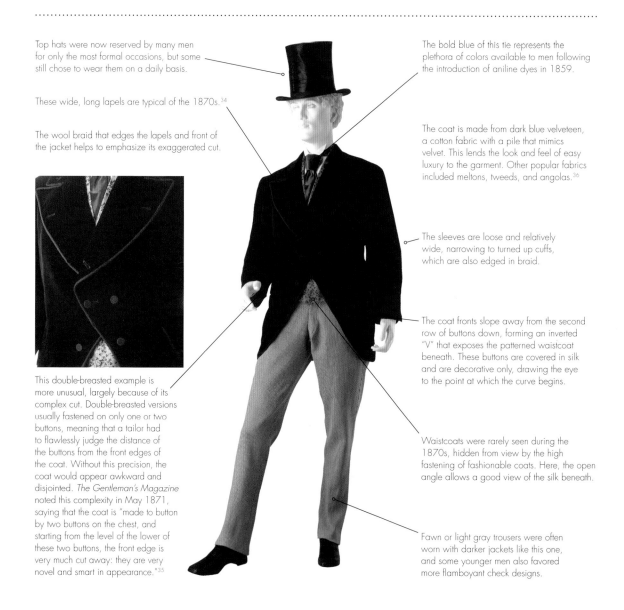

Top hats were now reserved by many men for only the most formal occasions, but some still chose to wear them on a daily basis.

These wide, long lapels are typical of the 1870s.[34]

The wool braid that edges the lapels and front of the jacket helps to emphasize its exaggerated cut.

This double-breasted example is more unusual, largely because of its complex cut. Double-breasted versions usually fastened on only one or two buttons, meaning that a tailor had to flawlessly judge the distance of the buttons from the front edges of the coat. Without this precision, the coat would appear awkward and disjointed. *The Gentleman's Magazine* noted this complexity in May 1871, saying that the coat is "made to button by two buttons on the chest, and starting from the level of the lower of these two buttons, the front edge is very much cut away: they are very novel and smart in appearance."[35]

The bold blue of this tie represents the plethora of colors available to men following the introduction of aniline dyes in 1859.

The coat is made from dark blue velveteen, a cotton fabric with a pile that mimics velvet. This lends the look and feel of easy luxury to the garment. Other popular fabrics included meltons, tweeds, and angolas.[36]

The sleeves are loose and relatively wide, narrowing to turned up cuffs, which are also edged in braid.

The coat fronts slope away from the second row of buttons down, forming an inverted "V" that exposes the patterned waistcoat beneath. These buttons are covered in silk and are decorative only, drawing the eye to the point at which the curve begins.

Waistcoats were rarely seen during the 1870s, hidden from view by the high fastening of fashionable coats. Here, the open angle allows a good view of the silk beneath.

Fawn or light gray trousers were often worn with darker jackets like this one, and some younger men also favored more flamboyant check designs.

Morning suit,

1880, Los Angeles County Museum of Art, Los Angeles, California

◆

The 1880s marked a somewhat transitional period for the elegant morning coat, originally worn by gentlemen as a riding coat. It was worn from c.1850 as formal wear, and by the end of the century had replaced the frock, worn for business and semi-formal as well as the most formal occasions. The example shown here illustrates a few differences in cut from that which would follow in the 1890s–1910s.

The coat is cut with simple V-notch lapels to match those of the waistcoat beneath.

Trousers, coat, and waistcoat were now usually all made from the same, or very similar fabric, nearly always black or dark gray. Waistcoats were mostly single-breasted, as shown here, with the only flash of diversion being a gold watch-fob.

Flapped pockets are set into a low waist seam. They are edged with black braid to match the rest of the coat.

Front edges are cut away in a gently sloping line towards the rear, the most recognizable aspect of the morning coat. Their rounded sides meet, and sit snugly over, the wearer's hips. Two covered decorative buttons top the tails at the back of the waist seam.

Due to the high buttoning of the coat and waistcoat, not much of this dove gray **cravat** can be seen.

This style was unique in retaining a top left breast pocket, an element that would disappear in morning coats during the last decade of the century.[37]

The 1880s morning coat featured three to five buttons placed high on the chest, starting just below the lapels and ending above (or at) waist level. On most occasions, only one or two (often those in the middle) would be fastened.

By the 1880s, the morning coat had replaced the frock or tail as appropriate attire for a groom. Note the similarity between the morning coat to the left and this wedding suit from 1885, Philadelphia Museum of Art.

Trousers taper very slightly toward the ankle, but in the main were cut fairly straight. The example here show a hint of a crease down the front of each leg, but this would not be common until the 1890s.

Seersucker suit,

c.1880s, RISD Museum, Providence, Rhode Island

◆

This three-piece "ditto" suit has a nautical feel about it, which is appropriate since it was made as lightweight summer leisure wear. It was owned and worn by James Adams Woolson, a leather merchant from Boston who, as the museum puts it, had an "understanding of fine textiles and materials" that was honed throughout his career. The impeccable cut and finish of this ensemble illustrates that knowledge and perfectionism.[38]

The suit is made from **seersucker**, a thin, lightweight linen or cotton fabric with Indian origins. The word comes from a Hindi corruption of the Persian phrase "shir shaker," meaning "milk and sugar." The puckered texture of this fabric, with a surface both smooth and rough, illustrates this description.

The result of the weaving technique used, known as slack-tension, meant that the fabric had a striped effect, and different colors could be applied (although gray/white and blue/white were by far the most common).[39] At the time of this suit's manufacture, stripes were especially popular in men's leisure wear.

Seersucker contributed important developments to the ease and accessibility of fashion—for example, due to its wrinkled appearance, it did not need pressing. It was also a cheap option, and therefore a popular fabric for ready-to-wear, mass-produced suits that could be finished in the simplest ways possible. This suit differs in that respect, due to its owner's knowledge and style, and features matching covered buttons and impeccably finished seams. This last detail was also often seen when a suit was made specifically for wear in hot countries. In colonial India, for example, the seersucker suit was popular for its heat dissipation and would have been made without a lining. British men living in India at this time—of relative wealth and status—would have had their suits made with flawless seams, a detail which would show more clearly without a lining.[40]

Various features mark this out as a lounge jacket, in particular the curved fronts, high revers, and lack of a waist seam.

Carte de visite, c.1880s, Philadelphia, private collection
Although the "ditto" seersucker suit was very popular, men did not have to choose a matching coat, waistcoat, and trousers in this fabric. This photograph, from around the same timeframe, shows a seersucker coat and waistcoat with plain black trousers.

Metropolitan Museum of Art, New York

The suit shown here is on trend for the 1880s in terms of cut, but the use of seersucker in menswear was by no means new in the late nineteenth century. The image to the left shows a blue and white seersucker summer coat, c.1795–99, made at another point in fashion history where stripes for men were popular.

Trousers are cut straight and wide to allow ease of movement.

Smoking suit,

1880s, Los Angeles County Museum of Art, Los Angeles, California

◆

The smoking suit—like the banyan before it—would only have been worn in the privacy of the home, in smoking rooms that men could retire to after dinner (nineteenth-century etiquette required them not to smoke in front of women). Outside the home, such suits were worn in environments like gentleman's clubs and railway sleeping cars. Similar in concept to a woman's relaxed tea gown, a smoking suit was looser in fit, and made from velvets, silks, and satins in a variety of colors—very different from the ever-encroaching black of daywear. Decoration could come in various forms, but military-inspired braiding and frogged closures (as seen on this example) were especially popular.

Towards the end of the century, discussions started to appear in fashion literature surrounding "smoking jackets" for women. "The term 'smoking jacket,'" said one Australian newspaper in January 1890, "does not strictly imply a garment supplied for comfort during indulgence in tobacco. It is rather a generic title for lounging dress, just as the tea-gown is."[41] At around this time it started to become fashionable for women's tea gowns to feature masculine influences such as the trimming, fabric, and detailing seen on a smoking or ornate dressing gown, and that is probably what this article refers to. An example is seen here in this c.1885 dressing gown from the Metropolitan Museum of Art.

The trousers shown here were made to be worn with the jacket, but the two parts did not always have to match: smoking jackets were also worn with day or evening trousers of a different shade, particularly from the very late nineteenth century onwards.

There is a thin line of braid, matching that on the jacket, on the outer edge of each trouser leg.

Slippers like these would usually have been made by a man's wife, daughters, or other female members of his family. **Berlin work** was a form of tent or cross-stitch embroidery, better known now as needlepoint. Master of the craft Mary Linwood wrote in the early nineteenth century that Berlin "wool" work was like "painting with a needle . . . the sister art of painting . . . the aim to produce as true a picture of nature as possible."[42]

Slippers, Europe or USA, 1850-1900, Los Angeles County Museum of Art

Smoking caps, often worn with a suit to complete the ensemble and to protect the hair from smoke, frequently took their inspiration from Near and Middle Eastern styles, however vague those might sometimes be.[43] This is seen especially in the elaborate silk knotted tassels dangling from the center of the crown of this cap, and the intricate glass bead work on each panel. Given this decoration and its red color, this example is not unlike a Turkish fez, which was also brimless and sat close to the head, its characteristic ornamentation being a single tassel in the center.

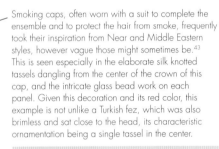

Alexandre Gabriel Decamps, *Turkish Guardsmen*, 1841, J. Paul Getty Museum

There is an undeniably problematic side to this appropriation of so-called "oriental" style. At the time it was deemed largely inappropriate as daywear, and only small hints of braiding or Indian-inspired prints, such as this c.1860–69 paisley waistcoat, for example, would be seen outside the privacy of the home.[44]

Vest, 1860–69, America, Metropolitan Museum of Art

Fashionable gentlemen in suits,

1890 (detail), GraphicaArtis/Getty Images

◆

These two suits (sometimes termed a "business" suit, although this phrase would not be commonly used until the early twentieth century) epitomize what most respectable, professional middle-class men were wearing by the last decade of the century: a three-piece ensemble derived from the sack style, comprising jacket, waistcoat, and trousers, with a white shirt and necktie. Since the late eighteenth century, wool had become a marker of the leisured classes, and now it remained as a practical and fashionable option, suitable for town and work wear as well as sports.

The jacket's top button now sits much lower, while that of the waistcoat beneath is higher. This means that a relatively large section of the waistcoat is visible below the shirt collar and necktie, a design change that gave some men the opportunity to experiment with bright and patterned fabrics for their waistcoats. For others, this experimentation stretched to neckwear only, as seen here.

The 1890s "re-design" of the frock coat (encouraged by Edward VII) was not universally accepted. Although it presented a more casual image, worn open or loosely fastened in front with linked buttons, it was fast becoming a garment associated with older and more conservative men. This suit illustrates what younger men favored: shorter jackets that could be fastened from top to bottom, front creases in trousers, and an altogether slimmer silhouette than the frock provided.[45] Popular newspapers and magazines of the period were quick to mock those younger men who still wore their frock coats: one short story, published in 1898, told of a young man whose hand-me-down frock was his pride and joy—his "one solace," giving him "recovered self respect." One day on meeting a group of acquaintances (dressed much like the example shown here) he accompanies them home with the intention of joining them for an evening out. However, the frock coat makes this impossible, and the young man instead stays at home to chat with his friend's old father, casting a rather pathetic figure in contrast to the professional, comparatively simple suits of his companions.[46]

Very tall, straight, starched collars were popular in the 1890s and into the turn of the century, reaching up to two and a half inches in height. Their appearance became so prevalent amongst working men that the term "white collar" (still in use today) came to be understood as a common reference for the professional middle-class man. A similar high, starched collar and tie can be seen in this portrait, c.1890s, Germany, private collection.

Sleeves are slender and taper toward the wrist. They are simply constructed of two pieces, with no curvature. White cuffs are visible below the jacket sleeves and would have been a common sight in the 1890s when white shirts were by far the most appropriate choice for daily attire.

Portrait photograph, c.1890s, private collection
This similarly dated image illustrates the realities of the different ways such a suit could be worn and accessorized. It shows a young man in a three-piece lounge suit, worn in a more casual manner and featuring trousers with a slight flare at the ankle.

Fancy dress ensemble in eighteenth-century style: Coat, breeches, and waistcoat, possibly American,

c.1870–99, Philadelphia Museum of Art, Pennsylvania

Fancy dress balls and parties became incredibly popular amongst the upper classes in the late nineteenth century. They coincided with a particularly strong theatrical trend for historically themed plays during the 1880s and 90s, both of revivals—such as Sheridan's *School for Scandal*—and historical melodramas written by contemporary playwrights, like Clyde Fitch's *Beau Brummell*, set in Regency London. The popularity of such plays, which often directly influenced the fancy dress costumes of the aristocracy, could have been partly down to the malaise of the fin-de-siècle (literally translating as "end of century"), a state of mind prompted by the fear of a new era in a time of already fast-paced social change. Basking in "historical escapism" also allowed less cerebral enjoyment for party-goers, who especially favored eighteenth-century costume because, for men, it gave permission to indulge their ancestral peacock fantasies. As a historically inspired costume that incorporates many other influences, it offers a unique opportunity to "read" a variety of styles.

The shoulders of this coat are far squarer than the soft, rounded slope of the eighteenth century.

These glass buttons, cut to look like crystals, line the fronts of the coat, the cuffs and waistcoat pocket flaps. They would have added to the shine and sparkle as the wearer moved in a candlelit ballroom, but are not especially representative of the eighteenth century.[47]

These wide cuffs and relatively short sleeves are similar to those seen on coats in the 1740s and 50s, before the longer, tighter, often cuff-less styles of the last half of the century became popular.

One of the surest giveaways that this is not an antique eighteenth-century suit is its bright magenta coloring. Until the development of synthetic dyes in the 1860s, such vibrant shades of pink would not have been achievable.

Fancy dress "advice" manuals from the late nineteenth century, such as Arden Holt's 1890s *Fancy Dresses Described; Or, What to Wear at Fancy Balls* offers a wide range of outfit choices deemed "Georgian." Styles are mainly named for fictional characters such as Sheridan's Charles Surface or Dick Turpin, both familiar and popular figures from the stage. These suggest either pastel silks with embroidery and an elaborate wig, or deep-colored velvet worn with a tricorne hat. Descriptions are relatively short on details, however: Charles Surface is, Holt declares, "always a most elaborate costume, the coat, waistcoat, and breeches made of light satin, and richly embroidered in gold and silver." With such guidance, a customer could choose almost any type of embellishment that caught his eye, whether it was "historically accurate" or not.[48]

This scrolling gold trim on the coat fronts is made from metallic *picot*, a flat, narrow decorative braid with looped edging. It is arranged in a series of loops in a vague appropriation of various influences, including European folk art.

Detail, fancy dress waistcoat, c.1870–99, Philadelphia Museum of Art

These turquoise scrolls are reminiscent of Greek and Chinese meander designs, edged with metallic gold trim that forms a scalloped fan shape along the front edges of the waistcoat and pocket flaps.

Man in an 18th century suit, c.1890s, New York, author's collection

This suit is an example of the common nineteenth-century practice of wearing antique clothing, including for fancy dress balls. Unfortunately, many existing eighteenth century suits and dresses in museum collections have been extensively altered and even damaged due to the practice. This photograph, taken in a New York studio, shows a man posing in his grandfather's suit. In this instance it does not appear to have been altered significantly, and is a nice example of the shape that this fancy dress costume is attempting to recreate.

Man's Waistcoat, Italy or France, c.1730, Los Angeles County Museum of Art

While the cut of the coat, with its fronts slightly sloping away, recalls the slim line of the 1770s and 80s, the waistcoat presents a mish-mash of eighteenth century trends. Its straight square edges, almost meeting in the center, are most akin to the cut of the earliest years of the century, although these were usually made with a slight curve and often finished at least at mid-thigh. The pocket positioning is closest to waistcoat fashions post-c.1760s, when flaps were placed nearer to the edges.

Chapter 5
1900–1939

"Black no longer satisfies the gay masculine butterflies," wrote the *Los Angeles Herald* in December 1905. "Men . . . are beginning to adopt clothing of a bright color and vivid patterns . . . Efforts to relieve the somberness of men's clothing have been especially directed toward the production of stylish fancy vests, and particular attention has been paid to buttons."[1] This article was one of many that gently encouraged a return to some degree of "fine plumage" at the turn of the century, as one women's fashion column put it. "One feels sure," the author wrote, "men will be warmly encouraged by our sex if they do break away from the conventional suit of solemn black."[2]

RIGHT
A young man c.1908,
USA, private collection

Six years after this piece was written, most men would be forced out of their somber black and into the khaki of the trenches. Nineteenth and early twentieth-century menswear is often regarded as a "uniform," so it could be said that men were merely swapping one for another when they adopted their khaki in 1914–18. Of course, this change cut much deeper, and, for many infantry, uniform came to epitomize the relentlessness and drudgery of training and then of war itself. Soldiers later remembered the feeling of being identical to every other man in their regiment through prescribed behavior, rigid timetables, and, significantly, indistinguishable uniform.

RIGHT
The window of
men's clothing store,
"P&Q," USA, 1919,
private collection

This chapter begins by examining some key styles from the turn of the twentieth century, which saw a new sartorial leader emerge in Queen Victoria's successor, her son Edward VII. He was not a young man when he took the throne, but along with wife Alexandra he was aware of the personal and political importance of fashion. British weekly magazine *Tit-Bits* declared in 1905 that "he is, by universal consent the best dressed man in his own dominions, and . . . has introduced more changes in the fashion of men's dress than any of his predecessors on the throne."[3] He is generally credited with the introduction of the countrified "Norfolk" suit, featuring a distinctive belted coat with deep pleats across front and back.

Several examples in this chapter will be dedicated to emerging leisure and sportswear, including the Norfolk suit, a golfing jacket with knickerbockers, a flannel "outing suit," and a bicycling outfit. Though some of these cut a different silhouette to what has previously been seen, they were nonetheless "suits" and would have been widely classified as such at the time. In recent years, more discussion has emerged surrounding the meaning of "masculinity" and "manliness" during the nineteenth century, particularly in its closing decades. Sports were a key player in this change of perception, as men were encouraged to join teams and associations as part of their leisure culture away from the domestic realm. For boys and young men in particular, sporting activity was seen as healthy, purifying and—crucially—as a way of diverting potentially deviant sexual energy. It was also no longer the province of the upper classes: middle class men increasingly used sports as a way of organizing their time, and as a way of casually associating with other men.

The clothing used for sports like football, rugby, and hockey "offered up the male body," as Varda Burstyn describes it, "to the male as well as the female gaze in ritual display and entertainment."[4] This book does not explore sporting uniforms of that type, but an understanding of their effect is useful when considering sports and leisure wear that corresponded more closely to the everyday "suit," and in particular the sporting and leisure styles described above.

Edward VII also helped to popularize the tailless evening coat known as the dinner jacket (in America, the tuxedo) in the 1880s while he was Prince of Wales (a period lasting from 1841 to 1901, when he took the throne). This was a hugely significant move away from a dress code that had dominated for an entire century, presenting "full dress" options that had never existed previously. "The dress-suit of to-day has never taken my fancy to any particular extent," wrote *To-Day* magazine in 1895. "you get a ball or banquet in a sea of black and white." The writer lamented that the only plausible alternative, a smoking jacket, was mainly worn at house-parties only, and, even then, "the inevitable swallow-tail ousted it."[5] The short, sharp dinner jacket presented a comparatively easy-wearing and casual new option, and it has since risen to become, paradoxically, the most formal garment that most men will ever wear. Edward's son George V did not exert the same influence, but the First World War (which

started four years after his coronation) halted any dramatic strides that may have taken place in men's fashion.

Up until this point, the dissemination of fashion information had developed considerably, as hand-colored fashion engravings were set aside in favor of full-color printing.[6] This led to the publication of fashion photographs in newspapers and magazines, allowing both women and men to learn about the latest established and burgeoning trends. It helped to further encourage a democratization of fashion, and after the war this enabled men to reacquaint themselves with civilian clothing and to keep up with new expectations. Returning to "civvy street" in 1918 meant fitting in with a radically altered society and stepping back into professional life on the back of a seismic shift.

For the many men who had enlisted in their teens, this meant deciding for the first time what work they wanted or were capable of doing. "In the trenches you know," *The Forsyte Saga's* Michael Mont dryly reminisces, "I used to dream of the Stock Exchange, snug and warm and just noisy enough."[7] The turn-of-the-century stock exchange conjures up images of a secure professional life, of dark frock coats and a gray respectability, no doubt a comforting dream for a solider in the nightmare of the front line. Before the war, entering the professional sphere also signified another rung on the ladder towards adulthood, coming as it did with a new set of clothes. From the ages of around four or five young boys were still "breeched" at the turn of the twentieth century, which meant swapping short dresses with trousers or knickerbockers, shirt, and coat. Essentially, this wardrobe altered little for the rest of a man's life, but once in the workplace his suit had to signify the level of his professionalism as well as his class. A plain black or gray three-piece lounge suit with immaculate collar and tie, plus newly popular bowler hat, became an almost universal symbol of what it meant to be a man, and cutaway coats with striped trousers were a popular city look.

As Nina Edwards astutely observes, the First World War is not a period we immediately think of in relation to sartorial care and details. However, "the pains people were prepared to go to for a stolen moment of luxurious indulgence," she says, "or perhaps just to retain some small aspect of home life, suggests that such pleasures were valued by the individual."[8] Years in the same uniform must have engendered an interest in colors, textures, and tailoring novelties for even the most aesthetically nonchalant man. We can see this tendency when examining the realities of how men felt about their "demob" suits at the end of World War Two: either a delight at being able to wear something new, or a disappointment that the garments were generally dark blues, browns, and grays in color.

The 1920s is frequently referred to as the "roaring twenties" and "the jazz age," a happy-go-lucky decade of recklessness and lax morals that, understandably, surfaced as a result of the anxiety and austerity of the war years. As one magazine commented in May 1919, there was a brief "reaction against drabness" in 1914, brought to an abrupt halt by "a world of drab and mud. And for nearly five years Art, Beauty, Joy, and Life have been things of no account."[9] However, as with any rose-tinted nostalgia, this perception is problematic, and the above quote more likely exemplifies a wish rather than a reality. The 1920s was certainly an era of comparative freedom and, for some, a time of optimism, excess, and experimentation. But for much of the world it was a time of continued poverty, discrimination, hardship, and inequality and, in some countries, colonial control. Given our knowledge of what would come in 1929 with the Wall Street crash, and the roots of fascism showing themselves across Europe, Carr and Hart's description of most people's experience as "a brief dance on the edge of a precipice" is poignantly appropriate.[10] Nevertheless, it is not an exaggeration to say that ideals of masculinity were irrevocably shaped during those ten years, influenced hugely by the manufactured appearance of film stars such as Rudolph Valentino and Douglas Fairbanks. The movie industry flourished in this atmosphere of burgeoning urbanization and consumerism, and fashion was inevitably influenced by such rapidly shifting worldviews. The drop waist and comparatively short skirt of female dress represented the greatest change, speaking to new notions of womanhood and equality.

Our popular image of corresponding menswear is, as Maria Costantino neatly summed up, embodied in a vision of "the young man casually and softly dressed in white flannel trousers, a white open-neck shirt, a brightly striped flannel blazer, and a straw boater."[11] While most women would adopt some form of the low-waisted sheath dress, the particular image evoked by Costantino's description is very specific to the upper classes. We have *The Great Gatsby*—especially its film representations—to blame for a perception of this aesthetic as widespread, although selected and distinct elements probably existed in the wardrobes of most urban men. Such soft, pink-and-white freshness also spoke to androgynous aspirations in fashion that existed for both men and women: a lean, svelte figure that prioritized youth above experience. This emphasis persisted for the rest of the twentieth century, with the pursuit of youth going hand in hand with that of less formal, more comfortable dressing. As *Vanity Fair* was keen to point out in 1922, "comfort" was certainly not synonymous with "carelessness," but if a happy medium could be met this was surely "the keynote of the modern man's wardrobe."[12] Such a combination expresses the increasingly fashionable aesthetic of the decade, a look that could potentially be achieved without the funds needed to commission made-to-measure clothing. Furthermore, small successes were celebrated by the Men's Dress Reform Party, introduced in the previous chapter. Whilst they recognized that striking changes to the formality of men's dress would not be seen for many years, they were able to acknowledge by 1921 that:

> Men have largely discarded long-sleeved, long-legged underwear both in summer and in winter; the once obligatory starched shirt and collar have collapsed before the soft varieties; high shoes have given place to low; and stiff derbies have yielded to soft hats or none at all.[13]

This chapter explores how these attitudes were expressed through menswear in the 1920s, showcasing the extreme silhouette of "Oxford bags" (which went on to influence trouser width more generally in the 1930s and 40s) and ordinary business wear and suits that retained the elite formality of the nineteenth century.

Youthful physiques continued into the following decade with a broad and tapered silhouette for men. Double breasted suits were especially popular as they emphasized the shoulders and chest, promoting an athletic "V"-shaped torso with slim waist and hips. Wide trouser legs hung from high waistlines, usually with deep pressed pleats down the front of each, and finished off with cuffed hems for more casual wear.

The basic proportions of this look have become exaggerated in the popular imagination, and this is largely thanks to the appropriation of the style by criminal groups and individuals such as Al Capone. The highly masculinized appearance of the fashionable 30s suit was ideal as an unspoken power symbol, creating a dominating presence that simultaneously aped

the dignity and respectability of the business suit. Semi-fictional gangsters such as Caesar Enrico Bandello (*Little Caesar*, 1930) and Tony Camonte (*Scarface: The Shame of the Nation*, 1932) helped to cement this association even further, although characterization was made most evident through the meticulous accessories sported by gangsters (interestingly, as Stella Bruzzi has pointed out, this attention to detail can be construed as overtly feminine[14]).

The similarity was not lost on society at large, though, and references to "gangster" style (often derogatory, when it was felt a particular individual had taken the look too far) abound in contemporary commentary. Meanwhile, this sharply masculine outline was being softened in sports and leisure wear. The sports jacket is referenced several times throughout this chapter, and a specific example is addressed in detail with an early 1930s "Palm Beach" style.

Throughout the early twentieth century, Chesterfield overcoats remained highly popular for their versatility. They could be made with either a single or double breast, a velvet collar or plain, varying numbers of outside pockets, a nipped-in waist or straight cut.[15] Ulster coats were worn to a lesser degree; more popular were raglan topcoats with a fly front fastening, rubberized cotton raincoats, and the relatively short-lived—but hugely popular—raccoon coat.

A favorite of Ivy League "soothsayers of fashion," as Deirdre Clemente termed Princeton students c.1910–1933, a genuine raccoon overcoat cost between $200 and $500—roughly equating to a staggering $7000 today.[16] "Since it takes from twenty to twenty-five skins for a coat of this kind, with prime skins selling at $18 apiece and the cutters demanding $100 a week, it is no wonder that prices are high," the *San Pedro Daily News* reported in January 1920.[17] Flamboyant, opulent and hard to miss in a crowd, these thick fur coats were the ultimate marker of wealth and style. They also remain unique in being the only fur coat, according to Harold Koda and Richard Martin, to be "ascribed fully to the modern male."[18]

As such the style is a perfect example of that aforementioned "brief dance on the edge of a precipice" that, for a lucky few, the 1920s represented. Paradoxically it also—within the already elite bubble of the university campus—offered a small peep of equality. In a world where the dividing line between black and white students ran deep, the wearing of a racoon coat "crossed and merged . . . racial and gender boundaries . . . to have similar relevance to each group within the collegiate context [showing] the pursuit of educational and personal progress."[19]

College style in general is an area worthy of mention during this period, since the universities unquestionably held significant sartorial sway. British influence is explored in this chapter with the example of Oxford Bags, a trend originating at Oxford University in the early 1920s. Various stories exist to explain how and why they became popular, and their reign was brief: but they arguably set the tone for the fashionably wide trousers that would dominate in the 1930s and 40s. In general, students at British universities wore

tailored garments and a certain level of uniformity was expected (explaining the outrage of a character in Waugh's *Brideshead Revisited* on finding the student protagonist wearing "an unhappy compromise between the correct wear for a theatrical party at Maidenhead and a glee-singing competition in a garden suburb."[20]) This approach was adapted by American college students at so-called "Ivy League" schools, including Princeton, Harvard, Yale, and Cornell, from the late nineteenth century onwards.

During the period under discussion, American students began to move away from the suit and embrace "odd" combinations such as a sports coat or blazer with flannel trousers (and frequently, no tie—even to class, where a certain level of formality had always been expected). Some universities became known for specific combinations of garments, which acted as a kind of uniform and badge of honor both on and off campus.[21] **Ivy League style** was to remain a significant influence on men's dress more widely throughout the United States, a strong marker of social prestige but also of the increasing demand for variety and flexibility.

Flannel outing suits, No. 9, The new Breakwater summer suit,

1900, The New York Public Library, New York, New York

◆

This flannel "breakwater" suit represents acceptable semi-formal wear at the turn of the twentieth century. The trade advertisement that originally accompanied the image made it clear how lucrative the summer clothing market was becoming: "We make with the greatest of care – the dressy summer man is the most particular of men. We want his trade; can't afford any shortcomings of fashion, fabric or making."[22]

A straw **boater** was the ultimate finish to any sporting or leisure outfit. Lightweight, affordable, and flattering to most men, it was suitable for use in active but gentle sport (e.g., boating and croquet) as well as a more passive, but highly fashionable, accessory. Its crown was usually encircled with ribbon in a shade matching the wearer's suit.[23] This sketch by Charles Dana Gibson, c.1901, shows a similar ensemble, worn at the beach and topped with a typical boater, private collection.

This striped shirt fits the "fancy" description ascribed to similar styles by *The World's News* (Sydney) in March 1903: "In warm-weather . . . most of the fancy shirts that remain on the market will be distinguished by stripes . . . [and will be] confined almost entirely to combinations of white with blue, brown, or black. Red . . . is declared to be growing more unpopular each year."[25] Here it is worn with a bow tie, the ends of which are tucked behind the turned-down collar.

The cut of this jacket is derived from the **reefer** (below), a double-breasted coat with wide lapels that had its origin in nautical attire. Later, it was appropriated by gentlemen for yachting, boating, and by those of an artistic and intellectual mindset. In its initial practical form, the garment was nearly always blue or black and relatively short, while this version has been given a leisurely lift with its distinctive stripes and hip length.

Flannel trousers would often be worn with a two-inch wide, light-colored belt.

Large, square patch pockets with rounded edges sit at each side of this jacket. Derived from nautical and military styles, they were practical and simple to construct and, on jackets like these, did not usually feature flaps or buttons.

Flannel, a brushed cotton or light woolen material, was the most common summer fabric, but one newspaper in 1896 sarcastically pointed out a drawback of the "flannel theory": "one of the surest and safest plans for keeping cool is to promote a moderate flow of perspiration. When you feel hot, tired, and thirsty this Summer, take a jug of iced water, and—throw it down the sink."[24]

The trousers are cut with a little slack, finishing loosely just below the ankle and ending in a deep turned-up cuff.

Man in a reefer jacket, c.1885–1910, Florida State Archives

Traveling suit,

c.1900–01, Sweden, Hallwyl Museum, Stockholm

◆

This three-piece suit was worn by its owner Walther von Hallwyl, a Swiss count who, on marrying into the influential Kempe family, later took Swedish citizenship. Along with his wife Wilhelmina and sometimes his daughter and son-in-law, Hallwyl travelled extensively across Egypt and Sudan at the beginning of the twentieth century.[26] This suit is an excellent example of a fashionable urban style reworked for the climate and conditions of North Africa.

By far, the item of clothing that most singles this out as a suit for foreign travel is the ubiquitous **pith helmet**, also known contemporaneously as a "sola topee" or "sun helmet."[27] Used first as a part of tropical military uniform, it was widely adopted by Europeans in India and in African countries to provide sun protection and quickly became a colonial symbol. Made from pith, a cork-like material, they did not provide much protection if horse riding, but were cool and light to wear and to transport. The veil provides extra sun protection to the face and back of the head.

Detail of von Hallwyl, wearing a very similar, if not the same, light-colored lounge or "sac" suit, 1890s, Hallwyl Museum.

For both men and women, lightweight woolen cheviot was a popular choice for travelling and summer clothes. In Perth, Western Australia, the summer months are hot and dry, reaching temperatures upwards of 40°C. *The Perth Daily News* remarked in 1902 that "The single-breasted sac suit in striped flannel, cheviot, or blue serge is the favorite for summer wear at present. The pockets should have flaps . . . the waistcoat shows a V above the jacket, if this is buttoned up."[28] This description, aside from the striped jacket and trousers, corresponds very closely to the cut of the suit seen here. The shirt and bow tie are striped, though in fairly restrained colors. As one newspaper mournfully pointed out in 1901, "stripes of yellow, green and red . . . have all passed out of fashion . . . the seeker for striking patterns is confronted by sober blue and white or pink and white stripes."[29]

Light-colored clothing has long been worn for summer and for travel in hot countries. *The Phrenological Magazine* claimed in 1881, "There is no doubt that white clothing retains the heat of the body for longer than dark clothing."[30]

This lounge suit, c.1910, was also owned by Walther von Hallwyl. The similarity in its cut and detailing shows how few concessions were made for travelling in a different culture and climate. It is a striking example of the complex and problematic approach of a colonial man on an exploration. Late nineteenth-century traveler Thomas Stinson Jarvis summed up the prevailing sartorial concerns, somewhat sarcastically, whilst in Lebanon in the 1870s: "I had but two suits with me . . . after considerable mending done in my own way . . . I thought at last that my appearance was intensely respectable . . . The wear and tear of riding and climbing, had created such devastation among the buttons so necessary to one's happiness and comfort, that we were constrained to sit on the divans and provide the necessaries for reuniting our garments. There is nothing more conducive to peace of mind than knowing that one's buttons are all right."[31]

Both of these suits display four buttons on the jacket, either left open or with only the top fastened, as was common for lounge suits. The rounded front corners of the jackets, too, mark this out as a typical turn-of-the-century lounge suit cut.

Summer whites,

c.1908–10, Atlantic City, New Jersey, Private Collection

◆

This photograph of a handsome couple was probably taken by "Dittrich Studios," one of the many photographers offering tintypes along the world-famous Boardwalk of Atlantic City. The man is appropriately dressed for a day at the beach: just as his companion wears her "whites" for summer, so does he, and the word "white" could apply to a broad range of light-colored fabrics.

He is wearing the conventional tall, stiff turn-down collar with rounded ends, which would have been made from celluloid and covered in linen.[32] Further examples of the style are seen in this advertisement from October 1910 (New York Public Library).

However, increasingly, other options were available. A 1910 edition of the semi-monthly *Men's Wear* catalog, produced for the clothing trade, described a "soft" collar made by "one of the interstate brands," which was "cut on lines which make a most comfortable summer collar without detracting from the style." It also advocated sporting variants, particularly the "Golfing," which featured a "low neckband in front at the place of buttoning . . . the spreading round points sit comfortably low, yet . . . preserve the dressy appearance so much sought."[33]

c.1908-10, private collection

This photograph, taken at around the same date, presents the stark contrast of a working-class couple in a combination of garments in similar color schemes, but there the likeness ends. It serves as a reminder of the quality of dress that much of the American population would have been wearing at this time, and the hardships they endured as part of the realities of daily life.

This is a lounge jacket with three outer pockets, three buttons at the front and with the slightly longer, wider lapels seen by around 1910.

A decorative **lapel pin** is worn on the coat. Though more associated with men's fashion, these could also be worn by women on blouses and bodices.

Until the early 1910s, it was usual for the waistcoat to be made in a lighter shade of fabric than the coat and trousers. By this date it was becoming common for the last one or two buttons of the waistcoat to be left undone; this man has not followed that example, but the two points at center front break up the waistline.

Peg-top trousers were a revival of a shape popular in the 1830s, cut wide at the hips and tapering to a close fit at the ankle. The cut became briefly fashionable again from around 1908, and while the example seen here is modest, such trousers could reach extreme proportions, especially amongst younger men and students. As one merchant tailor wearily remarked in 1910, "my trade consists mostly of . . . students. Of course [they] dress in the most extreme manner and want large chests and peg-top trousers that look like balloons, and these are the things that cause me a lot of trouble." He went on to describe that a major technical challenge lay in rendering the sought-after front creases into such wide trousers, because in those extreme cases, "the creases diverge outward at an angle of 45 degrees, more or less, from the bottom to the thigh."[34] Most peg-top styles would be creased at both the front and back of the legs, and would sometimes be cuffed (as here) on less formal occasions. [35]

Suit for cycling (full-length portrait of a young man),

c.1890–1910, Library of Congress, Washington DC

◆

With the development of cycling as sport in the late nineteenth century came new and ground-breaking garments. "Sportswear" was not only necessary, but also fashionable, and innovations could be dramatic—especially for women. The bloomer or bifurcated skirt costume quickly became notorious, illustrating the possibilities for the "new woman" and worrying men as much as it freed women. It is easy to overlook the developments in men's suits at this time, but significant strides were being made here, too, not least the increasing acceptability of sports clothing worn as ordinary daywear outside of the physical act of cycling. The outfit shown in this example is nevertheless still a "suit," and one that encompasses that notion of "practical elegance" promoted by the Prince of Wales in the late nineteenth century.

The collar is soft and turned down, worn with a tie knotted in a "four-in-hand" or "slip" knot, still common today. For sportswear it is likely that a ready-tied variety may have been worn; these had been available since close of the previous century and offered a quick, practical option.

The jacket shown here is representative of a single-breasted lounge or "sack" coat.

Cycling caps were advertised as a necessity, despite their complete lack of protection. The firm Arnold and Daniel of Philadelphia, declared in 1897 that "a Cycling Uniform is not complete without a Cap to match . . . [so] we have added a department to make same." Whilst riding, this young man would have worn a soft, flat example with a narrow brim, similar to that seen in the 1890s advertisement on this page.[36]

From the 1890s onwards, sporting suits seem to have been developed with an aim for flexibility. Usually consisting of an existing style of coat with specially made or ready-made "sports" trousers, the typical ensemble was something a man could potentially fashion from his existing wardrobe. A set of advertisements from 1897 describe various "combinations," including "bicycle and business" (a sack coat with "bicycle or golf" bloomers, also known as knickerbockers), a Norfolk jacket with "leggings," and "golf suits" (tweed sack-style coats worn with golfing bloomers). Social manners guide *Etiquette for All Occasions* (1901), stated that: "For cycling and general country sports, men wear knickerbocker suits of tweed, Norfolk or short jackets, heavy ribbed golf stockings, stout russet laced shoes and cloth caps."[37] Tweed is not shown here, but the flexibility and freedom provided by such an approach must have made the influence of a conservative etiquette guide increasingly obsolete.

This 1890s image shows how a similar jacket, knickerbocker, and socks combination could be worn with a more casual wool sweater (worn primarily to absorb perspiration), sometimes called a "bike sweater" and especially popular with boys and young men.[39]

New York Public Library

Advertisements of the 1890s–1910s displayed a wide array of shoes for the male cycling enthusiast, ranging from a brogue to a T-bar style, all with a fairly substantial heel as seen here. Boots were also worn, but, for obvious reasons, mainly in Britain and colder countries. A 1904 Australian newspaper regarded boots with stockings as "incongruous," and others held similar objections, but the debate seems to have been purely around aesthetics rather than practical concerns.[38]

The socks displayed here are plain, which was usual—but it was increasingly common to see colored, even garish, designs for sport (especially golf) which was a welcome change, adopted with much enthusiasm by many men. One newspaper even commented in 1909 that "Women are emulating men's love of gaudy socks by affecting stockings of colors as varied as the coat of Joseph."[40] Advances in high-speed knitting technology in the 1910s meant that such styles were far more readily available, but very long examples such as these (known as "stockings") were generally worn only for sport until the following decade. They would have been held up with garters worn on the calf.[41]

Norfolk jacket and trousers,

c.1910, Hallwyl Museum, Stockholm

◆

From c.1880 onwards, the **Norfolk** jacket, originally worn by the Rifle Corps in the 1859–60 Volunteer Movement, became popular for sportswear.[42] Its ascent was gradual, first adapted into the "Norfolk shirt" jacket in the 1860s and then, allegedly, getting its name from its popularity on the Duke of Norfolk's estate in the 1880s.[43] It has since become one of the most recognizable pieces of men's apparel from the mid-late nineteenth century, representative of the growing trend for leisure wear and as a welcome alternative to the all-pervading frock and lounge coats. Generally made from hardwearing, wool-based fabrics such as tweed, it was constructed with vertical box pleats at the sides and one at the back for ease of movement, and was held close to the body with a self-fabric belt. Although originally made for shooting (as seen here), it was also adopted for fishing, bicycling, and golf, and by the date of this Swedish example was dominating male sports and leisure clothing. In 1885, an American advertisement described "these new, inexpensive and exceedingly stylish jackets" as "suitable for general home wear, as well as for bicycling, lawn tennis and other out-of-door sports."[44]

This suit is made from brown cheviot, a fabric originally crafted of worsted wool from the Cheviot sheep. It is very hard-wearing, usually made as a twill weave with a dense, rough surface. For these reasons it is perfectly suited to country pursuits.

The number and style of pockets illustrate the many ways a Norfolk jacket could be modified according to its wearer's preferences. "So much, in fact, does it vary in its features," said the *Tailor & Cutter* in 1914, "that the term 'Norfolk' can almost be regarded as a misnomer."[45] This example shows four flapped pockets, making them a prominent feature. However, other coats from the same era were made with, for example, concealed breast pockets under the front pleats or straps (sometimes the box pleats were simulated), only two at the hips or, occasionally, no pockets at all.

In the 1950s, the Norfolk jacket made a comeback. The resurrection of very similar styles by certain high-profile figures such as Prince Philip, Duke of Edinburgh, led the American magazine *Gentry* to comment in 1953 that "Our fashion scouts have seen it worn in the country and at sporting events in recent months . . . Several custom tailors report that they are tailoring garments of this type at the request of individual clients."[46]

The Duke of Edinburgh with Princess Anne, c.1950s, GENTRY magazine (detail)

Tweed **flat caps** became an emblem of middle and upper class country sport and leisure pursuits, at the same time they continued to be worn daily by countless working class men and boys.

These buttons are made from cow or buffalo horn, a material introduced for the purpose from around 1812.[47]

The Norfolk's box pleats were sometimes made with openings that allowed the belt to pass through, leaving two strips of fabric covering it. Here, the reverse is shown, but both decorative options were popular.

The waistcoat beneath is single breasted, with seven buttons and three pockets.

Round, open cuffs were popular, though later examples sometimes featured a band at the wrist.

Norfolk jackets were very often worn with knickerbockers, particularly for golf, shooting, and walking. By the twentieth century it had become just as common to see them paired with trousers—usually in the same color and fabric, as seen here, but also made from flannel or knitted materials in differing shades.

"Full dress" evening suit,

1911, McCord Museum, Montreal

◆

At first glance this black-and-white ensemble may not seem vastly different from other examples of evening dress in this book, and in many respects it corresponds to the malaise that some men expressed about their eveningwear options prior to World War One. "The masculine dress suit," wrote a Californian newspaper in 1914, "is not beautiful, it is democratic . . . The vanity of male youth must express itself in socks or his ordinary attire. The democratic dress suit is sacred."[48] However, closer inspection reveals some small changes that, to early twentieth-century eyes, may have elevated both the attractiveness and the wearability of "full dress." As the Australian quote below demonstrates, some men did notice these changes and felt smart and satisfied in the current fashion.

"Evening dress is more becoming to the wearer than it was a few years ago," an Australian tailor declared in 1910. "The cut is smarter, the [figure is] displayed much more advantageously, and more liberty is allowed with regard to the waistcoat . . . the lower half (of the waistcoat) is cut away more than was the fashion formerly . . . I think you will find that most of the men who wear the correct attire do so because they like it [rather than from a sense of duty]."[49]

The front of the coat is cut away in a straight line at the waist. There is no waist seam in this example, although this was not a universal change.

From the beginning of the century, coat tails extended to the knee.

Evening trousers generally followed the line of day styles, and always matched the coat. They would never feature turnups at the cuff, but would often be made with some ornamentation in the form of braiding along the side seams. Braid could also, on occasion, edge the fronts, collar, and cuffs of dress coats, though this was less common.

The same tailor and "sartorial expert" quoted opposite commented that, by 1910, "the wearing of a black tie instead of the white is allowable more frequently than hitherto." This small degree of flexibility can be seen in the advertisement detail below, c.1909, showing three evening-suited men in varying combinations.

Arrow collars, Cluett shirts. Saturday evening post, Sept 25 1909, New York Public Library

This image also depicts men wearing either white or black waistcoats, another small element of choice that was open to them. The opening in the front of the waistcoat could be either a deep "V" or, as seen here, "U" shape.[50] It's possible this example may be slightly behind trend, as the *Tailor and Cutter* wrote in 1910, that "the really up to date vest is now made with a V opening."[51] Collars would usually be rolled (the edges rolled in a curve) with continuous lapels (i.e., no notch between the collar and the lapel). Most waistcoats were made with two small pockets, one on each side, and since dress coats were worn open, their fronts would usually be visible. Waistcoat buttons could be, as the semi-monthly *Men's Wear* suggested in 1910, "jeweled, or moonstones in simple settings, matching the shirt studs, or even gold . . . For ordinary evening wear, however, they should be plain mother-of-pearl or enameled." For black waistcoats, the most important thing was that buttons should be made "of the same material as the [waistcoat] . . . [and like] those which embellish the coat."[52]

Black wool wedding suit,

1914, Shippensburg University Fashion Archives and Museum, Pennsylvania

◆

Dress historian Jane Ashelford has pointed out that, by the eve of World War One, it was becoming far more difficult to tell a person's status in life by their clothes alone.[53] This wedding outfit is a good example of that change: its shape shows that it is a day lounge suit (now worn by most men, whatever their social status or profession) rather than the morning or tail ensemble that might be expected for formal occasions. In the previous century, only working-class bridegrooms would have worn a lounge suit on their wedding day. Its material, however, still signifies a special event: it is made from black wool, rather than the tweed or flannel that was usual for casual wear.

....

We are fortunate that some information about the couple has been retained. The suit belonged to David Raymond Fogelsanger (1889–1958), who married Lydia Hawbaker (1888–1935) in 1914. Her bridal gown is shown here in order to give an impression of the wedding aesthetic, and the role the suit would have played on the day.[54]

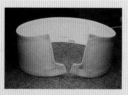

By the date of this suit, soft turned-down collars were worn widely, sometimes even for formal occasions such as weddings (as illustrated in this example). However, traditional tall, starched varieties like the one shown above were still favored by many men on their wedding day (c.1900-1910, author's collection).

This bowler hat dates to c.1910 and was purchased from "Mallory" on New York's Fifth Avenue. By c.1910, the bowler hat had largely replaced the top hat for all but the most formal social occasions.

Bow ties became popular for formal wear, as well as the standard long tie.

The waistcoat is cut very high with a V opening and six buttons. From c.1905 the final button would often be left undone, especially for less formal occasions.[55]

We can tell that this suit was made and worn at the very start of World War One, or possibly before war broke out. During the years of conflict lounge suits grew in popularity[56] but, due in part to fabric shortage, jackets finished higher up the thigh, had smaller, narrower lapels, and less emphasis on pockets and pocket flaps. This example does not conform to those changes. However, after c.1912 details such as hip pocket flaps and outer breast pockets were starting to become less fashionable generally, so this could be an older suit or perhaps one purchased by a groom who was not so concerned about being right on trend.

The trouser press had recently been invented (1890s). This meant that sleek, sharp creases down the center front of each trouser leg were now easily attainable and, therefore, very fashionable. From this date onwards it was rare to find trousers without the front crease.[57]

"Golfing" jacket and knickerbockers,

c.1917–22, Shippensburg University Fashion Archive and Museum, Pennsylvania

◆

This jacket, waistcoat, and knickerbocker suit presents marked differences to the previous Norfolk ensemble, most notably in its jacket's lack of pleats and belt and the use of knickerbockers rather than trousers. Nevertheless, this outfit was still made for sporting and country wear, most probably golf, given its use of tweed and the popular combination of tailored jacket with "knickers." Such suits were widely available as ready-to-wear items, making the sport as well as its clothing far more accessible. In Britain, golf had steadily risen to become the most fashionable sport played by the middle as well as the upper classes.[58] Across the Atlantic, as *Vanity Fair* discussed in June 1922, golf in America had gone from being the province of "rich people hunting novelty" to "the hands of the great middle class – professional and business men who sought health."[59] It is therefore not surprising that a wide range of options, frequently worn off the course as well as on, were available from the end of the 1910s.

Unlike many golfing jackets from the same era, this example does not utilize any shoulder vents or similar innovations for sporting flexibility.

Sleeveless pullovers superseded waistcoats for sporting suits during the 1920s, another aspect that helps us to date this example from the beginning of that decade, or probably slightly earlier.

We can see the beginnings of the fashionable "V" shape for the male silhouette: a defined waist, gradually broadening shoulders, and close-fitting hips.

Don'ts for Golfers in 1926 advised against wearing "a collar that is too high. Something about one inch in height is near enough the mark. Don't sport a necktie that flaps about. If you are wearing a long tie, see that it is fastened down securely." The neckwear shown here is commensurate with this advice; a bow tie being smart, fashionable and neat.[60]

Knickerbockers—essentially, loose fitting breeches—were originally designed for military wear. The flexibility they offered made them an obvious favorite for walking and sports, and various different styles emerged in the early twentieth century. Plus fours were one of these, termed as such simply because they were cut with an extra four inches of fabric that created an overhang just past the knee. Made with pleating, these could become exceptionally wide and reached their fashionable peak in the 1920s. The length and shape of these knickerbockers are one of the key ways we can date this suit. They are significantly narrower and closer-fitting than the plus fours shown in this 1925 photograph, suggesting that they are likely to be "plus twos" at the most; a style with two rather than four extra inches at the cuffs. This allows us to attribute a date of no later than 1922–23.

This image shows golfer Harry Vardon's grip, 1910–20. He is wearing a similarly cut jacket with plus twos and long woolen golf socks, courtesy Old Magazine Articles.

W.A. Fishbaugh, Golf course at the Miami Biltmore Hotel, Florida, 1925, State Archives of Florida

Jack Buchanan wearing an Oxford bags ensemble,

c.1925, Getty Images/Bettmann

◆

The term "Oxford bags" refers to these very wide trousers, often made from flannel, which originated at the University of Oxford in the middle of the decade. They could be worn with a sweater and flat cap or, as seen here, part of a more formal ensemble: this flexibility stems from students' wish to challenge the formal practice of changing dress several times a day.[61] The figure in this image is Scottish actor, dancer, singer, producer, and director Jack Buchanan (1891–1957). Buchanan was a fashion authority and the first to order a double-breasted **dinner jacket**, which became fashionable in the early 1920s, from a Savile Row tailor.[62] Although Oxford bags were a short-lived phenomenon, they set the trend for wider trousers, and their use by well-known figures like Buchanan makes them a firm feature of the decade.

Group of friends in Egypt, c.1920s, private collection
Oxford bags courted popularity in the most unlikely of places, including Egypt, where this image was taken in the mid 1920s. This was Robert Graves's experience when he took up a post at the Egyptian University, Cairo, in 1926: "My wide trousers, the first Oxford Bags to reach Egypt, interested them enormously, their own being still the peg-top sort . . . Soon everyone who was anyone wore Oxford Bags."[63]

The extreme width of these trousers was also frequently lampooned, especially in the press, with poems such as this one suggesting that the style could provide the wearer with significant aerodynamics:

> Oxford bags are all the go,
> The cuties like them too;
> They'll get the wind up them some day
> And sail up in the blue.
>
> Then have no fear in aeroplanes,
> If the engine stalls and fags,
> —Just step out and let her go—
> Come down in Oxford bags.[64]

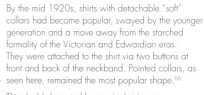

By the mid 1920s, shirts with detachable "soft" collars had become popular, swayed by the younger generation and a move away from the starched formality of the Victorian and Edwardian eras. They were attached to the shirt via two buttons at front and back of the neckband. Pointed collars, as seen here, remained the most popular shape.[66]

This double-breasted lounge jacket is very representative of daywear styles in the first half of the 1920s. We can't see the pockets, but it's likely there would have been two at hip level, either jetted or with flaps.

A requisite handkerchief peeks out of the breast pocket. Along with the likes of Winston Churchill, Cary Grant, and Noel Coward, Buchanan popularized this trend.[67]

Trousers were pleated at the waist to add volume, with a sharp fold continuing down each leg and allowing the trouser cuff to flare out over the wearer's shoes.

Leg width could be as much as 24 inches in diameter, accentuated by broad turned-up cuffs.[68]

Cambridge University rowing crew group, 1931, collection of Christina Bloom
It's possible that Oxford bags originated because students were forbidden from wearing knickers (short, baggy trousers) to class. Their solution was not to remove the knickers but to cover them with a pair of long, wide-legged trousers, enabling a swift change from lecture hall to sports hall.[65] They were also adopted as part of the uniform for rowing, as seen in this image.

Man modeling walking suit,

c.1925, Twyeffort Inc., New York, Library of Congress, Washington DC

◆

The name "walking" might at first seem to suggest a lounge suit or similarly casual ensemble. However, it actually refers to what is seen here: a formal cutaway or frock coat worn with waistcoat, standing collar, dress trousers, and, frequently, tan spats. The suit would usually be made from worsteds, tweeds, or cheviots, and could range in color from black to various shades of brown. As may be expected from the formality of this example, walking suits—or "English walking suits," as this style was specifically known, were ostensibly worn by the wealthy for "promenading," when the intention was more to display than to exercise. However, an outfit like this would also make up the common uniform of a wedding guest or for a day at the races. "Every well-dressed man should have an English walking suit in his wardrobe,"[69] said one clothing company in 1909; another said, "[This suit] on a man of a good figure is especially pleasing and especially well adapted to the dignified business man."[70] The suit shown here dates from the mid-1920s, but the fashion could be seen from the late nineteenth century until the start of the Second World War.

For formal occasions, most men would wear a detachable stiff **wing tip collar**. These would be attached to a narrow neckband, through small buttonholes located at the front and back.

While black or white bow ties were appropriate for evening wear, for formal day dress men could experiment a little more and choose a pattern for their tie; stripes or—as here—polka dots on a dark background were popular.

It is possible to see a section of the semi-stiff pleated front shirt or dickey, still known at the time as a "detachable bosom." For everyday wear, though, this look was becoming démodé for anything except the most formal wear. As Brisbane's *Daily Mail* commented in March 1923, "Stiff and semi-stiff bosomed shirts are seen now more upon the elderly men who remain true to the virtues of business attire, and are unwilling to take up anything new, regardless of the fact that it is more comfortable."[71]

After the First World War, and particularly as motor cars became more popular, the fashion for carrying a walking stick started to wane. However, they were still an essential accessory for more formal attire such as this.

Black silk top hats or "toppers" were worn for formal day dress, and would generally be around 12 to 13 centimeters in height. Early in the decade, gray variants became fashionable too, as discussed in Galsworthy's *The Forsyte Saga* when Winifred Dartie, preparing for a day at Ascot, asks her niece Fleur Forsyte: "Has your Father got a grey top hat? No? Oh! But he simply must wear one; they're all the go this year."[72]

A similar coat and gray pinstriped trousers, with one glove worn and the other carried, in this 1920s wedding portrait, private collection.

Business suit,

c.1926, McCord Museum, Montreal

◆

This olive-colored suit, classed as urban "business" wear, is a typical example of a mid- to late-1920s lounge jacket, waistcoat, and trousers. This kind of ensemble had been recommended for professional wear since the turn of the century and would have been readily available in department stores.

Looking back to the lounge or "sack" suit discussed previously, there are certainly recognizable features in this mid-1920s successor. Closer inspection, however, reveals some changes, and the 1860s predecessor will be referenced here for comparison.

Lapels are longer and narrower in 1926, and feature a rolled edge rather than the silk trim of the 1865 design.

The same slightly slanted left breast pocket remains.

While it was common for only the first button to be fastened in 1865, by the 1920s the middle one was favored. Partly because of this preference, it was still usual for lounge jackets to be made with only three front buttons.

The sleeves of the 1926 jacket are slimmer, with no trimming or cuff. Both would have been cut shorter than the shirt sleeves beneath (not illustrated in the 1926 example), in order to show that the wearer was a "gentleman," not a manual laborer, and that his profession would not dirty his white cuffs.

One of the most notable differences is the rounded collar, worn with a modern "full" necktie featuring the "four-in-hand" or slip fastening that is still used today.

In 1925, London's *Daily Chronicle* commented that the Prince of Wales would "continue to set the fashions . . . for men," and that to this end, "comfortable, loose fitting, formless English sack suits would be worn . . . Young men who went somewhat to the extreme would wear pleated trousers, with a one-button sack coat and a double-breasted waistcoat." If the suit shown here is anything to go by, only some of those predictions came to pass, but the lounge suit was certainly there to stay.[73]

There is a very defined pleat along the front of each trouser leg, ending in a small turned-up cuff.

This photograph of the Canadian architect Edward Maxwell, taken in 1893 (McCord Museum), is a good illustration of how sack suits had developed between the mid nineteenth century and the 1920s. It is made from a similar woolen fabric to the 1926 example, providing a more leisured "country" feel, but was still being chosen for formal occasions such as business, or this portrait sitting. Like the 1926 jacket, this 1890s ancestor sports deep curved fronts and a rolled lapel. Maxwell wears a turned-down collar with a sailor's knot, possibly purchased ready-made.

Evening/dinner suit,

1920s, National Museums Scotland, Edinburgh

◆

The development of the tailless dinner jacket (tuxedo), first introduced by the Prince of Wales in 1880s London, and then at Tuxedo Park in New York, was regarded by many as an affront to the stability and elegance of traditional "full dress," which was made up of a tail coat, white waistcoat, white shirt, detachable wing collar, white bow tie, and black trousers.[74] By the turn of the century, however, it was becoming widely accepted as an alternative—though it continued to inspire criticism. In July 1922 an article in *Vogue* (written from a woman's perspective) put forward the idea that it should have been a temporary fad: "During the war, because it seemed unfitting to dress formally for the evening, many men substituted in those years the dinner coat for the dress coat. And the majority of them, alas, have continued to do so . . . For most men . . . it is nothing more than laziness."[75] Nevertheless, the tuxedo only grew in popularity and has now turned full circle to be, for many men, the most formal garment in the wardrobe.

This silk bow tie corresponds to instructions set out by *Vanity Fair* in June 1921: "The bow should be generous and give the effect of spreading out at the end." [76] The tie is worn with a wing collar, which would be replaced by a soft stand-fall collar (for dinner jackets, not dress coats) by the 1930s.

Single-breasted styles were usually preferred for dinner jackets in the 1920s. This example is fastened at the waistline with a linked button. Using this technique, a second button would be added to a cord and passed through the buttonhole so that, when fastened, the effect was of two buttons side by side—somewhat like a cufflink fastening.

Evening wear advertisement, 1942 (detail), New York Public Library

Of course, one of the biggest changes of the dinner jacket was that it was cut without tails. This was a drastic departure for evening and formal wear, turning its back on centuries of tradition. Instead the jacket has the look of a business or lounge suit with its rounded fronts—a daytime garment with an evening sheen. The effect from the back, still with the long, lean silhouette but stopping at hip level, is seen in this illustration from the early 1940s.

Until the 1930s, dinner jackets were still worn with black or white waistcoats: the one shown here has a V-neck to match that of the jacket. Once these started to fall from fashion, the space was often filled with a **cummerbund**. "The smartest waistcoat," wrote *Vanity Fair*, "is cut straight across the trouser line and is high waisted . . . one reason (for the high waisted line) is due to the fullness of the new trousers which do not sit well with the long points of the old waistcoat." These trousers, the article continued, "are not unlike those of the early nineteenth century," being generously pleated or gathered across the waistline.[77]

Evening wear advertisement, 1942 (detail), New York Public Library

Dinner suits were always black until, in the 1940s, white became acceptable "for resort wear" and was popularized by the likes of Humphrey Bogart in *Casablanca* (1942). An article from November 1947 noted this trend, also offering some helpful tips to men who might be unsure whether to wear "full" or "semi" formal dress: "A dinner coat is definitely required for dining and dancing, at the theater, aboard a cruise ship . . . at bachelor dinners, at stag affairs . . . and when the woman you're escorting wears a dinner dress."[78]

"Palm Beach" suit,

c.1930–39, Fashion Institute of Design & Merchandising (FIDM), Los Angeles, California

◆

This wool and cotton ensemble represents a fantastically popular trend in 1930s America: the so-called "Palm Beach" suit, which was widely adopted as summer leisure wear and was favored by Wall Street throughout the decade. The name came from the popularity of Palm Beach in Florida as a place to "see and be seen" in new fashionable leisure wear. This particular example was purchased at Famous-Barr Co., a division of Macy's department store that was founded in Missouri in 1911.[79] The ease of purchasing such a suit demonstrates the growing acceptance of readymade clothing, while the brown check speaks of a continued English country aesthetic, popularized by the Prince of Wales (later Duke of Windsor).

The rounded "club" collar had its origins at Eton, but soft, attached and less formal versions became very popular during the 1930s for men of all ages—especially when pinned.[81]

The Palm Beach jacket was essentially a sports jacket, featuring the shaped, belted effect at the rear that was a feature of much men's leisure wear (see advertisement below, c.1932). As an "odd" jacket, it could be worn with different styles and colors of legwear (e.g., dress trousers, casual slacks, or even jeans) and a variety of shirts (this mismatched look was especially popular in the United States). Such options were also favored by younger men and, increasingly, teenagers. An advertisement by Goodall Tailoring appeared in *Boys' Life* in June 1938, specifically targeting a high school and student audience. "For school, play and parties . . . at graduation and the 'Big Prom' – you'll look your smartest in a new Palm Beach suit. Picture yourself in a sport back coat and pleated slacks . . . University-styled by the same experts who tailor Palm Beach suits for men."[80] The example here is on the more conservative side, worn with matching trousers and a light, bright—if relatively formal—shirt, collar, and bow tie.

The male silhouette of the 1930s began to mirror that of women, with a nipped-in waist and, most noticeably, broad and padded shoulders. In suit jackets this effect was accentuated by the use of a peak lapel, in which the lapel extends up past the collar and draws the eye toward the shoulder (open notches were also popular). The long, low-fastening lapels follow the line of the popular "Kent" double breasted style, popularized by the Duke of Kent.

First gaining popularity for holiday wear in the 1920s, the straw boater was a common accessory with a Palm or other leisure suit. Its fashionability waxed and waned, but a significant revival came in August 1936 when Edward VIII instigated a "straw hat summer." With the straw hat industry "in the doldrums," as one Australian newspaper put it, the King's enthusiasm meant that "2000 more people have found work."[82]

By this date, it was acceptable to wear either single or double-breasted jackets according to personal preference. Double breasted, as in this example, works to enhance the inverted triangular shape of the torso. Lapels extend down to the second set of buttons at the front, further emphasizing this "V" silhouette.

It would have been common for a fashion-conscious man to match his white collar with white French cuffs (closed with cufflinks)—here, a simple plain button fastening is shown.

In 1932, *The Santa Cruz Sentinel* described the fashionable cut and fit of men's trousers, closely corresponding with the style seen here, as "high-rise [with] vertical pleats at the front; considerable fullness over the hips and a gradual tapering . . . While this garment is loose it still creates a semi-shapely effect because of the figure-defining details at the waist and the trim cut of the trousers."[83]

Palm Beach ensemble advertisement (detail), 1932, courtesy Old Magazine Articles

Summer suit,

1931, McCord Museum, Montreal

◆

This light summer lounge suit carries on the developing leisure wear aesthetic of the early twentieth century. However, this example displays several contemporary details that allow us to confidently attribute a date of the early 1930s. At the same time it is markedly different to the previous "Palm Beach" example: there is less emphasis on the sharp, svelte "V" of the masculine torso and a softer, rounder finish to the jacket.

The presence of a waistcoat, clearly visible above the jacket lapels, elevates this ensemble to a three-piece, suitable for "business" as well as leisure wear.

The jacket features only two buttons, a design choice that recalls earlier sack styles and creates a loose, relaxed feel. Strictly speaking, single-breasted varieties at this time were intended more for morning and sporting wear than for town, although—as the waistcoat demonstrates—they could be combined with other accessories for a more formal finish. [84]

These patch pockets with rounded edges are reminiscent of those seen on the sporty Norfolk jacket, but also on military tunics: two above and two below the waist. The style recalls the relatively recent uniform of the First World War, whilst also highlighting the political uncertainty of the decade and, perhaps, anticipating the uniforms that would soon return to most men's wardrobes.

Portrait of solider, c.1914 (detail), private collection

This wedding portrait from 1936 shows a groom in a very similar jacket and trousers, complete with striped tie. Broader lapels and a nipped-in waist are indicative of the closing years of the decade, private collection.

"Now," wrote one newspaper fashion column in 1932, "(trousers) are loose about the hips, so that you can slip into them without the aid of a shoehorn." However, it was quick to point out, they were definitely "not peg topped."[85]

These trousers are not as wide as many fashionable styles typically seen throughout the decade, but some volume is provided through the turned-up cuffs. Those shown here are relatively modest, but trouser cuffs could reach quite significant depth and length, as one newspaper columnist recorded wryly in 1935:

> [My friend and I] were at a party one evening, and the hostess asked if he wanted an ash tray and he replied in the negative . . . and proceeded, much to her astonishment, to empty the ash into his cuff.[86]

Brown pinstriped suit,

c.1930s, Shippensburg University Museum & Fashion Archive, Pennsylvania

◆

This two-piece suit of brown pinstriped worsted wool was made by Glen Brooks for Dourtiches in Harrisburg, Pottsville. Pinstripes may have developed originally from urban bankers' wear in the nineteenth century, or from nineteenth and early twentieth century leisure and sporting wear. However it came about, by the 1930s the double-breasted pinstripe suit was ubiquitous, and this jacket and trousers are a fine example of a popular cut and color.

Double-breasted jackets usually had long lapels with a button or "flower" hole in each side.

This double breasted coat fastens with six one-inch brown plastic buttons, two of which fasten.

As evidenced in this jacket and in the photograph below, by c.1930 jackets were wider across the chest with squarer, boxier shoulders, the waist relatively high, with a close fit over the hips. As an article in a Melbourne newspaper put it in June 1935, the style comprised "wide shoulders and a distinct waistline, with the coat cut flat on the hips and trousers of medium width." Mr. Ernest Verey, a Sydney tailor who returned from a trip to London with this advice, also commented that "Oxford bags, and everything resembling them, have gone forever."[87] However, these trousers and the ones in this photograph are still noticeably wide, approximating around 18 inches at the cuff by the early 1930s.

In the 1930s neckties became wider, allowing for the display of bold, bright colors and patterns. As one newspaper described it in 1936, bright ties and pocket squares provided "(some tolerated) touch(es) of color" to increasingly "drab dress."[88] The tie shown here was made by "Beau Brummell," and presented to its owner on the "Don McNeill Breakfast Club" radio show.

Waistcoats were far less common during the decade, often worn only with eveningwear (and then often made without a back, in a kind of halter-neck construction). Instead of a waistcoat men took to wearing sleeveless, machine-knitted pullovers for warmth, but it was also acceptable to wear nothing at all between shirt and jacket. However, not everyone greeted this trend with pleasure. An issue of the *Colorado Eagle and Journal* from 1933 commented that "A vest . . . is useful because it has four pockets in which can be stored extra collar buttons, odd coins, stub pencils . . . keys, matches, cigarette holders . . . If we give up our vests I fear that we shall have to carry handbags, as the ladies do."[89]

Slim shaping over the hips was partly achieved by the lack of a center vent at the back of the jacket. Tapered lines at each side and a center back seam created a svelte, waisted silhouette.

Trousers were made with two pleats in the waistband, leading into a deep central crease down each leg. In the early-mid 1930s, newspaper and magazine fashion columns reported rather incredulously of the style being promoted for women. Often referred to as "Dietrich" trousers after the film star (who, to wide unease, chose to wear slacks—and bonafide men's suits—both on set and off), one paper described them as "worn with braces, almost a faithful copy of the masculine garment, with hip-pockets, pleated waists, creased legs, and turn-up hems." These were not widely adopted, but their very existence contributed to ongoing discussions around the suitability of trousers for women. In 1931 the revolutionary designer, Paul Poiret, spoke up in favor, though he declared that "you must not call the divided garment by that name [trousers] to women. They do not like it, but they will wear them just the same."[90]

Rear view of suit, c.1930s, Shippensburg University Fashion Archives & Museum

Evening suit,

c.1938, McCord Museum, Montreal

◆

Thanks in part to the films of Fred Astaire and the glamour of his "top hat, white tie, and tails," evening dress from the 1930s has become synonymous with style, grace, and effortless elegance. Its origins go back much further, of course, and the precision of the ensemble can be traced to Beau Brummell. There are also links to military exactness in the socially prescribed length, width, and placement of various components, as well as the strict sartorial codes surrounding the appropriateness of either a single or double-breasted waistcoat.[91]

Evening dress was worn with wing collars (in essence, stand collars with the points turned down).

Men could choose from a wide array of lapel styles and shapes on a dress waistcoat.

Single-breasted dress waistcoats usually had no more than three buttons, made in white or ivory to complement the fabric.

The Duke of Windsor revived Beau Brummell's favored color of midnight blue for evening dress (largely, in his case, because the shade allowed for greater enhancement of tailoring details in black and white photographs, but it was also noted that the color looked better in artificial light). However, black was still the commonly accepted—and often required—choice for coat and trousers.[92]

The more popular single-breasted evening waistcoat nearly always had pointed fronts, whilst the double-breasted were usually cut square across.[93]

By the early 1930s, coat tails reached below the knees (during the previous decade, they had generally stopped at knee length or just above). This gave a graceful and elegant line to the suit, and was a feature used to great effect by Fred Astaire (left), flaring out and moving with him as he danced.

Hulton Archive/Getty Images
Fred Astaire mid-leap, attired in clothing typical of films made during the 1930s and 40s.

Chapter 6
1939–1969

Once again, the specter of war threatened to halt any developments in men's fashion by putting most men between the ages of 18 and 41 into uniform. The fashion industry may not have come to a complete standstill, but new clothes were less of a priority, so most men—when out of uniform, at least—made do with suits they had purchased pre-war. In order to get a realistic overview of the key changes that did occur, the first part of this chapter illustrates the **zoot suit**, an iconic if short-lived style that represents some important social shifts. Its exaggerated proportions took a pre-existing silhouette to the extreme, rather than inventing something entirely new, but the suit flouted American wartime convention in its extravagant use of material. Some elements of this rebellious attitude, of a wanton disregard for rules that seemed so set in stone, must have been refreshing to young men in particular. As Harold Koda and Richard Martin expressed it, zoot suits represented "an ideal of adolescent rebellion: to enjoy the time of adulthood without its restraints."[1]

The second analysis focuses on a rather different social influence, but one equally unreachable to most men in the decade: that of Edward VIII, later Duke of Windsor. As well as his appeal to women ("You must understand," fashion designer Diana Vreeland commented, "that to be a woman of my generation in London – *any* woman – was to be in love with the Prince of Wales."), men wanted to emulate him.[2] On the same level as film idols such as Fred Astaire, Cary Grant, and Humphrey Bogart, the Duke was regarded as a style leader on both sides of the Atlantic. "What he wears," wrote one fashion column in late February 1941, "can be depended upon to become the current mode."[3] Although the Duke himself denied much of this influence—at least as intentional—it was palpable in the press and in contemporaneous fashion writing.

The concept of "austerity nostalgia" as discussed in the Introduction has a role to play in the ways in which 1940s clothing has since been discussed and deconstructed. It is also frequently placed under the banner of "classic style," which, Jay McCauley Bowstead has rightly pointed out, is problematic because it suggests that "the styles of this period had always existed (rather than being the result of a specific set of historical processes.")[4] Nevertheless, the Utility scheme that was in force in Britain during the War did demand so-called "classic" styles: suits that retained enough of a fashionable line to be appealing, but which would not date overnight. The third 1940s example of this chapter looks in detail at a British "Utility" government-issued suit from the early years of the decade. This is placed alongside a later "demob" ensemble, also government-issued, to men returning from active service. As the example will discuss, demob suits met with mixed reactions and what men were allocated seems to have been partly down to the luck of the draw. For most, the reality of returning to a civvy street wardrobe was about as far removed from the Duke of Windsor as it was possible to get.

The anti-climax of a late 1940s and early 50s return to some kind of normality was expressed most pertinently in menswear. "Drab," "conformist," "dull" are words often used in relation to the state of suits in this period, an atmosphere neatly summed up in Australian painter John Brack's *Collins St, 5pm* from 1955. Rows of bodies in tan, brown, black, and gray clothes walk in uniform lines to and from their places of work, their faces taut, against a backdrop of buildings in the same monochrome shades. Bare black skeletons of trees and lampposts break up the canvas, but our focus is on the figures and the clear monotony of their experience. Australia, too, was recovering from war and had the added pressure of continuing to define itself as, in some respects, a relatively "new" country. Brack's men (who display more conformity and rigidity than the few women in the piece) bear the burden of responsibility, and their identical long, brown overcoats scream loss of personal identity in the aftermath of world turmoil.

The Australian example in this chapter is, ironically, the furthest from Brack's image. Imbued with neo-Edwardian teddy boy influence, it is a bright red, leopard-lined stage suit belonging to singer Johnny O'Keefe. This of course does not represent the everyman experience (shown more accurately in the c.1950 Canadian example preceding it) but it does speak of a slowly shifting sartorial outlook and sense of what was acceptable for the modern twentieth-century man. It also shows the influence of the Teddy Boy who, like the zoot suit wearers that preceded him, was part of a small but hugely relevant subculture. The Teddy Boy (and to a lesser extent, the "Teddy Girl") presented a new vision of youth to a tired and disaffected post-war world. Their dress and attitude combined with popular music and dance to create the first wave of "youth culture," something that both shocked and bewildered the previous generation. No longer did boys suddenly become men; now there was an intermediary phase, a very real social and cultural phenomenon and also a valuable marketing concept. This was first introduced in America around 1944, and it was called "the teenager."

British teddy boys were a very visible embodiment of this new wave and were particularly prominent from c.1954-57, partly due to a number of violent incidents that sadly led to negative associations with the subculture as a whole. Known as "Edwardians" or "Working Class Edwardians," Teds reinterpreted the formal, tailored costume of their grandfathers with long "drape" jackets, peg-top or drainpipe trousers, and narrow or string ties. This was a pointed way of snubbing the wartime austerity of their fathers' clothing—a sartorial rebellion that was both daring and poignant and, as Steve Chibnall puts it, a marker of "fundamental disrespect for the old class modes and manners – a disrespect born of a romance with alien culture."[5]

Elements of this very British subset could be seen in America with the **rocker** style, influenced by figures such as James Dean, Elvis, and Marlon Brando, and characterized by jeans, t-shirts, leather jackets, and slick hair greased into a quiff. Into the 1960s, the British rocker (famously seen on the Beatles during their early, leather-clad Hamburg days) went head-to-head with a new subculture known as the **Mod**. Influenced by the dapper suits of the Teddy Boys before them, the Mods represented what they perceived as "modern" Britain: a combination of British and American culture and style that expressed itself through a scrupulous attention to detail and—most disturbing to older generations—an aspiration to live well, and to attain the heights of fashion no matter your social or economic background. For the men and women who fought to attain the longest period of peace and prosperity Britain had ever seen, this amounted to serious disrespect and ingratitude. As a reporter for *The Australian Woman's Weekly* found in 1964, "(the Mods were) reluctant to pose for pictures [for this article]. 'We don't want to pose in gear that'll be quaint old drag' . . . 'But it isn't old-fashioned, is it?' 'It will be by the time you get the pictures into print.' . . . The Mod word is swift, all right." The same article reported incredulously on the cost it took to be in fashion, especially for mod boys. "A boy could spend 25 guineas on the latest thing in suede jackets and find after three weeks that it is 'old frontier' – OUT."[6]

Stylistically, male Mods came to be recognized for the importance they placed on the suit. In the early 1960s, some appropriated a version of the "City Gent" look, even carrying umbrellas and wearing bowler hats. This brief fad had a longer-standing consequence in the adoption of the waisted suit, cut with a center-back seam that differentiated it from the previously popular Italian style propagated by designers such as Nino Cerruti and Ermenegildo Zegna (short, boxy jackets and narrow trousers worn with winklepicker shoes). John F. Kennedy, elected as President of the United States on November 8, 1960, was a high-profile promoter of the look. His suits made significant strides away from the preppy, wide-legged Ivy League fashions that had predominated for some time in America; instead, he capitalized on his svelte, athletic figure by donning longer jackets with nipped-in waists and a deep "V" front. Narrow trousers completed the look, which was often topped off *without* a hat: a daring change in an era when it was still the requisite for men to wear a hat outdoors.[7]

French designer Pierre Cardin played a pivotal role in popularizing this longer, waisted, slimline look—and propelled it to become one of the key styles of the decade. The Beatles initially set the fashion in stone with their shiny gray collarless stage suits (which will be examined in this chapter), a look that arguably contributed massively to their breakthrough. The suit affected their showmanship and on-stage presence whilst imbuing them with an elegance appreciated by young mod audiences and their parents alike. Professional men of all ages soon adopted variants of the suits popularized by these key sartorial players, as seen in a mid-1960s photograph of a group of Shell oil employees, and a family snapshot, c.1966.

John Lennon was apparently resentful that the Rolling Stones were able to achieve similar success while wearing whatever they liked, but the Beatles soon moved on from this more wholesome image. The late 1960s saw the return of the "peacock," a riot of color that had lain dormant in menswear since the eighteenth century. As if making up for lost time, it seemed that no colors, patterns, or textures were off limits. As with any seismic shift in fashion, this was of course about more than clothes and tied into strong and divisive political movements and ideologies. It also spoke to men on a very personal level, acknowledging a fundamental change in the perception of masculinity that had been brewing since the close of World War Two. As Delis Hill and others have cautioned, it is important not to assume that every young man succumbed to the peacock effect, and certainly the long hair, prewashed jeans, and flower print would have been unthinkable in most workplaces.

This may not seem very conducive to the suit, but more options for men did not mean that suits disappeared. On the contrary, the "peacock revolution" gave designers a golden opportunity to experiment with color, texture, pattern, and cut in new ways. Boutiques in London's Carnaby Street (known as "Peacock Alley") were famous for producing some of the decade's most outlandish designs, combined with impeccable tailoring and finishing. One of the best known, Mr. Fish, is represented in this chapter with a suit made from a velvet corduroy upholstering fabric. Its printed stripes create a rainbow of green, orange, red, yellow, brown, and beige, as well as darker red and green tones—a "peacock" effect if ever there was one. The cut of this, and many others like it, took inspiration from nineteenth and early twentieth century styles and promoted features such as exaggerated lapels and cuffs.

Influence also spread to Australia and New Zealand, and *The Australian Woman's Weekly* spoke in June 1966 of the "return of the dandy": a "new wave of English dandyism" with "foaming ruffles . . . velvet pantaloons . . . waisted jackets [and] tight trousers. There has not been such elegance, style and boldness in men's clothes . . . since Oscar Wilde."[8] The article interviewed Patrick Anson, 5th Earl of Lichfield, a photographer and "one of the best-dressed young Londoners." He believed that the time had come for people to dress as they pleased, with the influence of well-known "film stars, pop singers, hairdressers, photographers" to encourage them. "I have an idea," he declared in his closing words, "all men dress to be sexy like cock pheasants in the mating season." This concept of suits being "sexy," and that men should feel comfortable to express such aspirations for their clothes, summed up the daring and innovative mood of the time.

It was not only historicism that had a part to play in men's fashion. Multiculturalism and further opportunities to travel had broadened the outlook and perspectives of many. India, in particular, held a fascination for those interested in ideas of spiritualism, and this impacted the clothing of hippies significantly. It even affected the suit, which by the end of the decade had become a hippy's byword for all things conservative, stuffy, and traditional. The Nehru jacket's appropriation by the west may be problematic on several levels, but its rise can also be seen as a reaction of approval to the progressive nature of India's government under Jawaharlal Nehru, the country's first Prime Minister. The long, clean lines of the Nehru jacket, with its high standing collar and (usually) lack of surface ornamentation, allowed it to find an easy place within mod fashion. Later, its political associations and exoticism found favor with even the most fervent hippy.

The last example of this chapter discusses a suit that is equally problematic, but for different reasons. Mao Zedong's rise to power in 1950s China led to the traumatic outcomes of the Cultural Revolution (1966–1976). The plain militaristic suit, which also—as the analysis demonstrates—held very distinct traditional Chinese symbolisms, came to be regarded as a representation of the austerity and suppression of the revolution. In the early days of the People's Republic, wearing the suit was not mandatory, though utilitarian styles were strongly encouraged and, keen to either show their support or remain "safe," as Valery Garrett puts it, many soon changed their wardrobes.[9] As well as being classless, the suit is also widely regarded as promoting a kind of sexlessness. It was unisex in the strictest sense, though this term would not have been applied or even conceived of at the time, but "sexless" suggests the androgyny that these outfits embodied. Its subsequent western appropriation has largely been interpreted as male, though, with 1960s jackets for men featuring high Nehru-style or turned-down collars, Mao-style patch pockets, and center button fastening. Before the full horrors of the revolution were known outside of China, the suit was associated with idealistic socialist principles of equality and working together for the common good. For disaffected youths eager to find something to fight for and believe in, it is easy to understand the appeal. However, even in very recent years the suit has been reimagined by designers such as Yushan Li and Jun Zhou, the names behind the label Pronounce. Their pink Mao suit, with white stitching around its pockets and a detachable belt, presents a completely different impression stamped onto a recognizable shell. At the same time sober, dark examples, exquisitely cut to fit the twenty-first century "skinny suit" aesthetic, present an elegant and contemporary option that bears almost no relation to the original. The Mao suit has been included in this chapter as an acknowledgement of one of the most pervasive sartorial influences of the twentieth century, an amalgam of "suit" and "uniform" that has somehow endured, continuing to influence and intrigue.

In the previous chapters of this book, hats have been mentioned on the occasions that they appear in individual suit analyses. For centuries, the wearing of hats was so universal, so ingrained for men of every social level, that we can take it as read that a hat of some kind would have been worn whenever a man set foot outside. In the 1950s, however, that began to change. While many men still preferred to wear a hat outdoors—even during their leisure time—hat manufacturers started to express mounting concern that their industry would not survive. In 1950, British hatters launched a campaign called "Wear a Hat," and in 1956 the Felt Hatter's Union in Canberra took steps by proposing a "back to hats" campaign. This cry for help asked "big stores and firms employing large staffs to ask their workers to come to work 'hatted.'"[10]

The reason for this was identified as a "move toward flamboyance in a new direction," with young men choosing elaborate hairstyles and, as one newspaper reported in September 1950, "[an] ear-ring as a special adornment—a single trinket worn only on the right ear. Such a fashion, of course, demands no hat."[11] The influence of youth culture, which saw quiff-haired American teenagers rejecting suits in favor of denim worn with leather jackets, was undoubtedly a pivotal part of this gradual transformation. However, it was not until the inauguration of President John F. Kennedy in January 1961—with his boyish good looks and fresh presence in the White House—that a hatless future for men was more widely contemplated. By the end of his first year in office, it seems to have been accepted that his hat-wearing habits (or lack thereof) were unlikely to change. Hat companies and even fellow presidents tried—for example, in July 1962, when the Ecuadorian leader Carlos Julio Arosemena Monroy presented Kennedy with a Panama hat, a gesture deemed newsworthy by several publications.[12] Regardless, his steadfastness remained and contributed to growing levels of sartorial autonomy (although he was sometimes to be seen carrying a hat, in order, one newspaper concluded, to "yield to the pressure from the hat people").[13] Clair Hughes has suggested that rejecting the hat came easier to Kennedy than other men because, being "semi-royal," he "really had no need to show conformity with etiquette."[14] Nevertheless, as Neil Steinberg has pointed out in *Hatless Jack*, Kennedy was not in fact leading the fashion for going hatless: rather, he was following "in perfect step with his contemporaries."[15] His profile on the world stage inevitably made any fashion choice highly visible, and encouraged those who had already started to push their hats to the back of the wardrobe.

By the end of the decade, hat manufacturers were resigning themselves to the fact that "[a] rise in leisure hat volume is not buoyant enough to offset the tremendous thud caused by the plummet of the business hat," as an issue of trade magazine *Men's Wear* put it in 1969.[16] Into the 1970s and beyond, the predominant leisure theme continued, with men sporting baseball caps, flat caps, and casual versions of previous staples like the trilby and fedora. Soft, knitted, brimless variants such as beanies, berets, and balaclavas have wandered in and out of fashion, and are commonly worn by both men and women.

The overcoat or "topcoat" suffered a similar decline towards the end of this period. The 1950s saw a continuation of long raglan coats in the Chesterfield tradition, raincoats, and, towards the end of the decade, much shorter coats cut in a similar style. Waist-length windbreakers and duffel coats offered further alternatives that could be worn over casual clothes rather than business suits. One of the most notable trends of the 1950s follows on from a style introduced in the previous chapter, and demonstrates one of the first waves of "vintage" enthusiasm in contemporary fashion. The aforementioned raccoon coat enjoyed a brief but intense revival, particularly amongst students, with whom the fad first originated in the 1920s. One New York shop advertised extant raccoon coats "in magnificent disrepair," but copies were also available "[made] after those worn 30 years ago or else shortened to car coat length." This was part of what one newspaper described as "fashion's return to the Roaring 20's . . . especially for the campus and young career girl group."[17]

By the mid to late 1960s, overcoats were still a requirement for many men (especially in the professional realm) but there was an increasing demand to "liven" them up. In November 1967 reporter Walter Logan described some examples from the fashion house of John Weitz, including "a double breasted blue velour with an exaggerated collar . . . and a crimson lining; a single breasted French velour . . . with a very wide collar and . . . a double-breasted twill with extremely wide collar and lapels in a raglan cut."[18] This attitude exemplifies the experimental and sometimes daring sartorial mood of the 1960s, an outlook explored in this chapter alongside an acknowledgement of the convention and caution that, for many, characterized their clothing choices.

Rayfield McGhee in a "zoot suit,"

c.1942–43, Courtesy State Archives of Florida, Tallahassee, Florida

This photograph provides an important record of the lives and fashions of African American teenagers and young people in the early 1940s. It depicts Rayfield McGhee, a resident of Tallahassee, Florida, wearing an enigmatic zoot suit. Popularized by singer Cab Calloway, the style actually had its origins in civil unrest: more specifically, a spate of violence in Los Angeles in June 1943. Probably created by urban African American and Latino men, the zoot suit was present during the race-fueled riot and came to be associated with minority groups and working-class youth as much as it represented dance, song, and showmanship in the jitterbug age. This extreme, in-your-face jacket and trousers prompted much social commentary, even fear, and led to deeper political discussions around race relations, more recently becoming the trademark look of young South African tsotsis men.[19]

These suits were generally worn with a porkpie or wide-brimmed hat such as this one. It was often accessorized with a long feather, a feature that contributed to one psychologist's opinion of the craze as "an outward manifestation of adolescent neurosis . . . in a bizarre reversal of the normal male and female dress."[20]

The shoulders on men's jackets may have been wide throughout the 1930s, but the zoot suit at the start of the 1940s took width to a whole new level. With up to three inches of padding at each side, as well as gathers at the sleeve head to increase volume, the finished effect had a striking impact.

"Peg-top" zoot trousers have been described as high-waisted to the extreme (sometimes coming up to a few inches under the wearer's armpits), with three-inch wide **reet pleats** down the front of each leg that allowed up to 34 inches of fabric to swell out at the knees. The trouser cuff of the six-inch ankle could be up to five inches deep. However, this was merely fantasy for many zoot enthusiasts. Most men had to make do with less voluminous trousers such as those seen here, with navel-height waistbands, slimmer pleats and significantly narrower legs.[21]

Extremely wide and very peaked lapels further increase the appearance of breadth.

Although recognized as an American trend, the shape of the zoot suit is in fact an exaggerated version of the **English drape**, a cut that set a definitive silhouette for men in the twentieth century. It created the appearance of fullness across the chest through the cut and "drape" of the fabric, and a nipped-in waist accentuated this. Very few original zoot suits remain, partly because of strict wartime fabric restrictions that limited their production or enforced the re-use of material elsewhere. This photograph adds an extra element to the overview, however: the inclusion of its wearer gives a greater sense of the social and political backdrop to these extraordinary ensembles.

This image, also from the Florida State Archives, shows a group of young men who have accessorized their suits in various ways, including the wearing of a long watch chain on one side. The image shows a more casual side, too, and possibly a more realistic depiction of how "most" young people would have dressed "up" or "down" depending on the occasion, combining their wide trousers or broad-shouldered jackets with other wardrobe staples.

Unsurprisingly, zoot suits were mercilessly derided in the press. This cartoon accompanied a satirical article in a 1945 edition of *Yank: The Army Weekly* magazine, which considered the effect of American fashions on foreigners. "The only things that overwhelm me [about the US]," said one Egyptian delegate, "are the suits you call 'zoot' and some of the ties with great colorful markings . . . They would kill me on the street if I came back wearing one."[22]

Courtesy Old Magazine Articles

Suit worn by the Duke of Windsor,

c.1940s, Maryland Historical Society, Baltimore, Maryland

◆

King Edward VIII caused worldwide shock and scandal when he abdicated on December 11, 1938. This drastic action was taken in order to be with American divorcee Wallis Simpson, a match that was not permissible under the British constitution at that time. As Duke of Windsor, he was no less in the spotlight and had an especially strong influence on men's fashion throughout the 1940s, described at times as the "leader of men's fashion" whose sartorial choices could be "depended upon to become the current mode."[23] This suit is typical of his "look," beautifully cut in the English drape style. This example lacks the tweed that he (and his father before him) were so fond of, but his love for pattern was still expressed through accessories and, sometimes, the shirts that accompanied his suits.

Edward was a strong supporter of the "soft" unstarched collar, for evening as well as for day dress—a quiet revolution he termed "dress soft."[24]

The trousers are made with zip instead of button flies. By 1937, men's clothing designers started to experiment with zipper fastenings. *Esquire Magazine* praised the innovation as a means of avoiding "unintentional and embarrassing disarray."[25]

The Duke's suits were made by Scholte of Savile Row between 1919 and 1959. A stickler for perfection, Frederick Scholte had, in the Duke's own words, "rigid standards concerning the cut of a coat to clothe the masculine torso." Scholte certainly seemed to have some influence over his clients' choices, even when they were royalty. When the Duke came to a fitting wearing slightly wider trousers, the tailor is said to have remarked, "I hope you are not going in for those Oxford trousers." He may not have promoted Oxford bags, but into the 1930s and 40s he favored a trouser leg of the type seen here, which were wide over their full length and, worn with a long double-breasted jacket, gave the illusion of height to their 5'5" tall wearer.[26]

Along with most fashionable men of the 1940s, Edward, along with his brother the Duke of Kent, favored double-breasted jackets. It was Kent that originally popularized the four-buttoned style with long, sloping lapels that fastened below waist level. This was sometimes referred to as a "Kent" until the name was ousted in favor of his more famous brother.

Though he is generally credited with its invention, the Duke did not claim responsibility for the Windsor method of tying a tie. "[It] was I believe regulation wear for G.I.s during the war . . . I was in no way responsible for this," he claimed in his autobiography.[27]

The Duke and Duchess of Windsor aboard the ship 'Argentina', 1945, Keystone-France/Getty Images
As seen in this photograph as well as the suit under discussion, the Duke often wore cuffs on his trousers, a fashion that apparently enraged George V.[28]

Utility suit,

1940s, Great Britain, Victoria & Albert Museum, London

◆

From June 1, 1941, clothing was rationed in the United Kingdom. The intention, of course, was to limit new purchases, and many civilians were concerned about the effect this would have. However, this huge change did not deter designers or retailers, who still sought to provide fashionable, durable, inspiring clothes for men and women. By the following year, the mood of the British High Street had altered somewhat by the appearance of the Utility scheme for clothing. Recognizable for the logo "CC41," meaning "Civilian Clothing 1941," government Board of Trade–approved garments went on sale made from a small range of quality-controlled fabrics.[29] "There won't be the variety of 12 months ago," one newspaper wrote in January 1942, "but there will still be enough choice of colour and style."[30] That choice is illustrated in this double-breasted suit, which has been cleverly manipulated to suggest a fashionable line, and many of its concessions are not noticeable from the outside.

By the early 1940s, shirts generally had attached collars and cuffs. To align with rationing regulations, they were made without breast pockets.

Despite its Utility status and use of cheaper fabrics, this jacket still conforms closely to the fashionable silhouette of the early 1940s. Its relatively broad, peaked lapels and double-breasted cut maintain a style that remained popular throughout the decade, illustrated in this photograph from a 1947 wedding.

UK, private collection

Turn-ups on men's trouser legs were officially banned as part of the Utility Clothing scheme. However, this did not mean that they disappeared altogether: men were known to purchase pairs that were too long and create a cuff themselves with the excess fabric. When rationing was introduced into Australia in May 1942, *The Telegraph* rejoiced that "men are allowed to keep the crease down the middle of the trouser leg!" but did not seem particularly worried about the loss of the turn-up: "Its principal function is that of a repository for particles of fluff, and the occasional threepenny bit which mysteriously vanished when you dropped it one day in church."[31]

Ties made from wool and rayon acetate grew in popularity during the war years. This was largely due to the shortage in silk and, a 1950 magazine article suggested, their "adaptability for printing and hand screening."[32]

The single breast pocket is stay stitched into place. This technique is often used on curved or angled edges to prevent distortion. Here, it would have been chosen over interlining to save on fabric.[33]

More economy is hidden in the trouser pocket bags and waistband facings, both of which are made in low-priced, low quality cotton.[34]

The ban on waistcoats during the Second World War hastened the demise of three-piece suits, and waistcoats gradually came to be replaced with knitted versions, including sleeveless pullovers. These had been growing in popularity since the 1920s and 30s, but were adopted through necessity in the war years. A homemade example can be seen here, worn with a suit jacket, shirt, and tie, in 1939, private collection.

"Demob" suit,

c.1945, Imperial War Museum, London

◆

Between 1945 and 1946, millions of returning servicemen were issued ninety clothing coupons along with demobilization or "demob" clothing. This basic set comprised underwear, jacket and trousers, shirt, overcoat, a hat, two pairs of socks, and one pair of shoes.[35] These suits were generally of very high quality (partly because, as *The Daily Mail* pointed out in 1945, "there are not enough medium quality suits available [instead, servicemen will be given] superfine Scotch tweed suits which would cost 30 to 40 guineas in Saville Row"[36]). Not everyone, however, enjoyed the same quality: Sir Paul Bryan, who served with the Royal West Kent Regiment, commented in his memoirs that "Many never got worn because they were unwearable. Those that were worn were as immediately identifiable as 'demob suits' as those false teeth that stood out as 'National Health.'"[37] Other men were satisfied with the quality but met the scheme with a jaded skepticism, feeling that it was nothing more than a civilian uniform taking the place of their army one. However it was received, the demob remains a sartorial symbol of a return to peace, and a signal to a future "on civvy street."

....

Demob suits were issued with a plain white shirt and two additional detached collars.

Unlike the Utility example, this jacket embraces its double-breastedness, with an extra row of buttons that serve to widen the chest and torso even more.

Overall, the style of this suit is not hugely dissimilar to the previous Utility example. However, though the differences may be subtle, they were significant. Suits like this would include inside breast pockets, good quality lining fabrics and, most noticeably, well-made and high-quality materials for the jacket and trousers. This example is made from a gray pinstripe, a design that would become especially popular towards the end of the decade. Its fashionability did not suit all demobees, however, with one ex-soldier remarking that the pinstripe on his suit "fairly screams at you."[38] Another, returning home to Scotland after his service, remembered: "You had two choices: dark blue or brown, both pinstripe, single breasted or double breasted, wide lapels. I got a blue double breasted like a gangster's!"[39]

The peaked lapel here is broader than that of the previous example, extending further across the chest and almost meeting the shoulder edge.

The jacket is slightly nipped in at the waist, creating a svelte torso; nevertheless, it was reported in a London newspaper in October 1946 that "Despite rationing 'Civvy Street' has put an average of two inches on to the waistline of 'demobbed' men . . . [they are] now coming back to workshops to have an extra two inches put in the waist."[40]

Portrait in uniform taken towards the end of World War Two, Wales, private collection.

Two-piece suit,

1950, McCord Museum, Montreal

◆

Fashion historian Jennifer Craik has described 1950s males as, generally speaking, "incontrovertibly conservative in their choice of clothing," and the wearer of this unassuming suit probably fitted that description.[41] Whether or not a man wished to be conservative, post-war restrictions made frivolity largely inaccessible well into the 1950s. This Canadian example is useful because it provides an accurate view of what many working men would have been wearing on a daily basis in cities and towns.

Patterned ties—often very brightly patterned—were frequently the only splash of color in an otherwise somber ensemble. Some, however, still felt the options on offer were too garish. One 1954 newspaper quoted "a chap [speaking] of some of the vivid neckties being sold. He said there are some he would not be caught wearing at midnight at the bottom of a coalmine during a total eclipse of the moon!"[42]

It was usual for single-breasted jackets to feature no more than three buttons, with often only the first fastened, as seen here. Single breasted styles became far more popular than doubles into the 1950s, partly, it has been suggested, because returning servicemen had grown accustomed to its easy and simple fit during their time in uniform.

Part of ongoing rationing included as few pockets as possible. Here, and in the photograph to the right, the jacket has three pockets: two hip and one welted ("set-in," or cut into the garment) breast pocket.

A similar gray suit worn with patterned tie, c.1950, Wales, private collection.

As seen in the photograph above, trousers were still pleated at the front waist to create a fuller look, with the pleat continuing down the front of each leg. Later into the decade, trouser legs became significantly narrower.

Teddy boy, London,

1954, Tottenham, London, photo by Joseph McKeown/Getty Images, Picture Post

◆

Though inspired by elegant suits worn by upper-class Edwardians, the "Teddy Boy" or "Ted" style emerged as a sartorial rebellion amongst post-war, working-class British youth. Perhaps best described as a working-class dandy, the Teddy Boy, though a small subculture, has become one of the most recognizable cultural figures of the 1950s. Newspaper articles throughout the early to mid-50s convey stories of violence and fear relating to Teddy Boys, reflecting the dark side of the phenomenon. The similarity of the Teds' attire to earlier zoot suits, also associated with rioting and deviancy, was not lost on nervous social commentators. At the other end of the spectrum some found the Teddy uniform a welcome return to a more elegant time, and one article from 1955 even described it as a "mating call" of "modern young men who cut a fine figure."[43] As *The Picture Post* observed in 1954, these conflicting interpretations made "a confusing picture of exaggeration and distortion."[44] Nevertheless, this group's clothing was consistent and highly identifiable. A typical outfit consisted of what is seen here: a long drape jacket, a skinny or "Slim Jim" tie, and "drainpipe" trousers, finished off with long-toed winklepickers or "brothel creepers": shoes with large crepe soles.

Bootlace (known in the USA as bolo), "Slim Jim" ties, or those in the style of Bret Maverick, as seen here, comprised the most popular neckwear for a "Ted."

Step or "notch" collars were popular on neo-Edwardian jackets. An often-seen alternative was the low-rolling shawl collar. These were often faced in a darker contrasting color in the same fabric.[45]

Tight-fitting, ankle-length Italian-style trousers were given the name "drainpipe" because of their straight shape, and the trend was heralded by some mainstream London tailors as the next big thing. One declared in 1952 (before the name "Teddy Boy" had been officially coined) that "They look ridiculous, but we'll be wearing them." In the same year *The Tailor and Cutter* went so far as to suggest that men should get used to the idea of having to "point the toe" while dressing, "as you slide down the essentially narrow cylinders."[46] Despite fashion media forecasts like this, however, in the early 1950s these trousers were very much associated with adolescent Teds and the often confrontational image they projected.

The extreme narrowness of some styles was offset by larger turnups at the cuffs, as seen here.

Former Teddy Boy Mim Scala recalled in 2000 that "Shoulder pads [were] constructed to project eighteen inches outwards from each side of the neck . . . the ideal suit tapered from the extended shoulders to the trouser turn-ups." The width of these shoulders also inspired the nickname "wide boys," a term still in use today in Britain to describe a working-class man who lives by his wits, usually resorting to petty crime to fund his lifestyle.[47]

It is not visible here, but the Teddy Boy suit usually incorporated a waistcoat, often made in bright colors or a shiny brocade fabric. It was sometimes worn with a watch and chain.

The Teddy Boy interpretation of "Edwardian" relates to both early 1900s menswear and also the later 1940s revival of elements of that style. The influence of the original is clearly present in this 1908 fashion illustration of a well-dressed man in similar length coat with long lapels and trousers with a front crease on each leg, c.1908.

Man in Suit and Top Hat, 1908, USA, New York Public Library

Suit worn by Johnny O'Keefe,

c.1955–59, Powerhouse Museum, Sydney

◆

This eye-catching jacket and trousers was worn by Australian singer Johnny O'Keefe—"The Wild One" at the height of his fame. Reputedly made by his mother Thelma, it is a good example of his love for flashy stage wear and, with its drape cut and contrasting colors and textures, incorporates some stylistic elements reminiscent of the Teddy Boy image.[48]

O'Keefe often accessorized suits of this type with slim, wide bowties.

This long, narrow shawl collar is redolent of the neo-Edwardian look favored by Teddy Boys (see previous example).

There are no pockets in the jacket; all the flaps seen on the outside are shams. This highlights the fact that this is a performance piece, based on fashionable styles but with less need for utilitarian features.

Turned-up cuffs, also faced in leopard print, would add a flash of texture when the singer moved his arms on stage.

The jacket is lined in leopard-print velvet, which extends inside the jacket to the waist. Though by no means a new innovation for fashion, leopard print was still a relatively novel approach in the late 1950s following its appearance on Dior's runway in 1947. Dior used the print to accentuate contours in womenswear, an especially effective approach when the rest of the outfit was in a single shade, as seen in this menswear example.[49] The remainder of the decade would see the print becoming more and more popular, satisfying a post-war wish for some exoticism in everyday life. By the end of 1953, *The Sydney Morning Herald* was describing the use of leopard print as "a craze," particularly in America, and that although it was the most popular, other "even more dazzling" animal prints were being promoted in Paris, zebra and tiger stripes amongst them.[50]

Slightly curved edges to the jacket are reminiscent of the Edwardian styles that so strongly influenced 1950s menswear.

Each trouser leg is hemmed, giving the appearance of a turned-up cuff.

"Wash and Wear" suit,

c.1959, USA, Museum at the Fashion Institute of Technology, New York, New York

◆

This unassuming-looking jacket and trousers represents a ground-breaking advance in not only fashion technology, but in the way menswear was manufactured and consumed. The rage for labor-saving devices in the 1950s extended to clothing, with the new possibilities inherent in synthetic materials like nylon. *The West Australian* newspaper reported from a trade fair at London's Royal Festival Hall in 1954 of a suit that "can be thrown into the weekly wash without doing any harm. The suit can be taken from the wash-tub, hung out to dry, then worn without having to be ironed." Not only this, but unlike natural fibers such as cotton and linen, nylon and polyester (terylene) did not require dry cleaning, making them perfect for the man "on the go."[51] This example was made by the American company "Wash n' Wear" and is constructed from a gray seersucker nylon.[52]

....

By the last few years of the decade, jackets were cut with long notched lapels, fastening low—almost at waist level—with one or two buttons. A slim tie enhanced this lean look, as seen in these contemporary photographs taken in Missouri, USA (left) and Greece (right) in 1959.

This suit is shown with a plain white shirt and tie in a darker gray, but by the middle of the decade colorful accessories for men were enthusiastically promoted. One newspaper fashion column in October 1956 suggested always buying a gray suit, "because you can wear almost any color accessories with it."[53] Gray also had the advantage of not "show[ing] every speck of lint or dust," although, as the writer concludes, "with many of today's fabrics, less time and effort is required in care and upkeep."

Portrait, private collection   Wedding snapshot, private collection

Despite bold claims that wash and wear suits were resistant to wrinkles, this suit demonstrates that, to some degree, that was clearly not always the case. Nonetheless, advertisements from the mid-1950s onwards promised that "the suit will never crease, nor shrink or shine," and even that it could be washed whilst being worn.[54]

The looseness of this hip-length jacket, with its rounded corners and patch pockets, is typical of the late 1950s.

Seersucker nylon is a lightweight fabric, suitable for summer wear. Styles like this, however, could be worn all year round due to great advancements in home heating systems and an improvement in transport. This meant that warmer materials were no longer needed by as many people, and they were gladly cast aside in favor of clothing that may not have been as resilient but that was lighter and easier to wear on a daily basis.

Throughout much of the decade, trousers remained relatively baggy and straight-cut, nearly always featuring the ubiquitous front crease.

John Lennon's stage suit,

1963–64, National Museum, Liverpool

◆

In Beatles lore, various stories abound surrounding the origin of the famous collarless suits. The basic shape was certainly inspired by the designs of Pierre Cardin, though evidence suggests that Astrid Kircher, girlfriend of "fifth" Beatle Stuart Sutcliffe, made him a similar prototype.[55] Another influence could have come from that fact that the Beatles—including John Lennon, who wore this example—had admired the American rock n' roll act Jan and Dean, who wore a version of the collarless look in 1963.[56] However it came to be "theirs," this analysis will focus on the history of the style and its precedents in menswear, considering how and why it became so iconic in fashion as well as music history.

This clean-cut look, tying neatly into the **mod** movement of the early 1960s, was the result of a radical—but gradual—departure for the band after their nine leather-clad months in Hamburg. Manager Brian Epstein tidied up their image in part to make them acceptable to their fans' parents. It worked, and it didn't quell their audience's passion for them or, indeed, their own identity as a group. As Paul McCartney commented in 1969, "If you look at the pictures, you won't find anyone looking uncomfortable in those suits. They looked very smart and we looked proud of it all."[57] Lennon is reputed to have felt slightly differently, but as with everything the band promoted, the suits became a firm part of popular culture and were adopted by all kinds of wearers for all kinds of purposes—as seen in this 1963 wedding portrait.

Collarless suits with round necklines were by no means new in the 1960s. For much of the eighteenth century, fashionable men wore collarless coats, and several examples can be seen in chapter two. The necklines often sat much higher or dipped to a slight "V" in the center, but the overall effect was similar.

There are also prominent non-Western inspirations attributed to the style, most notably the Nehru jacket—which itself became a fashion staple later in the decade, and a version similar to this was worn by the Beatles at their Shea Stadium concert in 1966, Philadelphia Museum of Art.

Rounded jacket edges corresponded to several styles throughout history, seen particularly in lounge or "sack" suits of the mid- to late-nineteenth century and in burgeoning sportswear styles into the twentieth. This single-breasted cut, and use of only three buttons, is also reminiscent of the lounge and later sports jacket.

Keystone-France/Getty Images

Stephen Osman/Getty Images
The Beatles in collarless suits with their tailor, Dougie Millings, who made around five hundred garments for the group.

Suit by Mr. Fish,

1968, England and USA, Victoria and Albert Museum, London

◆

Mr. Fish, located near London's Bond Street, is a recognizable name in the history of 1960s fashion and consumerism. Although it catered to a wealthier clientele, its products reflected styles that could be purchased on the more affordable Carnaby Street, and founder Michael Fish's sartorial philosophy— "Clothes should not reflect how 'They' or 'I' think you should look. Clothes should reflect how you want to look"—certainly blended into the sentiments of the young, swinging, and fashionable in 1960s Britain.[58] The bold stripes of this suit are very typical of the psychedelic craze of the decade, but the fabric itself has an unexpected provenance, being made by U.S. furnishing manufacturer Hexter.[59]

This very wide, exaggerated collar is representative of fashionable styles at this date and also forecasts a trend that would be taken to the extreme in the 1970s. Frequently referred to as "Regency" style in the press, it is easy to make associations with 1790s coats, in particular, with their short lapels and wide, pointed collars.

Very high-fastening coats like this were often worn over a plain turtle-neck sweater, rather than a shirt.

Towards the end of the decade, double-breasted fastenings became popular once again, having been largely ousted in favor of single-breasted for around 15 to 20 years.[61]

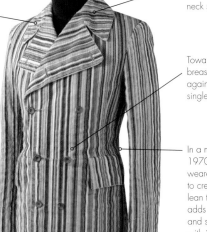

In a manner that would continue into the 1970s, this jacket is closely shaped to the wearer's body, featuring contoured seams to create a nipped-in waist and long, lean torso. The wide collar simultaneously adds breadth to the chest and shoulders, and similar effects were often accentuated with internal padding towards the end of the 1960s—much as they were in the early-mid nineteenth century. In May 1969, a Californian newspaper summed up this focus succinctly as "an almost universal approach to men's clothing—shape."[62]

Coat, 1790s, France (detail), Los Angeles County Museum of Art

The term "Regency" was particularly common in relation to collars that stood up at the back, also known as the "highwayman" style in the 1960s.

Corduroy was a style staple for men throughout the 1960s and 70s, described by one fashion column in 1966 as "going on forever, it seems . . . blossom[ing] out into all the current looks."[60]

References to "Edwardian" inspiration were frequently applied to menswear, and the length of this jacket is certainly an indicator of that period. However, one publication acknowledged the danger of relying too much on terms such as "Regency" or "Edwardian" for an "accurate" comparison, remarking that: "Many people have been confused by the terms, and so have manufacturers who are likely to sew six or eight buttons on a double-breasted suit and call it 'Edwardian' when more accurately [it] might be called a throwback to the 1920 jazz era."[63]

Dinner (tuxedo) jacket and trousers,

c.1960s, Shippensburg University Fashion Archives and Museum, Pennsylvania

◆

From the 1940s it had started to become acceptable for men to wear white tuxedo jackets for certain social occasions. However, it was not until the 1960s, when weddings and other highly formal events became more relaxed, that the popularity of the white dinner jacket grew substantially.[64] By 1968, even this had become "too formal" for some events, as one American newspaper explained in May of that year. Asking its readers whether it was "true" or "false" that "a white dinner jacket is the only acceptable summer substitute for the black tuxedo jacket," the reply came: "False . . . madras plaids, solid colors, and prints are all summery and attractive."[65]

Formal dress usually called for a black bow tie, which would ideally be hand tied rather than bought assembled. An attempt was made in the late 1960s to abolish bow ties from evening wear altogether, replacing them with a white polo-necked shirt, but this only ever achieved a very small following.[66]

Formal dress shirts retained detailing that had been seen for generations; narrow vertical tucks, as seen here, were especially common. Plain white piqué (a fabric with raised designs in the surface, also known as marcella) was often suggested as a suitable alternative in newspaper fashion advice columns. Mother-of-pearl was the most usual choice for dress shirt buttons.

Fashion columns and etiquette guides advised that trousers worn with a white dinner jacket should always be black—and that remains the case in the twenty-first century. It is also still common for such trousers to feature a decorative black silk or satin band (or sometimes, a length of cord) down the side of each leg. The pair shown here do not have this feature, nor do they correspond to Elizabeth Post's 1965 recommendation that "'Cuffed' trousers are not good form." This manual was revised and expanded from her grandmother Emily's works in the early twentieth century, when the dinner jacket was already a social staple for many men. The fact that largely unaltered advice (aside from a few relaxations) was being reprinted fifty years on is testament to the success and longevity of the style. The rest of the outfit aligns with the author's instructions: "The dinner coat has no tails and is cut like a sack suit except that it is held closed in front by one button at the waist line . . . [it is worn with] a black tie instead of a white one."[67]

The "shawl" collar, derived from smoking jackets, was the prevalent cut for dinner jackets. The following decade it became popular on a wider variety of jacket styles, including knitwear. According to *Harper's Bazaar* in 1972, "The shawl collar is back, looking great on jackets, toppers, and especially, wrapcoats. Its gently curving lines carry out the softer look so prevalent in Fall '72 fashions, and it looks marvellous."[68]

State Archives of Florida
A group of young men dressed in white dinner jackets outside Florida State University, Tallahassee, in 1963.

Black patent shoes or pumps were customary footwear with a tuxedo.

Suit by Jacques de Montjoye,

1968–69, McCord Museum, Montreal

◆

The designer of this jacket and trousers, Jacques de Montjoye, was best known for his womenswear and for the strong political statements imbued in some of his clothes—most notably, his 1967 dress entitled "Vietnam," which featured a red patch cut in the shape of a blood stain from a gunshot wound.[69] However, he made his name in menswear through dressing several well-known Canadian television personalities and artists, with ready-to-wear suits and casual clothing available for consumers at his Montreal store. A long-standing interest in sportswear stemmed from his early work in that field in Quebec, and can be seen in the easy formality of this ensemble.[70]

The jacket is made from plain-weave chambray, a lightweight cotton fabric that was originally (as far back as the fourteenth century) made from linen, and first known as "cambric" or "batiste." From the early twentieth-century onwards it was frequently used for military uniforms, and has since been embraced by designers such as Ralph Lauren and Tommy Hilfiger.[71]

The placket covering the jacket's button fastening is a significant design feature, creating a streamlined front that brings to mind the ongoing space-age, futuristic influence of the decade, plus further inspiration from the costumes of popular television shows *Star Trek* and *Space 1999*.[72]

Since the nineteenth century, patch pockets on civilian wear have been used to suggest leisure. They were to become even more fashionable the following year, when Yves St. Laurent would adapt his "Saharienne" women's collection for men.[73]

Flared trousers had been gaining popularity since the mid-1960s, but it was not until the following decade that they would become universally popular. By then, the wide hems would be even more pronounced than shown here, with the trousers close-fitting to the knees and then flaring out over the shoes.

This exaggerated collar, faced in the same brown plaid as the trousers and pocket flaps, forecasts the very wide collars that would dominate the 1970s. As with the previous example, it would be worn with a turtle-neck sweater or, by this date, a shirt with similarly-shaped collar, spread over the lapels.

High-fastening lapels mean that even if a tie were worn with this jacket, it would barely be visible. In 1968 an Australian newspaper reported the growing trend for going tie-less, which, they claimed, was a move originated in Italy. "Almost all sports and leisure suits and many day suits have woolly or silk polo-necked sweaters," the article claimed, although this would not have been an option in most professional circumstances.[74] Nevertheless, so prominent and popular was the change—in leisure wear, at least—that even stalwarts of the tailoring world such as Savile Row were forced to sit up and take notice, adapting their approach to various designs in light of the wishes of fashionable and influential clients.

As seen throughout this book, plaids, checks, and tartans have remained consistently popular throughout the history of menswear. Here, the use of brown-toned plaid represents a popular choice for sports and leisure wear throughout the 1950s and 60s, and the contrasting mustard-colored body of the coat makes these checked splashes all the more eye-catching.

Idealized portrait of Mao Zedong towering over the Yangtze river,

c.1960–70, Michael Nicholson/Corbis via Getty Images

—

What is now universally known as the "Mao" suit actually originated with his predecessor, Sun Yat-Sen, who led a revolution against China's Qing Dynasty and established the Republic of China on January 1, 1912. The plain, militaristic design was commissioned (but not designed) by Yat-Sen himself and given his name after his death in 1925.[75] However, when Mao Zedong later announced the foundation of the People's Republic of China in October 1949, the suit became an international symbol of his regime, and of Communism more generally. As this analysis will show, the suit combined a mix of Chinese and foreign influences, and although worn by both sexes, it remains very much associated with one male protagonist, going on to influence menswear in the decades since.

....

A young engaged couple at the close of WW1, private collection
The original Yat-Sen suit drew heavily on western military uniforms for inspiration,[76] and its Mao successor carried on that aesthetic, which can be clearly seen in this British uniform from the First World War, above (1918). The turn-down collar was of a type seen on both British and German uniforms, and the flapped patch pockets of Mao's jacket are almost identical to those in the image above.

The suit could be made in a range of muted tones, most popularly blue, green, or gray.

Despite its similarity to western military uniforms, the individual details on this jacket (including the placement and number of its pockets and shape of their flaps, and the number of buttons at center front), relate to very specific and symbolic traditional and revolutionary Chinese principles.

Four pockets, placed at equal distance above and below each other, embody the Four Cardinal Principles of conduct, cited in the *Book of Changes (I Ching)*:[77]

> Propriety
> Honesty
> Justice
> A sense of shame

A higher number of pockets could signify greater political status in the Party.

Five buttons at the center represented the five branches of the constitution of the Communist government: legislation, supervision, examination, administration, and jurisdiction.[78]

Mao's version of the suit, modified by tailor Tian Atong, was inspired in part by traditional Chinese peasant tunics, trousers, and black cotton shoes.[79] This reference to proletariat, working-class garments spoke directly to one of Mao's most fervent beliefs: that it was the peasants of the country who would

Chinese peasant painting, c.1990 (detail), private collection

"rise like a mighty storm . . . They will send all imperialists, warlords, corrupt officials, local tyrants and evil gentry into their graves."[80]

Chapter 7
1970–2000

With more options available to men than ever, it can be tempting to view this period as the beginning of the end for the traditional suit. However, as Tim Edwards explains in his exploration of fashion, masculinity, and consumer society, "There is very little evidence to support this hypothesis, as sales of suits since the so-called casual revolution of the 1960s and 1970s have remained comparatively constant."[1] The suit has never ceased to be an important garment, still worn daily by many men, and its continuing dominance amongst so many choices is testament to its ability to adapt and develop. It is perhaps this broader spectrum of menswear that has enabled designers to produce increasingly subversive output, one of which—Vivienne Westwood's "bondage" suit—is discussed in this chapter. It seemed that nothing was off-limits for the suit in this thirty-year time span, and long-held ideas around what constituted a "suit" in the first place were being questioned.

On the face of it, suits were no longer the province of men alone. Not only had trouser suits for women begun to gain traction since the 1960s, but increasingly, unisex design elements crept into menswear during the 70s. An example can be seen in this chapter with a plum-colored, Australian-made corduroy suit from 1973. The slim hips and nipped-in waist of the jacket, coupled with a broad belt to heighten the effect, has obvious feminine connotations. However, even this example does not suggest that "unisex" meant the appropriation of female elements into menswear, or vice versa—but rather the development of a purposefully androgynous aesthetic. Prominent figures such as David Bowie and Marc Bolan promoted this blurring of the sexes as expressed through fashion, makeup, and hairstyle, and this was to influence the succeeding New Romantic movement in the 1980s.

Nevertheless, there seems to have been a lack of consensus as to what "unisex" really meant. Kansai Yamamoto, who designed stage costumes for Bowie, explained that "I approached Bowie's clothes as if I was designing for a female."[2] Androgyny, then, was based around men adopting traditionally female practices, such as makeup. Bowie, however, was a rarity. As Jo Paoletti explains, the "peacock revolution" of bright colors and patterns for men was brief, and "for the most part, 'unisex' meant more masculine clothing for girls and women. Attempts to feminize men's appearance turned out to be particularly short-lived."[3]

It is interesting that "attempts to feminize men's appearance" still seem to have been based largely around that most male of garments, the suit. And no matter how it is cut or accessorized, there is perhaps a safety in the suit: a feeling that however it may be played with, it is still, in essence, a masculine institution. Even women's adoption of pieces of men's clothing in the 1970s and 80s, particularly following the success of *Annie Hall* in 1977, did not make the suit in any way a feminine garment. On the contrary, as Stella Bruzzi explains, "By not being fitted and not accentuating the feminine curves the distance between the masculinity of the clothes and the femininity of the body became magnified."[4]

Elsewhere during the decade, particularly in America, a more conservative feel reigned with "preppy" style, a reinterpretation of the Ivy League look that had been so popular in the first half of the century. Preppy suits were generally gray flannel and, ideally, made by classic companies like Brooks Brothers. Though plain, they were beautifully cut and accessorized with quality items, highlighting the elite and privileged backgrounds of the original New England prep-schoolers.

By 1970, the popularity of overcoats as a part of daily professional wear was on the wane. That year a study of "future market prospects" of textile industries in the United Kingdom predicted that "styles, particularly in overcoats and rainwear, are becoming much more casual."[5] Wealthy bankers in the 1980s reversed this trend within a small sector of society by favoring—in particular—Harris tweed and Burberry overcoats as outward signs of their success and prestige. In the following decade, sports coats and activewear became more fitted, suitable for both exercise and (crucially for this period) commuting. This versatility meant that men now had a far broader gamut in terms of what went over their suits, and the implementation of temperature-regulating materials ended, in Valerie Steele's words, "the need for bulky layering . . . [by creating] outer garments that could function as personal thermostats."[6]

The New Romantics combined a range of styles into their repertoire. The look was originally inspired by the London club scene after the demise of punk,[7] and early exponents were sometimes known as "New Dandies"—an appropriate epithet given their clothing's clear links to the early nineteenth century and original "Romantic" aesthetic. Suits featured, particularly towards the end of the movement, but there was no single cohesive silhouette. As well as the nineteenth-century romantic element, influences included the French Revolution, zoot suits of the 1940s, seventeenth-century Puritanism, and 1930s Hollywood chic. Such a mish-mash of styles was a reaction against the so-called "antifashion" of the punk movement, the style of which was described by Dick Hebdige as "the sartorial equivalent of swear words."[8] Neither movement embraced the conventional, and neither let the suit fully into their ideology (indeed, in terms of punk, not at all).

The 1980s, however, would usher in a period dominated by what came to be known as "power dressing"; where punk had sought to challenge class identity, mainstream fashions of the decade worked to reflect consumerism, elitism, and corporate ambition. Giorgio Armani was a key player in this approach, and here enters the paradoxical nature of 1980s menswear. His late 1970s Hollywood glamour-inspired garments made way in the early 80s for a soft, contoured, and, in the words of many, "feminine" breed of suit. Jackets were unstructured, with little lining and no padding, and made from lightweight fabrics not traditionally associated with male tailoring. His work on Paul Schrader's *American Gigolo* (1980), in which Richard

Gere plays a male prostitute, catapulted the suit to fame. Yet, as John Potvin explains, Armani was dressing a character who "is consumed as much as he consumes," who is "dependent on a woman to save him" and therefore emasculated, his traditional male power removed.[9] Christopher Breward also comments on the character's "narcissism" as being indicative of the 1980s New Man, a narcissism innately connected with immaculate dressing that, simultaneously, appears effortless.[10] Gere's costumes were unmistakably Armani, meaning any man that could afford to would be able to purchase this vision of masculinity—which, as Tim Edwards described it in the 1990s: "[is] no longer simply an essence or an issue of what you do, it's how you look . . . in a society . . . where traditional productive and work roles for men are undermined, the emphasis on appearance must increase, and does so relentlessly."[11] So, while women's power dressing emulated the "power-broking masculine look," as Delis Hill describes it, conceptions of masculinity were at the same time even less neatly defined than in the previous decade.[12]

The 1980s was without doubt an eclectic decade and one in which fashion did not rely solely on European and American talent. The cataclysmic influence of Japan during this decade cannot be overemphasized, and the work of two key designers, Kenzo Takada and Mitsuhiro Matsuda, will be analyzed in this chapter.

Until trade links with Japan were opened in 1854, the exchange of influences was almost nonexistent, to any commercial end, at least. From the last half of the century onwards, however, Europe and America saw an influx of design inspiration and, in turn, western dress became increasingly popular in Japan. As well as direct imports of furniture, textiles, and decorative arts, Japanese influence in the west was appropriated into the movement known as "Japonisme." This presented a romanticized, idealistic representation that could veer into patronizing territory: theatrical works such as Gilbert and Sullivan's *The Mikado* (1885) and Belasco and Long's *The Darling of the Gods* (1902) demonstrate how the west commonly perceived the east. While some Japanese men and women began to wear three-piece suits and bustle dresses, Europeans and Americans did not adopt kimono or the male "monsuke," except as strictly informal at-home dressing or tea gowns, and even then they were modified to fit a western aesthetic. Japanese clothing was still viewed very much as costume, and was a firm favorite at fancy dress parties of the elite. Japanese style was also frequently referred to as "Chinese" or generically "eastern," largely ignoring the traditional, subtle Japanese artistic approach of symmetry, balance, perspective, and an affinity with the natural world.

By 1970, Japan was beginning to infiltrate the internationally renowned French fashion scene. Japanese fashion, though more "westernized" than traditional, had developed its own distinct personality that seemed to transcend cultural boundaries. At the same time, it often subtly integrated Japanese aesthetic with, as Bonnie English has described in relation to Miyake, Yamamoto, and Kawakubo, "the concept of the kimono and the traditional Japanese way of packaging in which everything is somehow folded, wrapped, revealed and shaped."[13] This is particularly evident in the Matsuda suit of this chapter, with its use of complex pleating and draping to create one fluid, sophisticated sheath. Simultaneously, this suit incorporates very English nineteenth- and twentieth-century sportswear references, in a manner that is not immediately discernible but impossible to ignore once noted.

The Kenzo suit discussed here is a very different example, illustrating the boldness and diffidence that made this designer stand out in the 1970s and 80s. Kenzo "reconstructed Western clothing" and his flair for mixing patterns and textures created, as Yuniya Kawamura expressed it, "a combination that no Western designers ever imagined."[14] His infiltration of the Parisian scene enabled successors Kawakubo and Issey Miyake to change the landscape of fashion in the 1980s for both men and women.

Moving into the 1990s, the dominance of Japan continued. Some designers can even be said to have "attacked" traditional western menswear in an attempt to subvert it and create something new. In 1994 Rei Kawakubo, designing for Comme des Garçons, produced a suit that was, quite literally, deconstructed. Her fabrics often contained intentional flaws, but this suit (now in the collection of the Metropolitan Museum of Art) has raw, slashed edges where a collar should be, rendering an otherwise unassuming business jacket into an angst-ridden sartorial statement. This example perfectly illustrates the theory and practice of deconstructivism, an ideology pioneered by Kawakubo and Yohji Yamamoto during the 1980s. It confronted traditional tailoring techniques by displaying unfinished edges, and even left lines of tailoring chalk visible on fabric.[15]

The 1990s introduced Belgian designers Ann Demeulemeester, Martin Margiela, and Dries Van Noten as principal exponents of the movement, and elements of their vision— particularly a certain apathy and disenchantment with the fashion industry—filtered down into mainstream menswear. Societal concerns surrounding the economic recession of the early 1990s fueled, Elizabeth Wilson has suggested, a type of "aestheticisation of dystopia" when it comes to fashion.[16] Postmodern malaise could be regarded as a type of second-wave fin-de-siècle that had engulfed certain sections of society at the close of the nineteenth century: an intense anxiety that was partly discernible through dress and dress habits.

However, more generally speaking, suits in the 1990s moved away from the wide, brash 1980s silhouette to form a simpler, minimalist, more easygoing appearance. In part this was due to the dawning realization that, as Jill Nelmes has expressed it when writing about film, "capitalism was not infallible" following the yuppie's glory years of the 1980s.[17] As Nelmes observes, the decade ushered in a palpable crisis of masculinity, one that could perhaps be seen in the safe, wholesome image of wildly successful manufactured boy bands such as the Backstreet Boys and Boyzone. Clean white suits worked to create the kind of unthreatening, fashionable look of 1960s bands, but, cultural theorist Janice Miller has asserted, the boy band of the 90s was "less a music experience than a marketing one."[18] The image of Boyzone does illustrate an important and, as many would see it, positive shift in menswear and expectations of male style during the decade. It gradually became acceptable to wear a business suit without a tie, and with the top shirt button left open. Shirts for the office could be in any color but white, and, on increasingly popular "dress down Fridays," men paired denim jeans with t-shirts and casual waistcoats.

ABOVE
Men in white suits: Boyzone
at Pavarotti's concert,
Modena, Italy, June 1999,
Eric Vandeville/Getty Images

This soon expanded to become what was referred to as "casual business wear," famously championed by Bill Gates in the 1990s, which often included knitted polo shirts, blazers, and chinos. In April 1994 *The Canberra Times* summed up this trend as "Comfort . . . combining with classics, contemporary siding with casual and creativity with loose construction as men are being encouraged to warm up by softening up."[19] This "changing attitude" allowed men more freedom, the article wrote, in all areas of life but particularly—and most notably—the workplace. The fact that more workplaces were open to such relaxation gave designers a new challenge, which Australian brand Country Road said resulted in the "fluidity and texture of the 'split suit' as well as in the more traditional three-piece outfits." The "split suit" might consist of a suit jacket or blazer with jeans, or formal trousers with a sports jacket.

By the late 1990s, this kind of approach had become commonplace in many organizations, with the majority at least offering a "dress down Friday." As the Bureau of National Affairs (Bloomberg BNA) reported in January 1998, "traditional formal business attire typically is required only of top managers and executives. More than two-fifths of the responding employers . . . expect top officials to wear suits or dresses, but far fewer organizations mandate such formal dress for other workers."[20] However, this "liberation" was not unanimously popular, and many men—particularly those who only owned suits and preferred the lack of choice they were offered each day—struggled to adapt.

The trend waxed and waned, and some felt it illustrated a strong correlation between fashion and the economy. Erynn Masi de Casanova's work on "white collar masculinity" interviewed a former vice president of a Fortune 500 company who believed that "In the 1990s boom years, people were dressing very casually. Then the crisis hit, and people started dressing up." De Casanova suggests that this is because, in times of crisis, "men were compelled to focus on their physical appearance, one thing that they could control."[21] The connection of the suit to control, formality, stability, and respectability was still there nearly 400 years after its story began, and the last example in this book does not refute that—but it does offer a rebellious twist.

On the face of it, the "Sanderson" suit by New Zealand fashion label WORLD is a bright, unusual-looking two-piece suit. Its use of a bold floral pattern offers immediate historical parallels as well as a subversion of the "expected" male aesthetic, and the use of upholstery fabric suggests that a suit's composition can (indeed, should) be taken from unexpected sources. The energy of the print fits with the aesthetic of a casual workplace, but the cut and shape of the suit, plus its accompanying shirt and tie, speak of more formal expectations. At the same time, hidden from view is a subversive message: "At last I've Found my Sex Machine!" inscribed onto the jacket's lining. This defies all conventional associations with the suit, and the fact that it is a secret between the jacket and its wearer might imply that this 400-year-old institution is not quite brave enough—yet.

This book finishes at the year 2000, with the above-mentioned late 1990s example showing tremendous change but also tremendous staying power. At the time of writing, the skinny suit—in many respects a 1960s incarnation—tops the fashion charts, a nod to the cyclical nature of fashion but also to the way a suit can reflect rapidly shifting understandings of what "masculinity" really means. In the twenty-first century this seems to come down to individuality, with many men still embracing the suit, some repurposing it to fit their lifestyle, and still more resolutely ignoring it, as the conversation quoted at the beginning of the Introduction illustrates. All these options are now increasingly accepted, but our image of "the suit" as an historical, cultural, and social staple for men remains.

Suits: left, 1970, Bill Blass, and right, c.1970s, Thelma Finster Bradshaw,

Philadelphia Museum of Art, Pennsylvania

◄

Bill Blass, the first American designer to put his name on a fashion label, opened his own company in 1970—the date of these distinctive suits. During the 1960s Blass was especially well known for his womenswear, which frequently incorporated aspects of male tailoring, but later he became one of the first major American designers to offer a whole line of men's fashions.[22] The left-hand suit retains a standard silhouette of the late 1960s, but makes a bold statement with its eye-catching, multi-colored patterning. The suit to the right, made by Thelma Finster Bradshaw for her father, the artist Howard Finster, is another example of jacket and trousers made from a double-knit blend. In shape it is very similar to the Blass, but it embodies some different details and influences.

....

Polyester was immensely popular during the 1960s and 70s—a durable, high-tech, easily produced fiber that represented modern society. In the1960s, textured polyester was combined with wool to create the kind of double-knit fabric that this suit is made from. Double-knits paved the way for exciting new avenues in the textile industry, although eventually supply outstripped demand and the combination fell from its pedestal.

Fashion columns in the early 1970s highlighted the presence of "narrower chests and higher armholes" since 1970, and both become increasingly obvious in the following two examples of this chapter.[24] This incredibly bright, bold print with its wavy stripes and horizontal laddering pattern represents the "peacock" mood for menswear. Speaking of "black men's flamboyant fashions," *Ebony* magazine summed up the aesthetic of the period at large in 1972: "Bright, bold, basic peacock colors . . . reflect the personality of the individual rather than the pressures of society to conform . . . Nothing's taboo and the only restrictions are in the mind."[25]

Slanted pockets with flaps provide easy access, and in shape and practicality recall leisure and equestrian wear from the start of the century.

In the first year of the decade, the distinctive 1970s flare is becoming evident in these trousers. Cuffed hems heighten this focus.

Both coats are made with medium-wide notched lapels, a traditional yet popular cut. The Bradshaw suit is shown with a plain black t-shirt, but both would have been worn with either a shirt/shirt and tie combination or turtle (polo-neck) sweater.

Three-piece suit, France, c. 1765, Los Angeles County Museum of Art

These pocket flaps are cut in a scalloped shape, with three points connected by concave arches. This design is reminiscent of eighteenth century men's pockets after about 1720. The use of metal buttons on Finster's suit was also a feature of eighteenth-century coats, and is illustrated in the photograph above.

Like men's leisure wear throughout the late nineteenth and early twentieth centuries, both these jackets sport deep, curved fronts.

Wool blend suit,

1972, McCord Museum, Montreal

◆

This black-and-gray houndstooth check suit, with its neo-Edwardian feel, also features very wide lapels, a long body, and bell-bottom trousers, making it absolutely typical of the early years of the 1970s. The youth movements of the late 1960s and early 70s somewhat threatened the continuation of the suit amongst young men, but examples like this illustrate the way designers managed to keep formal jackets and trousers in step with developing trends.

Very wide lapels are a key marker of the decade. For more casual occasions, jackets like this would often be worn with an open, spread shirt collar to further enhance the breadth.

Even for business wear, it was becoming acceptable to wear a colored rather than plain white shirt. This example has a black body with white polka-dots, a design matched on the pocket square to the left. The contrasting white collar is reminiscent of separate, stiff collars of the nineteenth and early twentieth centuries.

The black and white polka dot theme continues inside the jacket, with a synthetic twill lining in the same design.[26]

Fashionable ties extended to at least 4 inches at their widest point. This example is made from white synthetic moiré, cut on the bias, with a pointed end.[27]

The basic shape of the formal suit remained fairly static throughout the 1970s. The middle-end of the decade brought a change, however, with the return of the three-piece suit, a style staple that had been out of fashion since the 1930s. This image from 1978 shows a suit with a similar aesthetic to the one shown here—note the equally wide lapels and shirt collar—but worn with a matching waistcoat. Note that the lowest button is fashionably undone.

Suit jackets could be either double or single-breasted, although the latter was more popular during the early years of the decade. In 1971 the *Australian Women's Weekly* published an article entitled "The Art of Updating your Husband," with a photograph of a man wearing a similar suit to the one shown here. The writer declared that the fashionable jacket "for now, and probably for many years to come, owes much to a hacking jacket."[28] This similarity can be seen in the close fit, shaped around the chest and waist, and angled pockets, "preferably with flaps."

Trousers are cut relatively close to the figure (and probably sit on the hips rather than waist), ending in a slight flare at the ankle. At this date the cuff circumference was usually up to about 18 inches, and several names for the style abounded, from "parallels" to "bell-bottoms" to "loons."[29]

Trouser turn-ups were becoming popular once again, but were not—as evidenced here—a universal attribute of the fashionable suit.

Wedding guests, 1978, private collection

Suit by Mr. John,

1973, Sydney, National Gallery of Victoria, Melbourne

◆

This wine-colored suit represents several important shifts in men's fashion of the early 1970s, and is a good example of forward-moving Australian fashion. The suit came from a chain of boutiques called "The House of Merivale and Mr. John," established in Sydney in the 1960s by husband-and-wife team Merivale and John Hemmes. When the duo opened their fifth store in Canberra in 1975, *The Canberra Times* described their clothing as "individual, and great attention is paid to detail with coordination carried through to the accessories. Only a limited number of each garment is made in a range of colors."[30]

In mid-1950s America, a so-called "pink revolution" began, principally amongst young college men. Pink shirts and accessories became incredibly fashionable alongside ubiquitous gray flannel suits, and were widely adopted by those young and daring enough to alter their wardrobes.[31] Less than 20 years later, pink could be seen everywhere—not just as an accessory but as the color of an entire suit. Its use on this shirt complements the dark cerise of jacket and trousers.

To twenty-first century eyes, there is a feminine element to the cut of this jacket, with its nipped-in waist accentuated by a broad, self-color belt. This type of shaping was frequently referred to by clothing advertisers in the early 1970s as "the fashionable 'waisted' or 'shaped' look."[32] However, in many ways this jacket is highly masculinized, accentuating narrow hips and a broad torso and shoulders. The popularity of suits shaped to the body in this way would continue throughout the decade, ideally suited to the toned and healthy body of young men. In many respects, they could be said to encourage men to exhibit themselves, to display their sexuality in similar ways to women. In some respects, suits like this validate James Laver's 1964 prediction that soon, men's clothes would "reacquire an erotic principle that they have lost for the last 200 years."[33]

These striking peaked lapels are cut with a curved edge, a very prominent and popular feature of the 1970s. They are so wide that their tips touch the edge of each shoulder.

There are two slanting pockets at each hip, also seen on the other 1970s examples in this chapter. However, these are jetted (a technique in which thin strips of fabric tape each side of a slit) rather than made with flaps. In this case, the aim would have been to maintain as slim an outline to the jacket as possible.

The cut and fit of these flares corresponds to a now trend for 1973, known colloquially as **baggies**. Rather than sit on the hips, these were high-waisted and gradually became wider from the knees down (up to as much as 22 inches at the knee, finishing with an impressive 28 at the bottom). They usually ended in a 2- to 2.5-inch turned-up cuff, and they were worn by both sexes.[34]

Palm Beach 'sand bags' from 1932 advertisement, (detail), courtesy Old Magazine Articles
At around the same time, there was a resurgence of the front trouser pleat. It fell largely from favor during the 1960s, but from the Oxford bags of the 1920s to the Palm Beach "sand bags" of the following decade, the recurring theme is another illustration of the deeply cyclical nature of fashion for both sexes.

Leisure suit,

1970s, Shippensburg University Fashion Archives & Museum, Pennsylvania

◆

Although it lacks the patch pockets and belt of the safari suit, this shirt and shorts combination maintains other hallmarks of that style. Its loose, easy, unpadded structure and fit are vital signifiers of the "leisure" aesthetic, but the more formal label of "suit" would still be applied to these garments when worn together.

Raglan sleeves were popular for sporting and casual wear, being flexible and relatively simple to produce, as no shaped armholes were required. They originated in around 1855 and were named for Lord Raglan, a British Army officer especially known for his involvement in the Crimean War.[35] In the twentieth century they were also a common feature of topcoats, as seen in this advertisement from 1942 (New York Public Library).

Model No. 1·
Young Men's Double
Drape Topcoat

Very dressy three-button
two to
Note fu
chest ar
heads. I
lefts. Fo
back a
unless
ord

The collar is cut with simple notched lapels, one of the earliest forms and also one of the easiest to create. It is not possible to wear this shirt with a tie, giving it a relaxed yet still tailored appearance. If worn with a jacket, this would probably be in a short sports style.

The rear of the shirt features in-built "action" pleats, reminiscent of those on the earlier Norfolk jacket. These were included to allow ease of movement, and can be seen appropriated into a formal business suit later in this chapter.

The buttoned hem of the shirt (simulating side belts), along with its angled slit pockets recalls gabardine—popularly known as "gab" jackets of the 1940s and 50s. These were named for the material most commonly used, but the term has come to be associated with this sports-influenced, easy-fitting style that was particularly fashionable amongst young men.

'Sportsman's Choice', March 31, 1945 (detail), courtesy Old Magazine Articles

The slim belt of the shorts and its two front pleats also correspond to 1940s styles, particularly evident in this advertisement for gabardine casual clothing, c.1945.

Technically, breeches could be termed an early version of "shorts" (and the evening or "dress" variety were occasionally called this)—simply because they were a shorter version of the trouser or pantaloon. However, shorts as we recognize them today are very differently worn and constructed, and irrevocably linked to ideas of sports and leisure. This is because their earliest iteration came about in the 1930s for outdoor leisure activities such as hiking. In subsequent decades, they became increasingly popular for casual wear outside the office, but very rarely in it: a notable exception is Bermuda shorts, and then only in a very specific place and for a very practical reason. However, as G. Bruce Boyer has discussed, Bermudian shorts can be credited with changing the way society has viewed the appropriateness and flexibility of the garment. He even describes shorts as "the first casual business wear" that stemmed from college students' "walk shorts" of the post-war years to an increased military influence in men's fashion.[36] This is an arguable idea; it does partly reflect the aesthetics of this example, with its smart gray polyester suiting fabric, welted pockets, self-fabric belt and covered buttons. However, the belt buckle suggests a recreational, sporting emphasis by featuring a nautical design of ship's steering wheel and yacht.

Suit by Giorgio Armani,

1982, Fashion Institute of Technology Museum, New York, New York

◆

In the world of twentieth-century tailoring, no name is perhaps more synonymous with power, prestige, and progression than Giorgio Armani. At a time when anything Italian was all the sartorial rage, the designer capitalized on his background and aesthetic to produce classic yet unstructured designs that are remarkable for their quality and innovation. Armani's own way of living life, as *New York Magazine* described it in 1996, with "discipline and indulgence" is illustrated in this outwardly reserved wool two-piece suit, which is remarkable for its lightness and intimacy. It exemplifies one of his comments on the state of fashion, and of its probable future: "Too much has been done too fast, with everyone always looking out for something new; so every season everything was changing very quickly . . . And this is the negative side of fashion, in a sense, that has made it look a bit ridiculous today, I think."[37] The year of this suit's production, 1982, was also the year that Armani featured on the cover of *Time* magazine, praised within for popularizing non-traditional menswear.

The museum describes this suit as one of Armani's key 1980s pieces, redefining "the look of the modern dandy."[38] The dandy of the 70s and 80s has been described as a "tastemaker for the general population," providing influence for high-end designers such as Armani, and enthusiastically consuming fashion in a manner previously associated more with women.[39] These complex ideas are caught up with the concept of the "New Man," a label that emerged in the 1980s in response to, as some have claimed, second-wave feminism's attack on traditional masculinity. The New Man was sensitive, creative, and introspective, interested in the self and the portrayal of self, someone the media recognized as ripe and ready for a "new look" and bodily transformation. At the same time he could be viewed as narcissistic, hyper aware of his physicality, and driven by consumerist desires.[40]

This ensemble shows the attention to detail displayed by the archetypal "New Man"—an interest in, and knowledge of, fashionable trends and accessories. In the 1980s, the influence of British designer Paul Smith with his vibrant color schemes encouraged men to pair darker suits with light, bright shirts and ties. It was now becoming acceptable for suited city workers to cast off plain white shirts for something more personal, like the sky blue shown here.

This depiction shows a slightly more formal look, but it became common for Armani suits to be worn with shirts with banded collars, eradicating the need for a necktie. When worn, ties were narrower than they had been the previous decade, and skinny knit varieties were popular for casual wear.[41]

Armani's "unstructured" suits combined formality with comfort, rejecting the very wide and padded shoulders that were fashionable throughout the decade. In an unprecedented move he reinvented the business suit by removing padding and interlinings, dropping the shoulders and lowering the button stance (or keeping it neutral). Here, this latter detail helps to create a very low, slim V down the front of the torso and a looser, softer finish.[42]

The use of only one button to close the jacket contributes to the easy fit Armani was aiming for: the idea that a suit could be looser (achieved by experimentation with the "drape cut" of the 1930s) as well as smart.[43] In essence, he wanted men to feel "in tune" with their clothing—for them to wear a suit rather than it wear them.

These trousers are loosely cut around the knee and thigh, tapering towards the ankle. They feature deep pleats at the front of each leg, and all of these elements recall 1930s and 40s styles.

Paul Smith ensemble worn by Patrick McDonald, 2007–2012, Rhode Island School of Design
Paul Smith's influence continued into the twenty-first century with exceptionally bright and bold combinations such as this Merino wool suit with shocking pink silk tie, 2007–12.

Three-piece suit by Kenzo,

1984, Philadelphia Museum of Art, Pennsylvania

◆

Kenzo Takada exploded onto the French fashion scene in 1970, the first Japanese designer to show his work in Paris. Along with Kansai Yamamoto and Issy Miyake, Kenzo quickly made a name for himself as one of Japan's rising fashion stars: but it was his bright and youthful clothing, in particular, that really made an impact and cemented him as one of fashion's greats.[44] This suit, one of Kenzo's early forays into menswear, was made in the early 1980s when his reputation was firmly established—but it still embodies that flair and vivacity that made him so sought after in the 1970s.

Relatively short and narrow lapels are another indicator of early 1980s style.

Suits made entirely from a plaid fabric were not unique to the 1980s, or even to the twentieth century. As shown in chapters three and four, tartan designs for menswear were making a statement in the early years of the nineteenth—and not just as small splashes of color in the form of a waistcoat (although this was extremely popular for a time; see the 1850–59 morning vest below. (Metropolitan Museum of Art).

The silhouette of this jacket is typical for the 1980s with its very broad, powerful shoulders and loose fit around the torso. Moving down, the outline becomes narrower, with a slimmer waist and hips and straight trouser legs. This corresponds to what one men's magazine in 1980 described as the "Y-line" silhouette for menswear, recommending "the ready-to-wear end of the market" for purchasing trousers to achieve this look: "straighter and without the fullness of recent years."[45]

The use of three round-edged, square patch pockets is reminiscent of styles seen on leisure wear since the late nineteenth century (see chapter four). Their inclusion here demonstrates the flexibility of suits at this time, the acceptance of more casual styles for both work and leisure wear. As *The Canberra Times* described it in 1982, patch pockets helped to add "a softer silhouette . . . for casual elegance" to suits and separates.[46]

The top-heaviness of this suit is emphasized when we see the tapered cuffs of its trousers, which sit very close to the leg and contrast strongly with the broad shoulders above.

Like the 1830 tartan suit earlier in this book, this example uses the same bright fabric for jacket, trousers and waistcoat, creating an overwhelming but utterly cohesive whole. At the beginning of the decade there were reports of "elegant" jackets in "giant checks and plaids in boldly contrasting colors or harmonizing neutrals" seen on the catwalk for autumn/winter 1981, but not yet widely available as ready-to-wear styles. Indeed, the look seems to have been an inspiration for high-end designers throughout the decade, with Vivienne Westwood's tartan and punk collaboration. Later, however, any hint of couture elitism was lost when tartan became a popular element of **grunge** style.

Mitsuhiro Matsuda suit, wool twill weave,

1986, RISD Museum, Providence, Rhode Island

◆

Western fascination with Japanese aesthetics is certainly not new, but, until the opening of Kenzo's Paris boutique in 1970, fashion was principally concerned with re-shaping Japanese design to suit European and American lifestyles. The term **Japonisme**, which developed at the end of the nineteenth century, could be said to imply an appropriation rather than a mutual appreciation. With Kenzo, Miyake, and others, however, came a gradual but genuine assimilation into the French fashion scene, in particular, resulting in Japanese design ranking amongst the top in the world and challenging preconceived western norms. As Bonnie English points out, these designers embrace new technologies whilst creating clothing imbued with "meaning and memory."[47] This suit by Matsuda is a perfect example of that blend of style; its laser sharp modernity is coupled with allusions to early twentieth-century leisure wear and sportswear.

The mid-1980s professional man had a range of shirt options available to him. In 1984, the manual *Color for Men* offered a system to help men achieve harmony in their dressing, providing four "seasonal palettes" that men could match their hair, eye, and skin color to. There were certainly more options than white alone, and colored shirts with contrasting white collars were very fashionable for all "seasons." For businesswear, a tie was always recommended.[48]

These very broad shoulders are typical of the male silhouette in the mid-late 1980s.

Lapels are now considerably narrower than in the previous decade. They are also very long, adding height to the torso.

This relatively high waist is more closely fitted than earlier in the decade. Its svelteness combined with the broad torso illustrates a comment made by bodybuilder Mike Mentzer in 1983: "For men, the ideal body of the 1980s is a cross between the slimness of the marathoner and the musculature of the bodybuilder."[51]

Detail of jacket from *Vanity Fair*, 1916, courtesy Old Magazine Articles

At the back, the jacket shows two long, pleated sections running vertically down each shoulder. This 1916 image from *Vanity Fair* illustrates the pivot sleeve and shoulder pleat of a golfing jacket, the very practical purpose of which was to expand the fabric and allow the player to swing more easily. The rows of pleats on Matsuda's jacket are stitched down, but clearly show traces of this early twentieth-century influence. During the 1980s "action backs" did make a return in sports jackets and sportswear, with one newspaper describing them as the "new look" of 1980.[49] Matsuda's use of the detail both subverts the traditional premise of the business suit and highlights the extent of the craze for active wear in the decade. As the designer commented in 1982, "My fashion ideas come from everyday life."[50]

These slanting pocket flaps recall equestrian clothing, particularly hacking jackets. They were originally placed in this way to enable easier access while the rider was seated.

The soft cigar color of this jacket and trousers is in line with its countrified influences. In the fall of 1986, checks, tweed, and "brawny" shades proliferated for sports coats, while dominant colors for business suits included "taupe, tan, toast and nutmeg."[52]

"Plain trousers are in the majority," wrote stylist Luciano Franzoni in June 1986, "but the ice has definitely been broken for fuller, pleated styles." He had seen "more than 10 percent of suits . . . [sold] with pleated pants that are narrower at the bottom." Some designers took inspiration from the 1940s zoot suit, and elements can be seen here in the pleated and cuffed trousers, wide shoulders, and relatively long jacket. The suit also corresponds to this same article's description of basic fashionable shapes in menswear: "slight waist suppression, two button closings . . . Lapels remain moderate, between 3 to 4 inches wide."[53]

Suit by Paul Smith,

1988, Victoria & Albert Museum, London

◆

Paul Smith's "Paul Smith man" presented a new breed of masculinity to 1980s Britain. The designer promoted an unashamed sartorial consciousness amongst young men, clothing the yuppies with their Filofaxes while also offering a flexibility and eccentricity that gave his clothes an edge. Elegance and Britishness were reinterpreted, as Suzy Menkes described it in 1982, "in a modern idiom."[54] A European influence (particularly from Milan) contributed to what has been described as Smith's "vast, endlessly recombinant jumble sale" of influences—aided by his appreciation of global idiosyncrasies, but also a jumble sale in which, cyberpunk author William Gibson put it, "all of the artefacts of his nation and culture constantly engage in a mutual exchange of code."[55] Among all this, we can see here a suit very much of its time—an example of the power dressing that so captivated young professionals in the 80s as well as a casualness that is not immediately apparent.

Worn as shown here, this suit embodies the advice given to ambitious, up-and-coming young professionals in John Molloy's influential *Dress for Success*, first published in 1975 and updated in 1988. Founded on a strong, conservative aesthetic, he advised men to "memorize the rules, dress the same." Molloy employed computerized surveys to put together his wardrobe recommendations, and to some extent the results could be individualized. However, he was quick to emphasize that cool, calm, and conservative wins the day: "Eighty-five percent of the executives we questioned in our research still think of 'fashionably' dressed men as incompetents, as lightweights. The style that executives admire is conservative, coordinated, high-powered and traditional." He cited figures such as Ronald Reagan and Chrysler boss Lee Iacocca, whose clothes "lend credibility." For women, political figures such as Nancy Reagan and Margaret Thatcher embodied the concept of "power" in dressing.[56]

Ronald and Nancy Reagan, c.1981–89, Mark Foley Collection, Florida Memory.

From this perspective, the jacket is entirely suitable for a corporate environment with its wide, strong shoulders, navy pinstripe and double-breasted fastening that adds breadth to the torso. However, a small concession to more relaxed attitudes exists in the tie-less shirt: but this is only a small hint at the scope of this suit. It was designed to be worn for both work and play with the jacket open, the shirt untucked, and the outfit accessorized with a jeans-style leather belt and canvas plimsolls.[57]

With a date of 1988, this suit's casual flexibility offers a bridge between the rigid structure of 80s power dressing and the self-conscious informality of 1990s "dress down Fridays" in the workplace (the popularity of which led to some companies reinstating stricter dress codes in the early 2000s).

Man's "bondage suit," Vivienne Westwood,

1990, Philadelphia Museum of Art, Pennsylvania

◆

This suit, while representative of the fashionable line of the early 1990s, is most remarkable as a piece of iconic Westwood. Subversive and shocking, it perfectly illustrates the boundary-crossing agendas of Westwood and her partner, fellow designer and impresario Malcolm McLaren, and complicates common conceptions about a suit's function and design. At the same time, this design both reinforces and negates the popular concept of the suit as a form of self-restraint. Variations of the design were produced from the 1970s–1990s, making this example one of the last iterations to be manufactured.

As a general rule, single-breasted jackets were more popular during the 1990s, but the double-breasted never went entirely out of fashion. Its use shows a crossing over from the broad power suits of the 1980s to the increasingly softer lines of the 90s. Here, the shoulders are still prominent but use less padding and do not dominate the silhouette.

There is a flapped **ticket pocket** on the left-hand side.

Red is generally seen as a powerful color that symbolizes boldness, even exhibitionism, and those associations are certainly appropriate here.

There are two long vertical zips running along the back of each trouser leg, as well as a front fly that extends up the back crotch seam.[58]

These peaked lapels, common with a double-breasted suit, maintain a fashionable 1980s aesthetic.

Westwood has explained that these trousers were born out of the punk aesthetic; they were a way of rebelling against the status quo and a "declaration of war," in McLaren's words, "against the consumerist fashions of the High Street."[59] Inspiration from both American pilot suits, which had straps and long zips for quick dressing and practicality, as well as bondage-wear straightjackets, have been cited.[60] There is certainly a strong erotic reference here, as well as a historical association that ties in to Westwood's interest in the "paradoxical empowerment of constriction in fashion." Whether it was at all empowering is open to debate, but these straps are strikingly similar to a short-lived trend first seen in womenswear of the early twentieth century.

This image from the *Los Angeles Herald* in November 1910 depicts the so-called "hobble garter." The "hobble" was a short-lived style consisting of a very narrow-hemmed skirt, forcing its wearer to take tiny steps—in essence, to "hobble" instead of walking naturally. In order to avoid accidentally splitting their skirt, some zealous women resorted to using the garter, a band of fabric worn just below the knees that held the legs together.

Sanderson suit, WORLD,

1997–98, National Gallery of Victoria, Melbourne

◆

The name "Sanderson" comes from the chintz fabric of this two-piece suit, a pattern of roses and peonies created by Sanderson, a design company founded in the nineteenth century by William Morris's contemporary, Arthur Sanderson. Bright, bold floral designs became a signature of his wallpaper and textile firm, and were strongly inspired by eighteenth- and nineteenth-century printed textiles.[61] The use of this print, more commonly associated with upholstery (although it is not unusual to find interior fabrics as clothing inspiration), is a striking choice on the part of New Zealand designers Denise L'Estrange-Corbet and Francis Long, but perfectly fits their "progressive" aesthetic. The suit was made for their Auckland-based fashion house, World.

Contrasting colors and patterns in one outfit were not unusual in the 1990s. The use of green and white check for this shirt, however, possibly ties into a more direct trend. The **grunge** subculture, associated with bands like Nirvana, popularized outsized, layered clothes worn with thick boots. These had a shabby appearance and the checked flannel shirt, worn loose, was a common staple. However, the look was taken up for business and semi-formal wear in the manner seen here; the tie, of course, was certainly not a typical grunge accessory.[62]

The jacket is lined in light pink acetate, with an inner ink inscription that reads: "At last I've Found my Sex Machine!!!" This fits with the provocative nature of L'Estrange's brand: in the early days of the World label, she and partner Francis Hooper would stage all-night shows in Auckland named "Sex," in a bid to promote and market the label. Along with other "avant-garde" designers such as Karen Walker and Elizabeth Findlay, L'Estrange was able to carve a niche for herself in the rather sparse fashion world of 1980s New Zealand.[63]

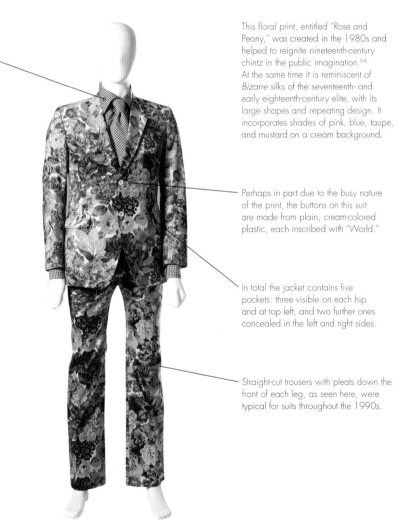

This floral print, entitled "Rose and Peony," was created in the 1980s and helped to reignite nineteenth-century chintz in the public imagination.[64] At the same time it is reminiscent of *Bizarre* silks of the seventeenth- and early eighteenth-century elite, with its large shapes and repeating design. It incorporates shades of pink, blue, taupe, and mustard on a cream background.

Perhaps in part due to the busy nature of the print, the buttons on this suit are made from plain, cream-colored plastic, each inscribed with "World."

In total the jacket contains five pockets: three visible on each hip and at top left, and two further ones concealed in the left and right sides.

Straight-cut trousers with pleats down the front of each leg, as seen here, were typical for suits throughout the 1990s.

Glossary of Terms

All the terms defined here are emboldened in the text.

Aesthetic dress (nineteenth and twentieth centuries): For men, the aesthetic dress movement—promoting 'artistic' medieval-style dress—was spearheaded by Oscar Wilde with his promotion of knee breeches and velvet coats.

Anglomania (eighteenth century): A term referring to the French appreciation of English culture and aesthetics, particularly fashion.

Armor (c. fourth–eighteenth century): Protective metal covering used in combat.

Baggies: High-waisted flared trousers popular in the mid-1970s.

Bag wig (eighteenth century): A wig featuring a small black silk bag, into which a section of hair (the *queue*) would be concealed. A black bow covered the bag and its drawstring fastening.

Baldric (sixteenth and seventeenth centuries): A belt worn across the chest, used to hold a sword.

Banyan (eighteenth century): A loose or fitted T-shaped gown, influenced by Indian and Persian styles. It was worn as an informal coat or as a dressing gown in the privacy of the home.

Berlin work (nineteenth century): An embroidery style similar to needlepoint, worked in a cross-stitch with wool onto canvas. It was used to decorate upholstery, bags, and shoes.

Bicorne hat (eighteenth and nineteenth centuries): A hat with two points featuring a turned-up brim, originally associated with military uniform. Sometimes decorated with a rosette or cockade.

Blazer (twentieth century–present): A tailored sports/leisure jacket with naval origins, often worn contemporaneously as part of a uniform.

Boater (nineteenth and twentieth centuries): A hard, flat-topped summer hat with a stiff brim, usually made from straw. It was commonly decorated with a ribbon band.

Boot cuffs (eighteenth century): Very large, wide coat cuffs that reached to the elbow.

Brandenburg: (seventeenth century): A long and loose-fitting overcoat decorated with cord and frogging.

Breeches (sixteenth–nineteenth centuries): Trousers finishing at knee-length or just below, worn by all men until the early nineteenth century when they became reserved for evening or very formal wear.

Canions (seventeenth century): Extensions to trunk hose that were worn on the calf, designed to add cover and interest to the exposed leg.

Carmagnole (eighteenth century): Famously worn by the *sans culottes* of the French Revolution, this short woolen cloth jacket had Italian peasant origins, hailing from Carmagnola in Turin.

Chatelaine (eighteenth and nineteenth centuries): A clasp with suspended decorative chains hanging from it, worn at the waist by both men and women. Watches, keys, wax seals, and other useful implements would hang from each chain.

Chesterfield: A full-length, tailored overcoat named after George Stanhope, 6th Earl of Chesterfield.

Cockade: A decorative rosette, usually worn on one side of a bicorne hat or the lapel of a coat.

Collar (sixteenth–twenty-first centuries): A piece of fabric, latterly stiffened, that fastens around the neck and is usually attached to a shirt or coat.

Cossack: Pleated trouser style derived from uniforms of the Russian cavalry; fabric is gathered into pleats at the waist to create fullness at the hips, but then tapers off significantly towards the ankles.

Cravat (seventeenth century–present): A neckband composed of a wide strip of fabric, wound around the neck with the ends tied in various styles. From the French *cravate*.

Cummerbund (nineteenth and twentieth centuries): A wide sash around the waist with evening dress, made in bright colors in the twentieth century. Used in lieu of a waistcoat.

Dandy (eighteenth and nineteenth centuries): A man who placed extreme importance on physical appearance, particularly dress. Englishman Beau Brummell is widely credited as the main instigator, although there were French models resulting from the politics of the Revolution.

Dinner jacket (nineteenth and twentieth centuries): A tailless jacket for informal evening wear, first introduced in 1888 as part of the tuxedo. In the twentieth century, it could be made in white as well as black—and in a variety of colors by the 1960s.

Ditto (nineteenth century): A suit in which each piece is made from the same fabric and pattern.

Doublet (sixteenth and seventeenth centuries): A waist or hip length fitted jacket with padding, worn over a shirt.

Dress coat (nineteenth and twentieth centuries): A formal cutaway tail coat, worn in the evening from the mid-nineteenth century onwards.

English drape (twentieth century): A jacket made with a cut that "drapes" across the chest, creating a wide-shouldered effect. Attributed to London tailor Frederick Scholte in the 1930s.

Falling band (seventeenth century): A white turned-down collar that was worn over the doublet, spreading out across the wearer's shoulders and usually trimmed with lace.

Flat cap (nineteenth–twenty-first centuries): A soft, rounded cap of English origin with a narrow stiff brim at the front. Often made from stiff, hardy woolen fabrics and can be traced back as early as the fourteenth century.

Frock coat: In the eighteenth century, this was the term for an informal coat with a turned-down collar and cuffed sleeves. In the early nineteenth century it evolved to become one of the main formal staples for men, cut with a waist seam, collar, lapels, and pockets.

Gown (sixteenth and seventeenth centuries): A loose, often calf- or knee-length garment worn over doublet and hose by professional and learned members of society. Often cut with wide, hanging sleeves and lined in fur during winter months.

Greatcoat (seventeenth–twentieth centuries): A calf-length woolen overcoat popular as part of military uniform. It often featured a distinctive layered cape around the shoulders.

Grunge (twentieth century): A music fusion between rock and heavy metal, originating in 1980s America. In terms of fashion, grunge was expressed through casual styling that incorporated denim, flannel shirts, layering, and distressed clothing. For men, Kurt Cobain was a major sartorial influence.

Habit dégagé or anglaise: A redingote (riding coat) cut away in front to display the waistcoat beneath.

Hanging sleeves (sixteenth and seventeenth centuries): In menswear, the oversleeves of a gown that hang open to the wrist or floor, the edges sometimes held together with ties.

Hedgehog (eighteenth century): In men's fashion, 'hedgehog' referred to a long, dishevelled hairstyle popular with the incroyables in the 1790s.

Incroyable (eighteenth century): With their female counterparts the *Merveilleuses*, these men belonged to an aristocratic subculture in post-Revolutionary Paris. Their dress was exaggerated, eccentric, and included long, unkempt 'hedgehog' hairstyles and accessories, including quizzing glasses, earrings, and bicorne hats.

Ivy League style (twentieth century): The predecessor to 'preppy' style, Ivy League was influenced by men's clothing worn on American college campuses in the early-mid twentieth century.

Japonisme/'Japonism' (nineteenth century): A surge of enthusiasm for Japanese textiles, painting, furniture, and interior design that flowed through Britain to America at the end of the nineteenth century. This developed in response to Japan's newly opened trade routes with Europe in 1854.

Jerkin (sixteenth and seventeenth centuries): A close-fitting, sleeveless jacket often made from leather and worn over a man's doublet.

Justacorps (seventeenth and eighteenth centuries): Three-piece suit worn by men. In French, literally means 'close to the body'.

Lapel (eighteenth–twenty-first centuries): The folded sections of fabric immediately below the collar on a coat or jacket.

Lapel pin (twentieth century): A decorative metal pin worn on the lapel, often used as a replacement for the boutonnière.

Macaroni (eighteenth century): A fashionable young man who affected exaggerated speech, postures, and dress. He was inspired by continental aesthetics and is often seen as a precursor to the nineteenth-century *dandy*.

Mackintosh (nineteenth – twenty-first centuries): A waterproof raincoat first made available in the 1820s, and named for its Scottish inventor Charles Mackintosh.

Mod (twentieth century): A 1960s term meaning "modern," "in fashion"— particularly in relation to clothes. Mod suits were close-fitting, often worn with slim ties and clean white shirts, reflecting a keen attention to detail.

Morning coat: Originally worn by men for their morning ride, this coat became popular as formal wear from c.1850. It featured a cutaway front and a tight fit around the hips to form tails at the back.

Muff (sixteenth century–present): A tubular, often fur-lined covering for both hands. Worn for protection and as a fashionable accessory.

Norfolk jacket (twentieth century): A loose-fitting, belted (or half-belted) jacket with box pleats, often made from tweed and worn for sporting and country pursuits. Its introduction is generally credited to Queen Victoria's son, Edward VII.

Open sleeve (eighteenth century): A wide cuff with a slit in the underside, through which frills of a shirt sleeve were visible.

Paned (sixteenth and seventeenth centuries): A technique used on sleeves and trunk hose. Constructed from several individual panels that, when worn, hang open and allow the rich (often contrasting) fabric beneath to be visible.

Pantaloons (nineteenth century): Named for a Commedia dell'Arte character named *Pantalone*, these early trousers were ankle length and relatively close-fitting around the leg. They were especially popular during the 1820s.

Passementerie (from the French *passements*): Elaborate, decorative trimming using braid, tassels, ribbons, and fringing.

Peascod belly (sixteenth century): A section of padding or bombast at the waist in order to produce an over-hanging section of fabric at the center. Starting above the waistline, the peascod tip would extend down slightly lower than the natural waist. Named for its visual similarity to a peapod.

Peg-top trousers (nineteenth and twentieth centuries): Peg-tops were cut wide at the hips and tapered to a very close fit at the ankles. They were initially popular for a brief time in the 1830s and were revived in the 1910s.

Phrygian cap (eighteenth century): Also known as the liberty cap or *bonnet rouge*, this was a soft cap with a pointed crown that was worn by the sans-culottes of the French Revolution.

Pith helmet (nineteenth and twentieth centuries): Head covering that provides sun protection made from pith, a cork-like material, staying cool and light.

Polyester (twentieth century): A synthetic, thermoplastic fabric made from polyethylene terephthalate. It became popular for men's suits in the mid twentieth century, often combined with wool to create a durable and maintainable modern fabric.

Raglan sleeve (nineteenth century–present): A sleeve that is cut in one piece, extending to the collar and joining a diagonal seam from the underarm to the neck. Associated with Lord Raglan, a British Army officer involved in the Crimean War (1853–56).

Reefer (eighteenth–twenty-first centuries): A heavy double-breasted jacket, usually made from wool, with nautical origins. Shorter versions were known as *pea coats*.

Reet pleats (twentieth century): Colloquial term for 'right', referring to the very deep pleats on the front of a zoot suit's trousers.

Rocker (twentieth century): A sartorial opposite to the *mod* style, rockers were influenced by motorcycle culture and wore leather and denim with a greased, swept-back hairstyle.

Sack suit (nineteenth and twentieth centuries): Known in England as the *lounge suit*, this comprised a loose, high-fastening jacket cut without a waist seam and tubular trousers.

Seersucker: A light, thin fabric made from cotton or linen and featuring a distinctive puckered texture. Very popular for summer suiting.

Shirt (sixteenth century–present): The closest garment to the skin, acting as a barrier between body and coat. Usually made in lightweight and light colored fabric with decoration in the form of embroidery, lace, or frills as fashions changed to display cuffs, fronts, and collars. Worn with a detachable collar throughout the late nineteenth and early twentieth centuries, and became front-fastening in 1871.

Shoulder knot (seventeenth century): A bunch of ribbon loops or cord worn on the right shoulder. After the seventeenth century, this decoration became part of a servant's livery.

Sidebody (nineteenth century onwards): A new development in coats in the late 1830s involving inserting an extra panel from below the armhole to the waist seam.

Solitaire (eighteenth century): Neckwear: a black ribbon worn over a stock that could vary in thickness. It could be tied, tucked into the shirt-front, knotted, or pinned according to preference.

Spencer: A short, tailless and skirtless coat that was briefly in vogue for men at the start of the nineteenth century. The style was instigated by its namesake, George John Spencer, the 2nd Earl of Spencer.

Steinkirk: A style of cravat that allegedly developed at the Battle of Steinkirk, Belgium, in 1692. Its ends were worn tucked into the buttonhole of the coat, creating an elegant yet relaxed appearance.

Stock (eighteenth and nineteenth centuries): A stiffened neckcloth usually made from linen and fastened at the back.

Stockings (sixteenth–nineteenth centuries): Close-fitting leg coverings worn with hose and breeches until the demise of the latter (except for very formal and court wear) in the nineteenth century.

Stovepipe hat (nineteenth century): A style of top hat with a very high, cylindrical, flat crown.

Sword knot (seventeenth and eighteenth centuries): A decorative bunch of ribbon and tassels, sometimes jeweled, that was hung from a sword's hilt.

Tartan: A (mostly) woolen fabric patterned in overlapping horizontal and vertical bands, variously colored on a solid background. Associated with Scotland, although early examples have been found outside of the United Kingdom.

Ticket pocket (nineteenth century–present): A small flapped pocket on the right-hand side of a man's coat, situated above the regular pocket. It became an integral part of men's tailoring after the advent of the railway in the 1830s, and the need for easily accessible ticket storage.

Tail coat (nineteenth century–present): A formal knee-length coat with only the rear of the skirt, known as the tails, intact.

Topcoat: A lighter version of an overcoat, cut in the same styles.

Top hat (nineteenth–twentieth centuries): A tall, flat-crowned hat with a broad brim turned up at the edges. It was worn as part of ordinary daily dress for much of the nineteenth century, and may have descended from the seventeenth century sugarloaf style.

Tricorne hat (seventeenth and eighteenth centuries): A hat with a broad brim that was held up in three places, creating the three points from which the name derives. This allowed elaborate and fashionable wigs to be seen at the sides and back of the head.

Trilby (nineteenth and twentieth centuries): A felt hat with a shallow brim and dip in the crown.

Trunk hose (sixteenth century): Voluminous padded hose that formed the upper part of a man's leg-wear, joined to the stocking beneath.

Ulster (nineteenth and twentieth centuries): An overcoat with a detachable cape, either single or double-breasted.

Voided velvet: A tufted fabric that is woven with a dense, discontinuous pile to produce blank areas that form a pattern.

Waistcoat (eighteenth century–present): A 'short coat' derived from the earliest seventeenth century styles that were worn first under a doublet, and then under a coat. Worn for warmth and as an added layer of protection for the shirt and coat. In the eighteenth and nineteenth centuries it also became a highly decorative garment, embellished to match the suit or to add color and pattern to a dark ensemble. In America, single-breasted versions often known as a *vest*.

Wing tip collar (nineteenth and twentieth centuries): A starched, formal collar with the tips pointed out to resemble wings.

Zoot suit (twentieth century): A suit with wide-legged, high-waisted trousers and a wide-shouldered, thigh-length jacket. An exaggerated version of the fashionable 1940s male silhouette, the suit was born out of conflicts between American servicemen and young Mexican American men in Los Angeles. It also had roots in jazz music and was famously worn by singer and dancer Cab Calloway.

Notes

Preface

[1] Antony, Michael, *The Masculine Century: A Heretical History of Our Time*, IN: iUniverse, 2008, p.45.

[2] Kuchta, David, *The Three-Piece Suit and Modern Masculinity: England, 1550–1850*, Berkeley: University of California Press, 2002, p.2.

[3] Gowing, Laura, *Gender Relations in Early Modern England*, London: Routledge, 2014, p.13.

[4] Veblen, Thorstein, *The Theory of the Leisure Class*, London: Penguin, (1899) 2005.

[5] Mikhaila, Ninya and Malcolm-Davies, Jane, *The Tudor Tailor: Reconstructing Sixteenth-Century Dress*, London: Batsford, 2006, p.18.

[6] Hollander, Anne, *Sex and Suits: The Evolution of Modern Dress*, London: Bloomsbury, (1994) 2016, p.45.

[7] Fisher, Will, *Materializing Gender in Early Modern English Literature and Culture*, Cambridge: Cambridge University Press, 2006, p.72.

[8] Vicary, Grace Q., "Visual Art as Social Data: The Renaissance Codpiece." *Cultural Anthropology*, 4, no.1 (1989): 3–25.

[9] ed. by Fletcher, Christopher, Brady, Sean, Moss, Rachel E., & Riall, Lucy, *The Palgrave Handbook of Masculinity and Political Culture in Europe*, London: Palgrave MacMillan, 2018, p.203.

[10] ed. by Jesson-Dibley, David, Herrick, Robert, *Selected Poems*, New York: Routledge, (1980) 2003, p.54.

[11] Stedman, Gesa, *Cultural Exchange in Seventeenth-Century France and England*, Oxon: Ashgate, 2013, np.

[12] *The Art of Prudent Behaviour in a Father's Advice to his Son, Arriv'd to the Years of Manhood. By way of Dialogue.* Mr Le Noble/Mr Boyer, London: Tim Childe, 1701, p.64.

[13] Frieda, Leonie, *Francis I: The Maker of Modern France*, London: Hachette, 2018, np.

[14] Yarwood, Doreen, *European Costume: 400 Years of Fashion*, Paris: Larousse, 1975, p.113.

[15] Hayward, Maria, *Rich Apparel: Clothing and the Law in Henry VIII's England*, Surrey: Ashgate, 2009, p.124.

[16] Amphlett, Hilda, *Hats: A History of Fashion in Headwear*, NY: Dover, (1974) 2003, p.1985.

[17] Sichel, Marion, *Costume Reference: Tudors and Elizabethans*, Plays, Inc., 1977, p.17.

[18] Mikhaila and Malcolm-Davies, 2006, p.19.

[19] Ashelford, Jane, *A Visual History of Costume*, London: Batsford, 1983, p.15.

[20] Hayward, 2009, p.124.

[21] Forgeng, Jeffrey L., *Daily Life in Elizabethan England*, CA: ABC-CLIO, 2010, p.129.

[22] Downing, Sarah Jane, *Fashion in the Time of William Shakespeare: 1564–1616*, London: Bloomsbury, 2014, p.39.

[23] ed. by Furnivall, Frederick J., Stubbs, Philip, *Anatomy of the Abuses in Shakespeare's Youth AD.1573*, 1877, London: The New Shakespeare Society, p.55.

[24] Olsen, Kristen, *All Things Shakespeare: A Concise Encyclopedia of Shakespeare's World*, CA: Greenwood, 2002, p.137.

[25] *The London Shakespeare: The Tragedies*, London: Simon and Schuster, 1957, p.293.

[26] Forgeng, Jeffrey L., 2010, p.136.

[27] Lockhart, Paul Douglas, *Sweden in the Seventeenth Century*, Hampshire: Palgrave Macmillan, 2004, p.26.

[28] Cunnington, C. Willett & Phyllis, *Handbook of English Costume in the Seventeenth Century*, London: Faber & Faber, (proof copy) p.145.

[29] Museum object data, Livrustkammaren. T4386.

[30] Steele, Valerie, *Encyclopedia of Clothing and Fashion*, NY: Charles Scribner's Sons, 2005, p.194.

[31] Vincent, Susan, *Dressing the Elite: Clothes in Early Modern England*, London: Berg, 2003, p.84.

[32] Rothstein, Natalie, Ginsburg, Madeleine & Hart, Avril, *Four Hundred Years of Fashion*, London: V&A Publications, 1984, p.145.

Introduction

[1] Hollander, Anne, *Sex and Suits: The Evolution of Modern Dress*, London: Bloomsbury, (1994) 2006, p.26.

[2] *You and Yours*, (2016). [Radio programme]. Radio 4: BBC.

[3] Jenss, Heike, *Fashioning Memory: Vintage Style and Youth Culture*, London: Bloomsbury, 2015, np.

[4] Hatherley, Owen, *The Ministry of Nostalgia*, London: Verso Books, 2017.

[5] *You and Yours*, (2016).

[6] Perry, Grayson, *The Descent of Man*, London: Allen Lane, 2016, np.

[7] Ibid.

Chapter One

[1] ed. by Le Gallienne, Richard, Pepys, Samuel, *Diary of Samuel Pepys: Selected Passages*, NY: Dover, 2012, p.164.

[2] Kuchta, David, *The Three-Piece Suit and Modern Masculinity: England, 1550–1850*, Berkeley: University of California Press, 2002, p.79.

[3] Field, Jacob F., *London, Londoners and the Great Fire of 1666: Disaster and Recovery*, NY: Routledge, 2017, np.

[4] Kuchta, 2002.

[5] Breward, Christopher, *The Suit: Form, Function and Style*, London: Reaktion, 2016, p.40.

[6] Claydon, Tony, and Levillain, Charles-Édouard, *Louis XIV Outside In: Images of the Sun King Beyond France, 1661–1715*, Oxford: Routledge, 2016, p.65.

[7] Pepys, Le Gallienne, 2012, p.166.

[8] Breward, 2016, p.40.

[9] Cole, Shaun, *The Story of Men's Underwear*, NY: Parkstone Press International, 2012, p.21.

[10] Uglow, Jenny, *A Gambling Man: Charles II and the Restoration, 1660–1670*, London: Faber & Faber, 2009, p.521.

[11] Breward, 2016, p.41.

[12] *The Art of Prudent Behaviour in a Father's Advice to his Son, Arriv'd to the Years of Manhood. By way of Dialogue*. Mr Le Noble/Mr Boyer, London: Tim Childe, 1701, p.63.

[13] de Winkel, Marieke, *Fashion and Fancy: Dress and Meaning in Rembrandt's Paintings*, Amsterdam: Amsterdam University Press, 2006, p.17.

[14] Ribeiro, Aileen, *Fashion and Fiction: Dress in Art and Literature in Stuart England*, New Haven: Yale University Press, 2005, p.1.

[15] Fuhring, Peter, Marchesano, Louis, Mathis, Remi and Selbach,Vanessa, *A Kingdom of Images: French Prints in the Age of Louis XIV, 1660–1715*, LA: Getty Research Institute, 2015, p.260.

[16] DeJean, Joan, *The Essence of Style: How the French Invented High Fashion, Fine Food, Chic Cafés, Style, Sophistication and Glamour*, NY: Free Press, 2005, pp.70–71.

[17] ed. by Bray, William, *Memoirs Illustrative of the Life and Writings of John Evelyn*, NY: G.P Putnam & Sons, 1870, p.751.

[18] Cunnington, Phillis Emily, *Costumes of the Seventeenth and Eighteenth Century*, Plays, Inc., 1970, p.20.

[19] Nunn, Joan, *Fashion in Costume, 1200–2000*, Chicago: New Amsterdam Books, 1984, 2000, p.61.

[20] Mansel, Philip, *Dressed to Rule: Royal and Court Costume from Louis XIV to Elizabeth II*, New Haven: Yale University Press, 2005, p.15.

[21] Cunnington, C. Willett & Phyllis, *Handbook of English Costume in the Seventeenth Century*, London: Faber & Faber, (proof copy) p.147.

[22] *Delphi Complete Works of Samuel Pepys (Illustrated)*, East Sussex: 2015, np.

[23] Mansel, 2005, p.11.

[24] McKay, Elaine in *Cutter's Research Journal, Volume 11*, United States Institute for Theatre Technology, 1999.

[25] http://collections.vam.ac.uk/item/O78912/wedding-suit-unknown/.

[26] Textile Research Centre, "Wedding Suit of King James II of Britain" in Secular Ceremonies and Rituals, trc-leiden.nl.

[27] Waugh, Norah, *The Cut of Men's Clothes: 1600–1900*, London: Faber & Faber, 1964, p.48.

[28] Earnshaw, Pat, *A Dictionary of Lace*, NY: Dover, 1984, p.180.

[29] Hart, Avril and North, Susan, *Historical Fashion in Detail*, London: Victoria & Albert Museum, 1998, p.80.

[30] Ibid, p.96.

[31] Epstein, Diana, *Buttons*, London: Studio Vista, 1968, p.15.

[32] Ewing, Elizabeth, *Everyday Dress: 1650–1900*, Tiptree: Batsford, 1984, p.24.

[33] McCallum, Paul in Ennis, Daniel James and Slagle, Judith Bailey, *Prologues, Epilogues, Curtain-Raisers, and Afterpieces: The Rest of the Eighteenth-Century London Stage*, Newark: University of Delaware Press, 2007, p.42.

[34] Spufford, Margaret, *The Great Reclothing of Rural England: Petty Chapman and Their Wares in the Seventeenth Century*, London: Bloomsbury, 1984, p.62.

[35] DeJean, Joan, *How Paris Became Paris: The Invention of the Modern City*, London: Bloomsbury, 2004, p.195.

[36] Turner Wilcox, Ruth, *Five Centuries of American Costume*, NY: Dover, (1963) 2004, p.111.

[37] Waugh, 1964, p.52.

[38] Staples, Kathleen A. and Shaw, Madelyn C., *Clothing Through American History: The British Colonial Era*, CA: Greenwood, 2013, p.313.

[39] Kelly, Francis M. and Schwabe, Randolph, *European Costume and Fashion, 1490–1790*, New York: Dover, 1929, p.169.

[40] Cunnington, C. Willett & Phyllis, (proof copy), p.158.

[41] Ibid, pp.154–5.

[42] Norberg, Kathryn, and ? Rosenbaum, Sandra, *Fashion Prints in the Age of Louis XIV: Interpreting the Art of Elegance*, Lubbock: Texas Tech University Press, 2014, p.154.

[43] Hughes, Clair, *Hats*, London: Bloomsbury, 2016, p.39.

[44] Russell, Douglas, *Costume History and Style*, NJ: Prentice Hall, 1983, p.265.

[45] Payne, Blanche, Winakor, Geitel, and Farrell-Beck, Jane, *The History of Costume: From Ancient Mesopotamia Through the Twentieth Century*, Harper Collins, 1992, p.376.

Chapter Two

[1] *The Whole Duty of Man*, 1770, London: John Beercroft, p.126.

[2] Hollander, Anne, *Sex and Suits: The Evolution of Modern Dress*, London: Bloomsbury, 1994, 2016, p.62.

[3] Perry, Gillian and Rossington, Michael, *Femininity and Masculinity in Eighteenth-Century Art and Culture*, Manchester: Manchester University Press, 1994, p.14.

[4] Yarwood, Doreen, *Illustrated Encyclopedia of World Costume*, NY: Dover, 1978, p.300.

[5] *The Miscellaneous Works of Oliver Goldsmith, M.B.*, London: Allan Bell & Co., 1834, p.225.

[6] Chazin-Bennahum, Judith, *The Lure of Perfection: Fashion and Ballet, 1780–1830*, NY: Routledge, 2005, p.31.

[7] Voltaire, *Letters Concerning the English Nation*, London: Tonson, Midwinter, Cooper & Hodges, 1778, p.2.

[8] Richardson, Samuel, *Clarissa*, 1748, ebook 2013.

[9] Yarwood, 1978, p.92.

[10] Doering, Mary D. in Blanco F., Hunt-Hurst & Vaughan Lee, *American Fashion Head to Toe: Volume One*, CO: ABC-CLIO, 2016, p.255.

[11] Flugel, J. C., *The Psychology of Clothes*, London: Hogarth Press, 1966, pp.110–11.

[12] Bolton, Andrew, *Anglomania: Tradition and Transgression in British Fashion*, NY: The Metropolitan Museum of Art, 2006, p.4.

[13] Cumming, Valerie, Cunnington, C. W., and Cunnington, P. E., *The Dictionary of Fashion History*, London: Bloomsbury, (1960) 2010, p.186.

[14] Bailey, Adrian, *The Passion for Fashion*, Dragon's World, 1988, p.28.

[15] Rudolf, R. de M., *Short Histories of the Territorial Regiments of the British Army*, London: H. M. Stationery Office, 1902, p.97.

[16] Chambers, William, *Chambers's Edinburgh Journal, Volume 1*, "Constantinople in 1831, from the journal of an officer," 1833, p.157.

[17] http://collections.vam.ac.uk/item/O13923/coat-and-breeches-unknown/

[18] *The Spectator: With Notes, and a General Index*, Vol.I, 1711, New York: Samuel Marks, 1826, p.189.

[19] Cunnington, C. Willett & Phyllis, *Handbook of English Costume in the Eighteenth Century*, London: Faber & Faber, 1964, p.52.

[20] http://collections.vam.ac.uk/item/O13923/coat-and-breeches-unknown/.

[21] Willett & Cunnington, 1964, p.52.

[22] Ibid, p.45.

[23] Waugh, Norah, *The Cut of Men's Clothes: 1600–1900*, p.55, p.52.

[24] Willett & Cunnington, 1964, p.56.

[25] Doran, John, *Habits and Men, with remnants of record touching the Makers of both*, London: Richard Bentley, 1855, p.198.

[26] Palairet, Jean, *A new Royal French Grammar*, Dialogue 16, 1738, p.249–50.

[27] "An Essay on Fashions, extracted from the Holland Spectator," *The Gentleman's Magazine*, July 1736, p.378.

[28] Willett & Cunnington, 1964, p.61.

[29] Ashelford, Jane, *The Art of Dress: Clothes and Society 1500 – 1914*, London: The National Trust, 1996, p.139.

[30] Cole, Shaun, *The Story of Men's Underwear: Volume 1*, NY: Parkstone International, 2012, np.

[31] Loudon, J.C., *The Magazine of Natural History and Journal of Zoology, Botany, Mineralogy, Geology, and Meteorology*, Volume I, London: Longman, Rees, Orme, Brown and Green, 1829, p.373.

[32] https://www.metmuseum.org/art/collection/search/79048.

[33] Harrison Martin, Richard, and Koda, Harold, *Two by Two*, New York: The Metropolitan Museum of Art, 1996, p.12.

[34] Yarwood, Doreen, *English Costume from the Second Century BC to 1967*, London: Batsford, 1969, p.189.

[35] Harrison Martin, Richard, *Our New Clothes: Acquisitions of the 1990s*, NY: Metropolitan Museum of Art, 1999, p.43.

[36] Kisluk-Grosheide, Daniëlle, *Bertrand Rondot, Visitors to Versailles: From Louis XIV to the French Revolution*, NY: The Metropolitan Museum of Art/New Haven: Yale University Press, 2018, p.68.

[37] Heck, J. G., *Iconographic Encyclopaedia Of Science, Literature, And Art: Volume III*, New York: D. Appleton and Co., 1860, p.106.

[38] Ilmakunnas, Johanna in ed. Simonton, Deborah, Kaartinen, Marjo, Montenach, Anne, *Luxury and Gender in European Towns, 1700–1914*, NY: Routledge, 2014, np.

[39] *The London Saturday Journal*, March 12, 1842, p.125.

[40] Ilmakunnas, 2014, np.

[41] Pastoureau, Michel, *Red: The History of a Color*, NJ: Princeton University Press, 2017, p.148.

[42] Sichel, Marion, *History of Men's Costume*, London: Batsford, 1984, p.39.

[43] *Walker's Hibernian Magazine, Or, Compendium of Entertaining Knowledge, Part 2*, Dublin: Thomas Walker, July 1790, p.490.

[44] "Styling the Macaroni Male," June 8, 2016, Clarissa M. Esguerra, Assistant Curator, Costume and Textiles. https://unframed.lacma.org/2016/06/08/styling-macaroni-male.

[45] McGirr, Elaine M., *Eighteenth-Century Characters: A Guide to the Literature of the Age*, Hampshire: Palgrave Macmillan, 2007, p.141.

[46] McNeil, Peter, "Macaroni Men and Eighteenth-Century Fashion Culture: 'The Vulgar Tongue," *The Journal of the Australian Academy of the Humanities*, 8 (2017), pp.67–68.

[47] Philadelphia Museum of Art data: http://www.philamuseum.org/collections/permanent/45317.html?mulR=786324968|11.

[48] Leslie, Catherine Amoroso, *Needlework Through History: An Encyclopedia*, CT: Greenwood Press, 2007, p.40–41.

[49] Rijksmuseum data: http://hdl.handle.net/10934/RM0001.COLLECT.2317

[50] Hollander, Anne, *Sex and Suits: The Evolution of Modern Dress*, London: Bloomsbury, (1994) 2016, p.61.

[51] *The Analytical Review*, No.3, Vol.19, June 1794, p.309.

[52] Ed. by Sparks, Jared, *The Writings of George Washington, Volume II*, Boston: Ferdinand Andrews, 1840, p.337.

[53] Styles, John, and Vickery, Amanda, *Gender, Taste, and Material Culture in Britain and North America, 1700–1830*, Yale Center for British Art, 2006, p.226–8.

[54] Epstein, 1968, p.36–7.

[55] McClafferty, Carla Killough, *The Many Faces of George Washington: Remaking a Presidential Icon*, MN: Carolrhoda Books, 2011, p.77–78.

[56] Dickens, Charles, *All the Year Round: A Weekly Journal*, London: No.26, Wellington St, 1860, p.369.

[57] *Fashioning Fashion*, p.130.

[58] Alderson, Jr., Robert J, *This Bright Era of Happy Revolutions*, SC: University of South Carolina Press, 2008, p.213.

[59] Tortora, Phyllis G. and Eubank, Keith, *Survey of Historic Costume*, London: Fairchild Books, 2010, p.309.

[60] Roche, Daniel in Steele, Valerie, *Paris Fashion: A Cultural History*, London: Bloomsbury, (1998) 2001, p.46.

[61] Pastoureau, Michel, *The Devil's Cloth: A History of Stripes*, NY: Washington Square Press, 2001, p.49 & 52.

[62] Byrd, Penelope, *The Male Image: Men's Fashion in Britain, 1300–1970*, London: Batsford, 1979, p.82.

[63] Gibbings, Sarah, *The Tie: Trends and Traditions*, Studio Editions, 1990, p.35.

[64] Amann, Elizabeth, *Dandyism in the Age of Revolution: The Art of the Cut*, Chicago: University of Chicago Press, 2015, p.95.

[65] Dwyer, Philip, *Napoleon: The Path to Power 1769–1799*, London: Bloomsbury, 2008, np.

[66] Richmond, Vivienne, *Clothing the Poor in Nineteenth-Century England*, Cambridge: Cambridge University Press, 2013, p.34.

Chapter Three

[1] d'Aurevilly, Barbey, in Sadleir, Michael, *The Strange Life of Lady Blessington*, NY: Little, Brown and Company, 1947, p.46.

[2] Tortora, Phyllis G. and Eubank, Keith, *Survey of Historic Costume*, NY: Fairchild, 2009, p.245.

[3] Kelly, Ian, *Beau Brummell: The Ultimate Man of Style*, NY: Free Press, 2013, np.

[4] *Neckclothitania; or, Tietania: Being an Essay on Starchers, by one of the cloth*, London: J.J. Stockdale, 1818.

[5] Baudelaire, Charles, "The Dandy" from *The Painter of Modern Life*, 1863, in ed.by Tanke, Joseph J. and McQuillan, Colin, *The Bloomsbury Anthology of Aesthetics*, London: Bloomsbury, 2012, p.373.

[6] Barthes, Roland, *The Language of Fashion*, London: Bloomsbury, 2013, p.63.

[7] Harvey, John, *Clothes*, Oxon: Routledge, 2014, np.

[8] Sydney, William Connor, *The Early Days of the Nineteenth Century in England, 1800–1820*, Volume 1, London: G. Redway, 1898, p.93.

[9] Hollander, Anne. "FASHION IN NUDITY." *The Georgia Review*, Vol.30, No.3, 1976, pp. 642–702. *JSTOR*, www.jstor.org/stable/41397286.

[10] Jones, Vivien, Austen, Jane, *Selected Letters*, Oxford: Oxford University Press, 2004, p.4.

[11] "GENTLEMEN'S FASHIONS FOR MAY." (1831, September 24). *The Sydney Gazette and New South Wales Advertiser (NSW : 1803–1842)*, p.4. Retrieved July 17, 2018, from http://nla.gov.au/nla.news-article220272.

[12] ed.by Blanco F., José, Hunt-Hurst, Patricia Kay, Vaughan Lee, Heather, and Doering, Mary, *Clothing and Fashion: American Fashion from Head to Toe, Volume 1*, CA: ABC-CLIO, 2016, p.206.

[13] *The West-End Gazette of Gentlemen's Fashion*, Vol.6, No.65, November 1867, p.20.

[14] Greig, Hannah, *The Beau Monde: Fashionable Society in Georgian London*, Oxford: Oxford University Press, p.115–16.

[15] Schaeffer, Claire, *Claire Schaeffer's Fabric Sewing Guide*, Krause, 2008, p.277.

[16] Takeda, Sharon Sadako and Spilker, Kaye Durland, *Fashioning Fashion: European Dress in Detail 1700–1915*, NY: Delmonico, Los Angeles County Museum of Art, 2011, p.128.

[17] Hunt, Margaret R., *Women in Eighteenth Century Europe*, Oxford: Routledge, 2014, p.164.

[18] Calahan, April, *Fashion Plates: 150 Years of Style*, NH and London: Yale University Press, 2015, p.92.

[19] Sichel, Marion, *Costume Reference 5: The Regency*, London: Batsford, 1978, p.14.

[20] Fitzmaurice, Edmond, *The Life of Granville George Leveson Gower, Second Earl Granville, K.G., 1815–1891*, Volume 1, Chizine, (1915) 2018, np.

[21] Hollander, Anne, *Fabric of Vision: Dress and Drapery in Painting*, London: Bloomsbury, 2002, p.126.

[22] Backhouse, Frances, *Once They Were Hats: In Search of the Mighty Beaver*, Toronto: ECW Press, 2015, np.

[23] Ouellette, Susan, *US Textile Production in Historical Perspective: A Case Study from Massachusetts*, London: Routledge, 2007, np.

[24] Sichel, Marion, *Costume Reference 5: The Regency*, London: Batsford, 1978, p.8, p.16.

[25] Metropolitan Museum item information, Accession Number: 2009.300.2932 https://metmuseum.org/art/collection/search/157813.

[26] Waugh, Norah, *The Cut of Men's Clothes: 1600 – 1900*, London: Faber & Faber, 1964, p.116.

[27] Byrd, Penelope, *Nineteenth Century Fashion*, London: Batsford, 1992, p.95.

[28] Mortimer, Thomas, *A General Dictionary of Commerce, Trade, and Manufactures: Exhibiting their present state in every part of the world*, London: Richard Phillips, 1810.

[29] Simons, William, quoted in Makepeace, Margaret, *The East India Company's London Workers: Management of the Warehouse Labourers, 1800–1858*, Suffolk: The Boydell Press, 2010, p.24–25.

[30] Richmond, Vivienne, *Clothing the Poor in Nineteenth-Century England*, Cambridge: Cambridge University Press, 2013, pp.21–22.

[31] ed.by Hoffmeister, Gerhart, *European Romanticism: Literary Cross-çurrents, Modes, and Models*, MI: Wayne State University Press, 1990, p.231.

[32] Waugh, Norah, *The Cut of Men's Clothes: 1600 – 1900*, London: Faber & Faber, 1964, p.118.

[33] Johnston, Lucy, *Nineteenth century Fashion in Detail*, London: Victoria & Albert Museum, 2005, p.156.

[34] Waugh, 1964, p.82.

[35] ed.by Brown, Ian, *From Tartan to Tartanry: Scottish Culture, History and Myth*, Edinburgh: Edinburgh University Press, 2010, np.

[36] Epstein, 1968, p.40.

[37] https://hammond-turner.com/index.php/history

[38] *Highland Light Infantry Chronicle*, Vol. VII, No.1, January 1907, p.3.

[39] Rev Sinclair, John, *Memoirs of the Life and Works of John Sinclair, Bart*, London: William Blackwood & Sons, 1837 p.257.

[40] Frank, Adam, *The Clans, Septs & Regiments of the Scottish Highlands*, VA: Clearfield, 1970, p.535.

[41] "GENTLEMEN'S FASHIONS FOR MAY." (1831, September 24). *The Sydney Gazette and New South Wales Advertiser (NSW : 1803–1842)*, p.4. Retrieved August 29, 2018, from http://nla.gov.au/nla.news-article2202721.

[42] Walker, G., *The Art of Cutting Breeches*, Fourth Edition, London: G. Walker, 1833, p.25.

[43] Hart, Avril, *Ties*, London: Victoria & Albert Museum, 1998, p.46.

[44] Johnston, Lucy, *Nineteenth Century Fashion in Detail*, London: Victoria & Albert Museum, 2005, p.140.

[45] Davis, R. I., *Men's Garments 1830–1900: A guide to pattern cutting and tailoring*, CA: Players Press, 1994, p.90.

[46] "OBSERVATIONS ON FASHIONS AND DRESS." (1830, June 24). *The Sydney Gazette and New South Wales Advertiser (NSW : 1803–1842)*, p.4. Retrieved July 17, 2018, from http://nla.gov.au/nla.news-article2195384.

[47] Sichel, 1978, p.13.

[48] *Workwoman's Guide* By a Lady, London: Simpkin, Marshall & Co., 1840, p.55.

[49] "A YOUNG LOGICIAN." (1845, October 8). *South Australian Register (Adelaide, SA : 1839–1900)*, p.4. Retrieved December 7, 2017, from http://nla.gov.au/nla.news-article27451067.

[50] Davis, R. I., 1994, p.14.

[51] Couts, Joseph, *A Practical Guide for the Tailor's Cutting-Room; being a treatise on measuring and cutting clothing*, London: Blackie & Son, 1848, p.58.

[52] *The West End Gazette of Gentlemen's Fashions*, edited by a committee of the above society, Vol.III, London: Kent & Co., 1870, p.5.

[53] Davis, R. I., 1994, p.22.

[54] Epstein, 1968, p.44.

[55] Foster, Vanda, *A Visual History of Costume: The Nineteenth Century*, Volume 5, London: Batsford, 1984, p.23.

[56] "GENTLEMEN'S FASHIONS." (1840, November 12). *Launceston Advertiser (Tas. : 1829–1846)*, p.4. Retrieved August 6, 2018, from http://nla.gov.au/nla.news-article84750812

[57] Yarwood, Doreen, *Costume of the Western World*, Cambridge: Lutterworth, 1980, p.111.

[58] Hart, 1998, pp.53–54.

[59] Kelly, Stuart, *Scott-Land: The Man Who Invented a Nation*, Edinburgh: Polygon, 2010, np.

[60] "FASHIONS FOR APRIL." (1851, August 12). *The Sydney Morning Herald (NSW : 1842–1954)*, p.4 (Supplement to the Sydney Morning Herald). Retrieved January 17, 2018, from http://nla.gov.au/nla.news-article12929374.

[61] The Habits of Good Society: A Handbook of Etiquette for Ladies and Gentlemen, London: James Hogg & Sons, 1859, p.148.

[62] Tortora & Eubank, 2009, p.370.

[63] Hartley, Cecil B., *The Gentleman's Book of Etiquette and Manual of Politeness*, Boston: G.W. Cottrell, 1860, p.146.

[64] Johnston, Lucy, 2005, p.216.

[65] Mayhew, Henry et.al, *Punch, or the London Charivari*, Vol.XXVII, 1854, p.123.

[66] Houfe, Simon, *John Leech and the Victorian Scene*, Suffolk: ACC Art Books, 1984, p.142.

Chapter Four

[1] Harvey, John, *Men in Black*, London: Reaktion, 1995, p.23.

[2] "MEN'S FASHIONS." *The Goulburn Herald and Chronicle (NSW : 1864–1881)* 10 July 1867: 4. Web. 19 Aug 2018 http://nla.gov.au/nla.news-article100873801

[3] Perrot, Philippe, *Fashioning the Bourgeoisie: A History of Clothing in the Nineteenth Century*, NJ: Princeton University Press, (1981) 1994, p.70.

[4] Mayhew, Henry, *The Morning Chronicle Survey of Labour and the Poor: The Metropolitan Districts*, Volume 1, London: Routledge, np.

[5] "OLD CLOTHES, AND WHAT BECOMES OF THEM." (1865, February 4). *Sydney Mail (NSW : 1860–1871)*, p.8. Retrieved July 11, 2018, from http://nla.gov.au/nla.news-article166660809.

[6] *Generations of Style: Brooks Brothers, The First 100 Years*, p.21.

[7] Cockburn Conkling, Margaret, Lunettes, Henry, *The American Gentleman's Guide to Politeness and Fashion* , NY: Derby & Jackson, 1860, p.29.

[8] Lunettes, Henry, *The American Gentleman's Guide to Politeness and Fashion*, 1860, p.29.

[9] Hartley, Cecil B., *The Gentlemen's Book of Etiquette and Manual of Politeness*, Boston: G.W Cottrell, 1860, p.118.

[10] Lunettes, Henry, *The American Gentleman's Guide to Politeness and Fashion*; 1863, p.31.

[11] *Gossip for the Gentlemen*, Daily Alta California, Volume 19, Number 6245, 20 April 1867, p.6.

[12] "Men's Fashions." *Illawarra Mercury (Wollongong, NSW : 1856–1950)* 12 July 1867: 4. Web. 19 Aug 2018 http://nla.gov.au/nla.news-article135813592.

[13] Miller, Michael B., *The Bon Marche: Bourgeois Culture and the Department Store, 1869–1920*, NJ: Princeton University Press, 1981, p.3.

[14] *The West End Gazette of Gentleman's Fashions*, Vol.III, London: Kent & Co., June 1870, p.48.

[15] Hopkins, John, *Basics Fashion Design 07: Menswear*, Lausanne: AVA Publishing, 2011, p.88.

[16] Cole, Shaun, *The Story of Men's Underwear: Volume 1*, NY: Parkstone International, 2012, np.

[17] "ABOUT SHIRTS." (1874, May 13). *Wagga Wagga Advertiser and Riverine Reporter (NSW : 1868–1875)* Retrieved November 2018 from http://nla.gov.au/nla.news-article104115537.

[18] Wilde, Oscar in *The Pall Mall Budget*, Volume 32, 1884, p.32.

[19] Galsworthy, John, *The Forsyte Saga*, Surrey: The Windmill Press, (1922) 1950, p.410.

[20] Hunt-Hurst, Patricia Kay in Blanco F, José, *Clothing and Fashion: American Fashion from Head to Toe*, Denver, CO: ABC-CLIO, 2016, pp.184–220.

[21] Hartley, 1860, p.140.

[22] Breward, Christopher in Taylor, Lou, *The Study of Dress History*, Manchester: Manchester University Press, 2002, p.138.

[23] Minister, Edward & Son, *The Gazette of Fashion and Cutting Room Companion*, August 1, 1868, No.268, Vol.23, p.30.

[24] Woods, John, *A new and complete system for cutting Trousers*, London: Kent & Richards, 1847, p.7.

[25] *The West End Gazette of Gentleman's Fashions*, Vol.10, No.120, London: Kent & Co., June 1872, p.45.

[26] Sichel, Marion, *Costume Reference: The Victorians*, Plays, Inc., 1978, p.33.

[27] Foster, Vanda, *A Visual History of Costume: The Nineteenth Century*, Vol.5, London: Batsford, 1984, p.82.

[28] *The Athenaeum*, No.1537, April 11, 1857, p.466.

[29] *Beadle's dime book of practical etiquette for ladies and gentlemen*, New York: Irwin P. Beadle & Co., 1859, p.21.

[30] Kinsler, Blakley Gwen, *The Miser's Purse*, Piecework, November/December 1996, p.47–48.

[31] Yarwood, Doreen, *Illustrated Encyclopedia of World Costume*, NY: Dover, 1978, p.154.

[32] *The West-End Gazette of Gentlemen's Fashions By a Committee of the Above Society*, May 1872, p.44.

[33] Devere, Louis, *The Gentleman's Magazine of Fashion*, London: Simpkin, Marshall & Co., May 1871, p.4.

[34] Johnston, Lucy, 2005, p.30.

[35] Devere, 1871, p.4.

[36] Johnston, 2005, p.30.

[37] Byrde, Penelope, *Nineteenth Century Fashion*, London: Batsford, 1992, p.99.

[38] RISDM data: https://risdmuseum. org/art_design/objects/1705_suit_worn_ by_james_adams_woolso n_1829_1904

[39] Boyer, G. Bruce, *True Style: The History and Principles of Classic Menswear,* PA: Perseus, 2015, p.201.

[40] O'Byrne, Robert, *The Perfectly Dressed Gentleman*, London: CICO, 2011, np.

[41] "FASHION." (1890, January 10). *Fitzroy City Press (Vic. : 1881–1920)*, p.3 (Supplement to the Fitzroy City Press.). Retrieved May 12, 2018, from http://nla. gov.au/nla.news-article65678455.

[42] Ledbetter, Kathryn, *Victorian Needlework*, CA: Praeger, 2012, p.33.

[43] Hunt-Hurst, Blanco F, José, 2016, p.234.

[44] Breward, 2016, p.89.

[45] Shrock, Joel, *The Gilded Age*, CN: Greenwood Press, 2004, p.81–3.

[46] "HIS FROCK COAT." (1898, 17 September). *The Capricornian (Rockhampton, Qld. : 1875–1929)*. Retrieved August 20, 2018, from http://nla. gov.au/nla.news-article68205799.

[47] Philadelphia Museum of Art object data: 1996-19-11a—c/

[48] Holt, Arden, *Fancy Dresses Described: A Glossary of Victorian Costumes*, NY: Dover, (1896) 2017, p.305.

Chapter Five

[1] *Los Angeles Herald*, Volume 33, Number 84, 24 December 1905, p.7.

[2] *Morning Press*, 17 December 1908, p.5.

[3] *Tit-Bits* quoted in *Los Angeles Herald*, California, April 9, 1905, Page 35.

[4] Burstyn, Varda, *The Rites of Men: Manhood, Politics, and the Culture of Sport,* Toronto: University of Toronto Press, 2000, p.94.

[5] Dunkerley, W.A., *To-Day*, London, 1895.

[6] Blackman, Cally, *100 Years of Fashion Illustration*, London: Laurence King, 2007, p.9.

[7] Galsworthy, John, *The Forsyte Saga*, Surrey: The Windmill Press, (1922) 1950, p.553.

[8] Edwards, Nina, *Dressed for War: Uniform, Civilian Clothing and Trappings, 1914 to 1928,* London: I.B Tauris, 2015, p.73.

[9] *Current Opinion*, May 1919, "London's Literary Tailor: H. Dennis Bradley expresses his philosophy of clothes through the medium of the advertizement," Volumes 66–67, p.319.

[10] Carr, Richard, and Hart, Bradley W., *The Global 1920s: Politics, economics and society*, Oxford: Routledge, 2016, np.

[11] Costantino, Maria, *Men's Fashion in the Twentieth Century: From Frock Coats to Intelligent Fibres*, CA: Costume & Fashion Press, 1997, p.44.

[12] Art and Picture Collection, The New York Public Library. "For the well dressed man : comfort is the keynote of the modern man's wardrobe." *The New York Public Library Digital Collections.* 1922. http://digitalcollections.nypl. org/items/510d47e0-f013-a3d9-e040-e00a18064a99.

[13] *Vanity Fair*, "The Well Dressed Man in Winter," 1921.

[14] Bruzzi, Stella, quoted in Arnold, Rebecca, *Fashion, Desire and Anxiety: Image and Morality in the Twentieth Century*, London: I.B Tauris, 2001, p.38.

[15] Sichel, Marion, *Costume Reference 8: 1918–39*, London: Batsford, 1978, p.14.

[16] Clemente, Deirdre, "Showing Your Stripes: Student Culture and the Significance of Clothing at Princeton, 1910–1933." *The Princeton University Library Chronicle*, Vol.69, No.3, 2008, pp. 437–464. *JSTOR*, JSTOR, www.jstor.org/stable/10.25290/ prinunivlibrchro.69.3.0437, p.440.

[17] San Pedro Daily News, Volume 19, Number 16, 20 January 1920, p.8.

[18] Koda, Martin in Tulloch, Carol, *The Birth of Cool: Style Narratives of the African Diaspora*, London: Bloomsbury, 2016, p.67.

[19] Ibid.

[20] Waugh, Evelyn, *Brideshead Revisited: The Sacred and Profane Memories of Captain Charles Ryder,* London: Penguin, (1945) 2012, np.

[21] Tulloch, 2016, p.67.

[22] Science, Industry and Business Library: General Collection , The New York Public Library. "Flannel outing suits; No. 9. The new Breakwater summer suit." *The New York Public Library Digital Collections.* 1900.

[23] Hughes, Clair, *Hats*, London: Bloomsbury, 2016, p.198.

[24] "IN SUMMER-TIME." (1896, October 25). *Sunday Times (Sydney, NSW : 1895–1930)*: Retrieved December 2017 from http://nla.gov.au/nla.news-article130400893.

[25] "FEW CHANGES IN FASHIONS FOR MEN." (1903, March 7). *The World's News (Sydney, NSW : 1901–1955)*, p.19. Retrieved March 30, 2018, from http://nla. gov.au/nla.news-article128457052.

[26] Hallwyl Museum data: http://hallwylskamuseet.se/en/explore/family.

[27] Jackson, Ashley, *Mad Dogs and Englishmen: A grand tour of the British Empire at its height*, London: Quercus, 2009, np.

[28] "WHAT MEN ARE WEARING." (1902, November 15). *The Daily News (Perth, WA : 1882–1950)*, p.6. Retrieved April 9, 2018, from http://nla.gov.au/nla.news-article81322122.

[29] *Mariposa Gazette*, Number 42, 30 March 1901, p.2.

[30] Story, Alfred T., *The Phrenological Magazine*, 1881, p.175.

[31] Stinson Jarvis, Thomas, *Letters from East Longitudes: Sketches of Travel in Egypt, the Holy Land, Greece, and Cities of the Levant*, Toronto: James Campbell & Son, 1875, p.210.

[32] Hunt-Hurst, Patricia Kay in Blanco F, José, *Clothing and Fashion: American Fashion from Head to Toe*, Denver, CO: ABC-CLIO, 2016, p.216.

[33] *Men's Wear* [semi-monthly], Volume 28, October 1910, p.115.

[34] *The American Tailor and Cutter*, Volume 32, J. Mitchell Company, 1910, p.26.

[35] Bradley, Carolyn G., *Western World Costume: An Outline History*, N.Y: Dover, 2013, p.123.

[36] Arnold and Daniel, Philadelphia, 1897, via oldcycles.eu.

[37] Quoted in Alford, Steven E. and Ferriss, Suzanne, *An Alternative History of Bicycles and Motorcycles: Two-Wheeled Transportation and Material Culture*, London: Lexington Books, 2016, p.107.

[38] "Cycling." *The Evening Star (Boulder, WA : 1898–1921)* 13 October 1904: 4. Web.

21 Aug 2018 http://nla.gov.au/nla.news-article204535161.

[39] Stamper, Anita M. and Condra, Jill, *Clothing Through American History: The Civil War Through the Gilded Age, 1861 – 1899*, CA: Greenwood, 2011, p.355.

[40] "STOCKINGS OF MANY COLORS." (1909, May 8). *The Daily News (Perth, WA : 1882–1950)* Retrieved August 21, 2018, from http://nla.gov.au/nla.news-article77120933.

[41] Blanco F., 2016, p.216.

[42] Victoria & Albert Museum. Retrieved from http://collections.vam.ac.uk/item/O78848/norfolk-jacket-unknown/.

[43] Johnston, Lucy, *Nineteenth century Fashion in Detail*, London: Victoria & Albert Museum, 2005, p.162.

[44] *Sacramento Daily Union*, Volume 53, Number 124, 16 July 1885, p.3.

[45] *Tailor & Cutter*, Volume 49, 1914, p.168.

[46] *Gentry*, "Renaissance of the Norfolk Jacket," Spring 1953, p.105.

[47] *It's All Done with Buttons*, La Mode Division, B. Blumenthal & Company, 1949, p.4.

[48] *San Pedro News Pilot*, Volume 1, Number 175, 27 April 1914, p.2.

[49] "EVENING DRESS." (1910, August 2). *The Tumut Advocate and Farmers and Settlers' Adviser (NSW : 1903–1925)*, p.3. Retrieved March 7, 2018, from http://nla.gov.au/nla.news-article112262430.

[50] Payne, Winakor, Farrell-Beck, *The History of Costume: From Ancient Mesopotamia Through the Twentieth Century*, London: Harper Collins, 1992, p.550.

[51] The American Tailor and Cutter, Volume 32, 1910, p.iv.

[52] *Men's Wear*. [semi-monthly], Volume 29, 1910, p.64.

[53] Ashelford, Jane, *The Art of Dress: Clothes and Society 1500 – 1914*, London: The National Trust, 1996, p.303.

[54] Bohleke, Karin. *Titanic Fashions: High Style in the 1910's*. Hanover: Shippensburg University Fashion Archives and Museum, 2012.

[55] Sichel, Marion, *Costume Reference 7: The Edwardians*, London: Batsford, 1986, pp.8–12.

[56] Edwards, Nina, *Dressed for War: Uniform, Civilian Clothing and Trappings, 1914 to 1928*, London: I.B Tauris, 2015, p.48.

[57] "THE TROUSERS CREASE." (1914, June 13). *The Muswellbrook Chronicle (NSW : 1898–1955)*, p.6. Retrieved March 2, 2018, from http://nla.gov.au/nla.news-article107868473

[58] Anderson, Fiona, *Tweed*, London: Bloomsbury, 2017, p.89.

[59] Evans Jr, Charles, "The Americanization of Golf," *Vanity Fair*, June 1922.

[60] Green, Sandy, *Don'ts for Golfers*, A&C Black, (1925) 2008 p.39.

[61] Manlow, Veronica, *Designing Clothes: Culture and Organization of the Fashion Industry*, NJ: Transaction Publishers, 2007, p.64.

[62] Flusser, Alan J., *Clothes and the man: the principles of fine men's dress*, NY: Villard, 1985, p.124.

[63] Graves, Robert, *Goodbye to All That*, NY: Octagon, 1980, p.328.

[64] "Oxford Bags," by Moses, Jack, *Glen Innes Examiner*, NSW, March 10, 1928, p.5.

[65] Clemente, Deirdre, *Dress Casual: How College Students Redefined American Style*, NC: University of North Carolina Press, 2014, p.125.

[66] Tortora and Eubank, *Survey of Historic Costume*, p.480.

[67] Storey, Nicholas, *History of Men's Fashion: What the Well-Dressed Man Is Wearing*, South Yorkshire: Remember When, 2008, p.31.

[68] Lehman, LaLonnie, *Fashion in the Time of the Great Gatsby*, London: Shire/Bloosmbury: 2013, np.

[69] Borsodi, William, *Advertisers Cyclopedia or Selling Phrases, Economist Training School*, Binghamton, N.Y: D.C Race Co, 1909, p.1134

[70] America's Textile Reporter: For the Combined Textile Industries, Volume 18, 1904, p.208.

[71] About Shirts. (1923, March 25). *The Daily Mail (Brisbane, Qld. : 1903–1926)*, p.13. Retrieved May 22, 2018, from http://nla.gov.au/nla.news-article220567878.

[72] Galsworthy, John, (1922) 1950, p.635.

[73] Quoted in *The Morning News*, Wilmington, Delaware, January 8, 1925, p.1

[74] Takeda, Sharon Sadako and Spilker, Kaye Durland, *Reigning Men: Fashion in Menswear, 1715–2015*, NY: Prestel/Los Angeles County Museum of Art, 2016, p.256.

[75] *Vogue*, July 15, 1922: Francis de Miomandre, *The Case Against the Decline of Masculine Elegance*, p.62.

[76] *Vanity Fair*, "For the Well Dressed Man," June, 1921.

[77] Ibid.

[78] *Collier's Magazine*, "Black Tie," November 29, 1947, p.82.

[79] Kindell, Alexandra, Demers, Elizabeth S., *Encyclopedia of Populism in America: A Historical Encyclopedia*, Volume 1: A–M, CA: ABC-CLIO, 2014, p.176.

[80] *Boys' Life*, New York: The Boy Scouts of America, June 1938, p.43.

[81] Gavenas, Mary Lisa, *The Fairchild Encyclopedia of Menswear*, London: Fairchild Books, 2008, p.91.

[82] STRAW "BOATER." (1936, August 22). *The Longreach Leader (Qld. : 1923–1954)*, p.4. Retrieved February 1, 2018, from http://nla.gov.au/nla.news-article37360810.

[83] *Santa Cruz Sentinel*, Volume 86, Number 80, 6 October 1932, p.15.

[84] Chenoune, Farid, *A History of Men's Fashion*, New York: Flammarion, 1993, p.175.

[85] "WHAT WELL-DRESSED MEN WILL WEAR THIS YEAR." (1932, January 25). *News (Adelaide, SA : 1923–1954)*, p.9. Retrieved March 3, 2018, from http://nla.gov.au/nla.news-article128302095

[86] "AROUND the Town." (1935, December 21). *Barrier Miner (Broken Hill, NSW : 1888–1954)*, p.5 (SPORTS EDITION). Retrieved March 3, 2018, from http://nla.gov.au/nla.news-article46715062.

[87] Tailor On London Dress For Men (1935, June 26). *Barrier Miner (Broken Hill, NSW : 1888–1954)*, p.2. Retrieved July 2, 2018, from http://nla.gov.au/nla.news-article46696412

[88] *Santa Cruz Sentinel*, Volume 94, Number 113, 10 November 1936.

[89] "Why hide expensive tie under your waistcoat? Wearing vest offers advantages and trouble," *Colorado Eagle and Journal*, Number 3, 10 January 1933, p.1.

[90] "MEN'S TROUSERS FOR WOMEN." (1933, April 15). *Recorder (Port Pirie, SA : 1919–1954)*, p.2. Retrieved August 13, 2018, from http://nla.gov.au/nla.news-article95994673.

[91] Takeda and Spilker, 2016, p.161.

[92] Bolton, Andrew, *Anglomania: Tradition and Transgression in British Fashion*, NY: The Metropolitan Museum of Art, 2006, p.75.

[93] Sichel, Marion, *Costume Reference 8, 1918 – 1939*, London: Batsford, 1978, pp.13–15.

Chapter Six

[1] Martin, Richard Harrison and Koda, Harold, *Orientalism: Visions of the East in Western Dress*, NY: Metropolitan Museum of Art, 1994, p.39.

[2] Williams, Susan, *The People's King: The True Story of the Abdication*, London: Penguin, 2003, np.

[3] Duke Sets Color Fashions (1941, February 26). *The Sun (Sydney, NSW : 1910–1954)*, p.9 "LAST RACE ALL DETAILS." Retrieved July 18, 2018, from http://nla.gov.au/nla.news-article230944193.

[4] Bowstead, Jay McCauley, *Menswear Revolution: The Transformation of Contemporary Men's Fashion*, London: Bloomsbury, 2018, np.

[5] Chibnall, Steve, "Whistle and zoot: The changing meaning of a suit of clothes," *History Workshop*, no.20, 56–81.

[6] "IT'S A MOD, MOD WORLD." (1964, May 20). *The Australian Women's Weekly (1933–1982)*, p.5. Retrieved July 19, 2018, from http://nla.gov.au/nla.news-article51779808.

[7] Delis Hill, Daniel, *Peacock Revolution: American Masculine Identity and Dress in the Sixties and Seventies*, London: Bloomsbury, 2018, p.85.

[8] "Return of the Dandy." (1966, June 22). *The Australian Women's Weekly (1933–1982)*, p.11. Retrieved July 19, 2018, from http://nla.gov.au/nla.news-article44024618.

[9] Garrett, Valery, *Chinese Clothing: An Illustrated Guide,* Oxford: Oxford University Press, 1994, p.107.

[10] "News In Brief." (1956, July 24). *The Canberra Times (ACT : 1926–1995)*, p.3. Retrieved November 8, 2018, from http://nla.gov.au/nla.news-article91218521.

[11] "Men are throwing their hats away!" (1950, September 11). *The Sun (Sydney, NSW : 1910–1954)*, p.11 (LATE FINAL EXTRA). Retrieved November 9, 2018, from http://nla.gov.au/nla.news-article230475306.

[12] Desert Sun, Volume 35, Number 302, 24 July 1962.

[13] *Desert Sun*, Volume 37, Number 171, 21 February 1964.

[14] Hughes, Clair, *Hats*, London: Bloomsbury, 2017, p.104.

[15] Steinberg, Neil, *Hatless Jack: The President, the Fedora, and the History of an American Style*, London: Granta Books, 2005, p.210.

[16] *Men's Wear*, Volume 160, London: Fairchild, 1969, np.

[17] "Newest Fashion for Coeds Is As Old As the Flapper," *Desert Sun*, 1957.

[18] Logan, Walter, "The Topcoat Scene is Getting Livelier," *The San Francisco Examiner*, Sunday, November 5, 1967, p.108.

[19] Peiss, Kathy, *Zoot Suit: The Enigmatic Career of an Extreme Style*, Philadelphia: University of Pennsylvania Press, 2011, pp.1–3.

[20] "Sex psychology of a zoot suit." (1944, April 2). *The Sun (Sydney, NSW : 1910–1954)*, p.3 (SUPPLEMENT TO THE FACT). Retrieved May 16, 2018, from http://nla.gov.au/nla.news-article231822178.

[21] Obregn Pagn, Eduardo, *Murder at the Sleepy Lagoon: Zoot Suits, Race, & Riot in Wartime L.A.*, Chapel Hill: University of North Carolina Press, 2003, p.181.

[22] *Yank*: June 15, 1945, "Foreigners Observe American Culture," p.18 oldmagazinearticles.com.

[23] "Duke sets colour fashions," *Bay of Plenty Times*, Volume LXIX, Issue 13288, 14 March 1941.

[24] Edward VIII, *A Family Album*, London: Cassell, 1960, pp.108–09.

[25] Cole, David John, Browning, Eve, and Schroeder, Fred E. H., *Encyclopedia of Modern Everyday Inventions,* CT: Greenwood Press, 2003, p.121.

[26] Menkes, Suzy, *The Windsor Style*, London: Grafton, 1987, p.127.

[27] Edward VIII, 1960, p.116.

[28] Holden, Anthony, *Prince Charles*, NY: Atheneum, 1979, p.43.

[29] IWM data: https://www.iwm.org.uk/history/how-clothes-rationing-affected-fashion-in-the-second-world-war.

[30] "Utility Clothing." (1942, January 10). *The Daily News (Perth, WA : 1882–1950)*, p.21 (First Edition). Retrieved March 22, 2018, from http://nla.gov.au/nla.news-article78578072.

[31] "Notes on the News" (1942, August 1). *The Telegraph (Brisbane, Qld. : 1872–1947)*, p.3 (LATE WEEK END). Retrieved March 23, 2018, from http://nla.gov.au/nla.news-article172616485.

[32] *Men's Wear*, February 10, 1950, p.231 oldmagazinearticles.

[33] Victoria & Albert Museum data: http://collections.vam.ac.uk/item/O84102/suit-utility/.

[34] Ibid.

[35] Jobling, Paul, *Advertising Menswear: Masculinity and Fashion in the British Media since 1945,* London: Bloomsbury, 2014, p.12.

[36] "'Demob' Suits Of Best Scotch Tweed." (1945, September 4). *The Mercury (Hobart, Tas. : 1860–1954)*, p.5. Retrieved March 23, 2018, from http://nla.gov.au/nla.news-article26142068.

[37] Bryan, Sir Paul, *Wool, War and Westminster: Front-Line Memoirs of Sir Paul Bryan, DSO, MC.*, NY: Tom Donovan, 1993, p.169.

[38] Hutton, Mike, *Life in 1940s London*, Gloucestershire: Amberley Publishing, 2013, np.

[39] MacDougall, Ian, *Voices from War and Some Labour Struggles: Personal Recollections*

of War in Our Century by Scottish Men and Women, Mercat Press, 1995, p.255.

[40] "'DEMOBBED' MEN'S WAISTLINE GROWS." (1946, October 11). The Courier-Mail (Brisbane, Qld.:1933–1954), p.1. Retrieved March 27, 2018, from http://nla.gov.au/nla.news-article49362697.

[41] Craik, Jennifer, The Face of Fashion: Cultural Studies in Fashion, London: Routledge, 2003, p.184.

[42] "Colour Trend." (1954, August 13). Macleay Argus (Kempsey, NSW : 1885–1907; 1909–1910; 1912–1913; 1915–1916; 1918–1954), p.2. Retrieved February 16, 2018, from http://nla.gov.au/nla.news-article234555376.

[43] "Teddy suit is mating call." (1955, June 29). The Argus (Melbourne, Vic. : 1848–1957), p.2. Retrieved June 13, 2018, from http://nla.gov.au/nla.news-article71890618.

[44] Marchant, Hilde, "The Truth about the 'Teddy Boys' and the Teddy Girls," Picture Post, 29 May, 1954, London.

[45] Tyrell, Anne V., Changing trends in fashion: patterns of the twentieth century, 1900–1970, London: Batsford, 1986, p.128.

[46] "Narrow Trousers For Australians." (1952, January 6). The Sunday Herald (Sydney, NSW : 1949–1953), p.1. Retrieved June 13, 2018, from http://nla.gov.au/nla.news-article18488730.

[47] Scala, Mim, Diary of a Teddy Boy: A Memoir of the Long Sixties, Goblin Press, 2009, p.13.

[48] MAAS Museum data: https://collection.maas.museum/object/163411.

[49] Martin, Richard and Koda, Harold, Christian Dior, NY: The Metropolitan Museum of Art, 1996, p.18.

[50] "The Sydney Morning Herald." (1953, December 22) The Sydney Morning Herald (NSW : 1842–1954) Retrieved August 2018 from http://nla.gov.au/nla.news-article27520868.

[51] "Men To Wear Washable Suits Soon." (1954, March 15). The West Australian (Perth, WA : 1879–1954), p.15. Retrieved May 6, 2018, from http://nla.gov.au/nla.news-article49622749.

[52] FIT Museum data: http://fashionmuseum.fitnyc.edu/view/objects.

[53] "WHEN BUYING A SUIT BE COLOUR CONSCIOUS." (1956, October 26). Western Herald (Bourke, NSW : 1887–1970), p.15. Retrieved May 6, 2018, from http://nla.gov.au/nla.news-article104015373.

[54] "NEW WASHABLE SUIT IN U.K." (1954, March 6). Barrier Miner (Broken Hill, NSW : 1888–1954), p.2 (SPORTS EDITION). Retrieved May 6, 2018, from http://nla.gov.au/nla.news-article49418758.

[55] Davies, Hunter, The Beatles, London: Ebury Press, (1968) 2009, p.189.

[56] Kelly, Michael Bryan, The Beatle Myth: The British Invasion of American Popular Music, 1956–1969, NC: McFarland, 1991, p.109.

[57] Lewisohn, Mark, The Beatles – All These Years: Volume One: Tune In, London: Little, Brown, 2013, np.

[58] Newsweek, Volume 72, Part 2, p.672.

[59] Victoria & Albert Museum data: http://collections.vam.ac.uk/item/O7844/mans-suit-mr-fish/.

[60] Desert Sun, Number 17, California, 25 August 1966, p.6.

[61] Delis Hill, 2018, p.106.

[62] Desert Sun, Number 250, California, 23 May 1969, p.12.

[63] Desert Sun, Number 244, California, 16 May 1969, p.7.

[64] Robertson, Whitney A. J. in Blanco, Hunt-Hurst, Vaughan Lee and Doering, Clothing and Fashion: American Fashion from Head to Toe, Volume One, CA: ABC-CLIO, 2016, p.312.

[65] Arizona Daily Star, Tucson, Arizona, May 12, 1968, p.30.

[66] Byrd, Penelope, The Male Image: Men's Fashion in Britain, 1300–1970, London: Batsford, 1979, np.

[67] Post, Elizabeth and Post, Emily, Etiquette, Toronto: Harper Collins, 1965, np.

[68] Harper's Bazaar, Volume 105, Hearst Corporation, 1972, np.

[69] McGillis Ian, "McCord Brings Expo 67 Styles Back to Life," Montreal Gazette, 16 March 2017.

[70] McCord Museum data: http://museedelamode.ca/collection/designersquebecois-en.html.

[71] Lynch, Annette and Strauss, Mitchell D., Ethnic Dress in the United States: A Cultural Encyclopedia, NY: Rowman & Littlefield, 2015, p.67–68.

[72] Paoletti, Jo B., Sex and Unisex: Fashion, Feminism, and the Sexual Revolution, IN: Indiana University Press, 2015, p.51.

[73] Delis Hill, 2018, p.110.

[74] Ties disappear in Italy (1968, March 8). The Canberra Times (ACT : 1926–1995), p.13. Retrieved June 8, 2018, from http://nla.gov.au/nla.news-article107040704.

[75] Grace, Stephen, *Shanghai: Life, Love and Infrastructure in China's City of the Future*, CO: Sentient, 2010, p.132.

[76] Finnane, Antonia, *Changing Clothes in China: Fashion, History, Nation*, NY: Columbia University Press, 2008, p.184.

[77] Garrett, Valery, *Chinese Dress: From the Qing Dynasty to the Present*, VT: Tuttle Publishing, 2007, p.458.

[78] Breward, Christopher, *The Suit: Form, Function and Style*, London: Reaktion, 2016, p.100.

[79] Steele, Valerie and Major, John S., *China Chic: East Meets West*, Yale: Yale University Press, 1999, p.57.

[80] Mackerras, Colin, *China in Transformation: 1900–1949*, London: Routledge, 2008, p.135.

Chapter Seven

[1] Edwards, Tim, *Men in the Mirror: Men's Fashion, Masculinity, and Consumer Society*, London: Bloomsbury, (1997) 2016, p.55.

[2] Mallon, Jackie, *Designer Kansai Yamamoto talks all things David Bowie*, Monday, 21 May 2018, fashionunited.uk.

[3] Paoletti, Jo B., *Sex and Unisex: Fashion, Feminism, and the Sexual Revolution*, IN: Indiana University Press, 2015, p.6.

[4] Bruzzi, Stella, *Undressing Cinema: Clothing and identity in the movies*, Oxon: Routledge, 1997, p.177.

[5] *Hosiery and knitwear in the 1970s: a study of the industry's future market prospects*, H.M. Stationery Off., 1970, p.33.

[6] Steele, Valerie, *Encyclopedia of Clothing and Fashion*, NY: Charles Scribner's Sons, 2005, p.4.

[7] Blackman, Cally, *100 Years of Fashion Illustration*, London: Laurence King Publishing, 2007, p.258.

[8] Hebdige, Dick, quoted in Richardson, Niall, and Locks, Adam, *Body Studies: The Basics*, Oxon: Routledge, 2014, p.77.

[9] Potvin, John, *Giorgio Armani: Empire of the Senses*, London: Routledge, 2013, p.64.

[10] Breward, Christopher, *The Suit: Form, Function and Style*, London: Reaktion, 2016, p.205.

[11] Edwards, Tim, *Men in the Mirror: Men's Fashion, Masculinity, and Consumer Society*, London: Bloomsbury, (1997) 2016, p.55.

[12] Delis Hill, Daniel, *As Seen in Vogue: A Century of American Fashion in Advertising*, Lubbock: Texas Tech University Press, 2004, p.123.

[13] English, Bonnie, *Japanese Fashion Designers: The Work and Influence of Issey Miyake, Yohji Yamamoto and Rei Kawakubo*, London: Berg, 2011, p.20.

[14] Kawamura, Yuniya, *Fashioning Japanese Subcultures*, London: Berg, 2012, p.23.

[15] Kennedy, Alicia, Emily Stoehrer, Banis and Calderin, Jay, *Fashion Design, Referenced: A Visual Guide to the History, Language, and Practice of Fashion*, MA: Rockport Publishers, 2013, p.125.

[16] Wilson, Elizabeth quoted in Arnold, Rebecca, *Fashion, Desire and Anxiety: Image and Morality in the 20th Century*, London: Tauris, 2001, p.25.

[17] Nelmes, Jill, *An Introduction to Film Studies*, Oxon: Routledge, 1996, p.269.

[18] Miller, Janice, *Fashion and Music*, Oxford: Berg, 2011, np.

[19] "MORE TO LIFE." (1994, April 12). *The Canberra Times (ACT : 1926–1995)*, p.14. Retrieved August 6, 2018, from http://nla.gov.au/nla.news-article118112694.

[20] *Dress policies and casual dress days*, Bureau of National Affairs, January 1998, p.1.

[21] Masi de Casanova, Erynn, *Buttoned Up: Clothing, Conformity, and White-Collar Masculinity*, NY: Cornell University Press, 2015, pp.9–10.

[22] Blass, Bill, *Bare Blass*, NY: Harper Collins, 2003, np.

[23] ed. by Hall, Dennis R. & Susan G., *American Icons*, CT: Greenwood, 2006, p.567.

[24] "Men's Wear Is Off To Handsome Start This Decade," *Desert Sun*, Number 187, 12 March 1970.

[25] *Ebony* magazine, August 1972, p.156.

[26] McCord Museum collection data: M972.112.3.1–5.

[27] Sterlacci, Francesca and Arbuckle, Joanne, *Historical Dictionary of the Fashion Industry*, NY: Rowman & Littlefield, 2017, p.353.

[28] "THE ART OF UPDATING YOUR HUSBAND." (1971, June 2). *The Australian Women's Weekly (1933–1982)*, p.30. Retrieved May 18, 2018, from http://nla.gov.au/nla.news-article44798006.

[29] Reed, Paula A., *Fifty Fashion Looks that Changed the 1970s*, London: Conran Octopus, 2012, p.42–3.

[30] "HUSBAND, WIFE FASHION TEAM." (1975, December 5). *The Canberra Times* (ACT : 1926–1995), p.15. Retrieved April 9, 2018, from http://nla.gov.au/nla.news-article102190028.

[31] Lindop, Edmund, *America in the 1950s,* MN: Lerner, 2010, p.1964.

[32] Advertising (1972, April 11). *The Canberra Times (ACT : 1926–1995)*, p.12. Retrieved May 25, 2018, from http://nla. gov.au/nla.news-article102208991.

[33] Laver, James, quoted in Wills, Garry, *Values Americans Live by*, NY: Arno Press, 1978, p.565.

[34] Delis Hill, 2018, p.77.

[35] Sweetman, John, *Raglan: From the Peninsula to the Crimea*, South Yorkshire: Pen & Sword Military, 2010, p.338.

[36] Boyer, Bruce G., *True Style: The History and Principles of Classic Menswear,* PA: Perseus, 2015, np.

[37] *New York Magazine,* 16 Sep 1996, p.30–32.

[38] The Museum at FIT online collection data, 85.58.7.

[39] Warner, Helen, *Fashion on Television: Identity and Celebrity Culture,* London: Bloomsbury, 2014, p.127.

[40] Edwards, Tim, 2016, p.39.

[41] Blanco, Vaughan Lee and Doering, 2016, p.204.

[42] Boyer, 2015, np.

[43] Potvin, 2017, p.149.

[44] Polan, Brenda and Tredre, Roger, *The Great Fashion Designers*, Oxford: Berg, 2009, p.141.

[45] "TIMESTYLE." (1980, August 10). *The Canberra Times (ACT : 1926–1995)*, p.14. Retrieved May 25, 2018, from http:// nla.gov.au/nla.news-article125615279.

[46] "WOOL Tailored separates for men." (1982, March 16). *The Canberra Times (ACT : 1926–1995)*, p.16. Retrieved May 27, 2018, from http://nla.gov.au/nla.news-article12690988345.

[47] English, 2013, p.6.

[48] Jackson, Carole and Lulow, Kalia, *Color for Men*, NY: Ballantine Books, 1984, np.

[49] "The 1980 man." (1980, April 27). *The Canberra Times (ACT : 1926–1995)*, p.14. Retrieved May 9, 2018, from http://nla.gov. au/nla.news-article110593389.

[50] *Newsweek*, Volume 100, Issues 18–26, 1982, Page 98.

[51] Mentzer, Mike and Friedberg, Ardy, *Mike Mentzer's Spot Bodybuilding: A Revolutionary New Approach to Body Fitness and Symmetry,* London: Simon & Schuster, 1983, p.22.

[52] *San Bernardino Sun*, 13 July 1986, p.29.

[53] "Suitable for Fall," *The Cincinnati Enquirer*, Cincinnati, Ohio, Tuesday, June 24, 1986, p.20.

[54] Menkes, Suzy, *Forbes*, Volume 155, Issues 6–9, 1995, p.104.

[55] Sheridan, Jayne, *Fashion, Media, Promotion: The New Black Magic,* Oxford: Wiley-Blackwell, 2010, p.193.

[56] *San Bernardino Sun*, Volume 115, Number 45, 14 February 1988, p.58.

[57] Victoria & Albert Museum collections data, T.3&A-1988.

[58] Philadelphia Museum of Art object data: 2000-38-1a,b.

[59] Kelly, Ian and Westwood, Vivienne, *Vivienne Westwood*, London: MacMillan, 2014, np.

[60] Vermorel, Fred, *Vivienne Westwood: Fashion, Perversity and the Sixties laid bare*, NY: Overlook Press, 1993.

[61] Banham, Joanna, *Encyclopedia of Interior Design*, London: Routledge, 1997, p.1110.

[62] Steele, Valerie, *Fifty Years of Fashion: New Look to Now*, New Haven: Yale University Press, 1997, p.145.

[63] Molloy, Maureen and Larner, Wendy, *Fashioning Globalisation: New Zealand Design, Working Women and the Cultural Economy*, West Sussex: Wiley Blackwell, 2013, p.2004.

[64] Hillier, Bevis and McIntyre, Kate, *Style of the Century*, Watson-Guptill Publications, 1998, p.243.

Select Bibliography

Alderson, Jr., Robert J, *This Bright Era of Happy Revolutions*, SC: University of South Carolina Press, 2008.

Alford, Steven E. and Ferriss, Suzanne, *An Alternative History of Bicycles and Motorcycles: Two-Wheeled Transportation and Material Culture*, London: Lexington Books, 2016.

Amann, Elizabeth, *Dandyism in the Age of Revolution: The Art of the Cut*, Chicago: University of Chicago Press, 2015.

Amphlett, Hilda, *Hats: A History of Fashion in Headwear*, NY: Dover, (1974) 2003.

Anderson, Fiona, *Tweed*, London: Bloomsbury, 2017.

Antony, Michael, *The Masculine Century: A Heretical History of Our Time*, IN: iUniverse, 2008.

Arnold, Rebecca, *Fashion, Desire and Anxiety: Image and Morality in the Twentieth Century*, London: I.B. Tauris, 2001.

Ashelford, Jane, *A Visual History of Costume*, London: Batsford, 1983.

Ashelford, Jane, *The Art of Dress: Clothes and Society 1500–1914*, London: The National Trust, 1996.

Backhouse, Frances, *Once They Were Hats: In Search of the Mighty Beaver*, Toronto: ECW Press, 2015.

Bailey, Adrian, *The Passion for Fashion*, London: Dragon's World, 1988.

Banham, Joanna, *Encyclopedia of Interior Design*, London: Routledge, 1997.

Blackman, Cally, *100 Years of Fashion Illustration*, London: Laurence King, 2007.

Blanco F, José, *Clothing and Fashion: American Fashion from Head to Toe*, Denver, CO: ABC-CLIO, 2016.

Blass, Bill, *Bare Blass*, NY: Harper Collins, 2003.

Bohleke, Karin, *Titanic Fashions: High Style in the 1910's*. Hanover: Shippensburg University Fashion Archives and Museum, 2012.

Bolton, Andrew, *Anglomania: Tradition and Transgression in British Fashion*, NY: The Metropolitan Museum of Art, 2006.

Borsodi, William, *Advertisers Cyclopedia or Selling Phrases, Economist Training School*, Binghamton, NY: DC Race Co, 1909.

Bowstead, Jay McCauley, *Menswear Revolution: The Transformation of Contemporary Men's Fashion*, London: Bloomsbury, 2018.

Boyer, G. Bruce, *True Style: The History and Principles of Classic Menswear*, PA: Perseus, 2015.

Bradley, Carolyn G., *Western World Costume: An Outline History*, NY: Dover, 2013.

Bray, William, *Memoirs Illustrative of the Life and Writings of John Evelyn*, NY: G.P. Putnam & Sons, 1870.

Breward, Christopher, *The Suit: Form, Function and Style*, London: Reaktion, 2016.

Brown, Ian, *From Tartan to Tartanry: Scottish Culture, History and Myth*, Edinburgh: Edinburgh University Press, 2010.

Bruzzi, Stella, *Undressing Cinema: Clothing and Identity in the Movies*, Oxon: Routledge, 1997.

Bryan, Sir Paul, *Wool, War and Westminster: Front-Line Memoirs of Sir Paul Bryan, DSO, MC*, NY: Tom Donovan, 1993.

Burstyn, Varda, *The Rites of Men: Manhood, Politics, and the Culture of Sport*, Toronto: University of Toronto Press, 2000.

Byrd, Penelope, *The Male Image: Men's Fashion in Britain, 1300–1970*, London: Batsford, 1979.

Byrd, Penelope, *Nineteenth Century Fashion*, London: Batsford, 1992.

Calahan, April, *Fashion Plates: 150 Years of Style*, NH and London: Yale University Press, 2015.

Carr, Richard, and Hart, Bradley W., *The Global 1920s: Politics, Economics and Society*, Oxford: Routledge, 2016.

Chambers, William, *Chambers's Edinburgh Journal, Volume 1*, 'Constantinople in 1831, from the Journal of an Officer,' 1833.

Chazin-Bennahum, Judith, *The Lure of Perfection: Fashion and Ballet, 1780–1830*, NY: Routledge, 2005.

Chenoune, Farid, *A History of Men's Fashion*, New York: Flammarion, 1993.

Chibnall, Steve, 'Whistle and Zoot: The Changing Meaning of a Suit of Clothes,' *History Workshop*, no. 20, 56–81.

Claydon, Tony, and Levillain, Charles-Édouard, *Louis XIV Outside In: Images of the Sun King Beyond France, 1661–1715*, Oxford: Routledge, 2016.

Clemente, Deirdre, "Showing Your Stripes: Student Culture and the Significance of Clothing at Princeton, 1910–1933." *The Princeton University Library Chronicle*, vol. 69, no. 3, 2008, pp. 437–464.

Cockburn Conkling, Margaret, Lunettes, Henry, *The American Gentleman's Guide to Politeness and Fashion*, NY: Derby & Jackson, 1860.

Cole, David John, Browning, Eve, and Schroeder, Fred E. H., *Encyclopedia of Modern Everyday Inventions*, CT: Greenwood Press, 2003.

Cole, Shaun, *The Story of Men's Underwear: Volume 1*, NY: Parkstone International, 2012.

Costantino, Maria, *Men's Fashion in the Twentieth Century: From Frock Coats to Intelligent Fibres*, CA: Costume & Fashion Press, 1997.

Couts, Joseph, *A Practical Guide for the Tailor's Cutting-Room; Being a Treatise on Measuring and Cutting Clothing*, London: Blackie & Son, 1848.

Craik, Jennifer, *The Face of Fashion: Cultural Studies in Fashion*, London: Routledge, 2003.

Cumming, Valerie, Cunnington, C. W., and Cunnington, P. E., *The Dictionary of Fashion History*, London: Bloomsbury, (1960) 2010.

Cunnington, C. Willett & Phyllis, *Handbook of English Costume in the Seventeenth Century*, (proof copy) Faber & Faber, London.

Davies, Hunter, *The Beatles*, London: Ebury Press, (1968) 2009.

Davis, R. I., *Men's Garments 1830–1900: A Guide to Pattern Cutting and Tailoring*, CA: Players Press, 1994.

DeJean, Joan, *How Paris Became Paris: The Invention of the Modern City*, London: Bloomsbury, 2004.

Delis Hill, Daniel, *As Seen in Vogue: A Century of American Fashion in Advertising*, Lubbock: Texas Tech University Press, 2004.

Delis Hill, Daniel, *Peacock Revolution: American Masculine Identity and Dress in the Sixties and Seventies*, London: Bloomsbury, 2018.

Devere, Louis, *The Gentleman's Magazine of Fashion*, London: Simpkin, Marshall & Co., May 1871.

de Winkel, Marieke, *Fashion and Fancy: Dress and Meaning in Rembrandt's Paintings*, Amsterdam: Amsterdam University Press, 2006.

Dickens, Charles, *All the Year Round: A Weekly Journal*, London: No.26, Wellington St, 1860.

Doran, John, *Habits and Men, with remnants of record touching the Makers of both*, London: Richard Bentley, 1855.

Dwyer, Philip, *Napoleon: The Path to Power 1769–1799*, London: Bloomsbury, 2008.

Earnshaw, Pat, *A Dictionary of Lace*, NY: Dover, 1984.

Edward VIII, *A Family Album*, London: Cassell & Co., 1960.

Edwards, Nina, *Dressed for War: Uniform, Civilian Clothing and Trappings, 1914 to 1928*, London: I.B. Tauris, 2015.

Edwards, Tim, *Men in the Mirror: Men's Fashion, Masculinity, and Consumer Society*, London: Bloomsbury, (1997) 2016.

English, Bonnie, *Japanese Fashion Designers: The Work and Influence of Issey Miyake, Yohji Yamamoto and Rei Kawakubo*, London: Berg, 2011.

Ennis, Daniel James and Slagle, Judith Bailey, *Prologues, Epilogues, Curtain-Raisers, and Afterpieces: The Rest of the Eighteenth-Century London Stage*, Newark: University of Delaware Press, 2007.

Epstein, Diana, *Buttons*, London: Studio Vista, 1968.

Evans Jr., Charles, "The Americanization of Golf," *Vanity Fair*, June 1922.

Ewing, Elizabeth, *Everyday Dress: 1650–1900*, Tiptree: Batsford, 1984.

Finnane, Antonia, *Changing Clothes in China: Fashion, History, Nation*, NY: Columbia University Press, 2008.

Fisher, Will, *Materializing Gender in Early Modern English Literature and Culture*, Cambridge: Cambridge University Press, 2006.

Fitzmaurice, Edmond, *The Life of Granville George Leveson Gower, Second Earl Granville, K.G., 1815–1891*, Volume 1, Chizine, 1915.

Fletcher, Christopher, Brady, Sean, Moss, Rachel E., & Riall, Lucy, *The Palgrave Handbook of Masculinity and Political Culture in Europe*, London: Palgrave MacMillan, 2018.

Flusser, Alan J., *Clothes and the Man: The Principles of Fine Men's Dress*, NY: Villard, 1985.

Forgeng, Jeffrey L., *Daily Life in Elizabethan England*, CA: ABC-CLIO, 2010.

Frieda, Leonie, *Francis I: The Maker of Modern France*, London: Hachette, 2018.

Foster, Vanda, *A Visual History of Costume: The Nineteenth Century, Volume 5*, London: Batsford, 1984.

Furnivall, Frederick J., Stubbs, Philip, *Anatomy of the Abuses in Shakespeare's Youth AD 1573*, London: The New Shakespeare Society, 1877.

Galsworthy, John, *The Forsyte Saga*, Surrey: The Windmill Press, (1922) 1950.

Garrett, Valery, *Chinese Dress: From the Qing Dynasty to the Present*, VT: Tuttle Publishing, 2007.

Gavenas, Mary Lisa, *The Fairchild Encyclopedia of Menswear*, London: Fairchild Books, 2008.

Gibbings, Sarah, *The Tie: Trends and Traditions*, London: Barron's, 1990.

Grace, Stephen, *Shanghai: Life, Love and Infrastructure in China's City of the Future*, CO: Sentient, 2010.

Graves, Robert, *Goodbye to All That*, NY: Octagon, 1980.

Green, Sandy, *Don'ts for Golfers*, London: A&C Black, (1925) 2008.

Greig, Hannah, *The Beau Monde: Fashionable Society in Georgian London*, Oxford: Oxford University Press, 2013.

Harrison Martin, Richard, and Koda, Harold, *Two by Two*, New York: The Metropolitan Museum of Art, 1996.

Hart, Avril, *Ties*, London: Victoria & Albert Museum, 1998.

Hart, Avril and North, Susan, *Historical Fashion in Detail*, London: Victoria & Albert Museum, 1998.

Hartley, Cecil B., *The Gentleman's Book of Etiquette and Manual of Politeness*, Boston: G.W. Cottrell, 1860.

Harvey, John, *Men in Black*, London: Reaktion, 1995.

Hatherley, Owen, *The Ministry of Nostalgia*, London: Verso Books, 2017.

Hayward, Maria, *Rich Apparel: Clothing and the Law in Henry VIII's England*, Surrey: Ashgate, 2009.

Hebdige, Dick, quoted in Richardson, Niall, and Locks, Adam, *Body Studies: The Bascis*, Oxon: Routledge, 2014.

Heck, J. G., *Iconographic Encyclopaedia Of Science, Literature, And Art: Volume III*, New York: D. Appleton and Co., 1860.

Hillier, Bevis and McIntyre, Kate, *Style of the Century*, New York: Watson-Guptill Publications, 1998.

Hoffmeister, Gerhart, *European Romanticism: Literary Cross-Currents, Modes, and Models*, MI: Wayne State University Press, 1990.

Holden, Anthony, *Prince Charles*, NY: Atheneum, 1979.

Hollander, Anne. "FASHION IN NUDITY." *The Georgia Review*, vol. 30, no. 3, 1976, pp. 642–702. JSTOR, JSTOR, www.jstor.org/stable/41397286.

Hollander, Anne, *Sex and Suits: The Evolution of Modern Dress*, London: Bloomsbury, (1994) 2016.

Holt, Arden, *Fancy Dresses Described: A Glossary of Victorian Costumes*, NY: Dover, (1896) 2017.

Hopkins, John, *Basics Fashion Design 07: Menswear*, Lausanne: AVA Publishing, 2011.

Houfe, Simon, *John Leech and the Victorian Scene*, Suffolk: ACC Art Books, 1984.

Hughes, Clair, *Hats*, London: Bloomsbury, 2016.

Hunt, Margaret R., *Women in Eighteenth Century Europe*, Oxford: Routledge, 2014.

Hunt-Hurst, Patricia Kay in Blanco F, José, *Clothing and Fashion: American Fashion from Head to Toe*, Denver, CO: ABC-CLIO, 2016.

Hutton, Mike, *Life in 1940s London*, Gloucestershire: Amberley Publishing, 2013.

Jackson, Ashley, *Mad Dogs and Englishmen: A Grand Tour of the British Empire at Its Height*, London: Quercus, 2009.

Jackson, Carole and Lulow, Kalia, *Color for Men*, NY: Ballantine Books, 1984.

Jenss, Heike, *Fashioning Memory: Vintage Style and Youth Culture*, London: Bloomsbury, 2015.

Jesson-Dibley, David, Herrick, Robert, *Selected Poems*, New York: Routledge, (1980) 2003.

Jobling, Paul, *Advertising Menswear: Masculinity and Fashion in the British Media Since 1945*, London: Bloomsbury, 2014.

Johnston, Lucy, *Nineteenth Century Fashion in Detail*, London: Victoria & Albert Museum, 2005.

Kawamura, Yuniya, *Fashioning Japanese Subcultures*, London: Berg, 2012.

Kelly, Francis M. and Schwabe, Randolph, *European Costume and Fashion, 1490–1790*, NY: Dover, 1929.

Kelly, Ian, *Beau Brummell: The Ultimate Man of Style*, NY: Free Press, 2013.

Kelly, Ian and Westwood, Vivienne, *Vivienne Westwood*, London: MacMillan, 2014.

Kelly, Michael Bryan, *The Beatle Myth: The British Invasion of American Popular Music, 1956–1969*, NC: McFarland, 1991.

Kelly, Stuart, *Scott-Land: The Man Who Invented a Nation*, Edinburgh: Polygon, 2010.

Kennedy, Alicia, Emily Stoehrer, Banis and Calderin, Jay, *Fashion Design, Referenced: A Visual Guide to the History, Language, and Practice of Fashion*, MA: Rockport Publishers, 2013.

Kindell, Alexandra, Demers, Elizabeth S., *Encyclopedia of Populism in America: A Historical Encyclopedia, Volume 1: A–M*, CA: ABC-CLIO, 2014.

Kinsler, Blakley Gwen, *The Miser's Purse*, Piecework, November/December 1996.

Kisluk-Grosheide, Daniëlle, *Bertrand Rondot, Visitors to Versailles: From Louis XIV to the French Revolution*, NY: The Metropolitan Museum of Art/New Haven: Yale University Press, 2018.

Kuchta, David, *The Three-Piece Suit and Modern Masculinity: England, 1550–1850*, Berkeley: University of California Press, 2002.

Ledbetter, Kathryn, *Victorian Needlework*, CA: Praeger, 2012.

Lehman, LaLonnie, *Fashion in the Time of the Great Gatsby*, London: Shire/Bloosmbury: 2013.

Leslie, Catherine Amoroso, *Needlework Through History: An Encyclopedia*, CT: Greenwood Press, 2007.

Lewisohn, Mark, *The Beatles – All These Years: Volume One: Tune In*, London: Little, Brown, 2013.

Lindop, Edmund, *America in the 1950s*, MN: Lerner, 2010.

Lockhart, Paul Douglas, *Sweden in the Seventeenth Century*, Hampshire: Palgrave Macmillan, 2004.

Logan, Walter, "The Topcoat Scene is Getting Livelier," *The San Francisco Examiner*, Sunday, November 5, 1967.

Lynch, Annette and Strauss, Mitchell D., *Ethnic Dress in the United States: A Cultural Encyclopedia*, NY: Rowman & Littlefield, 2015.

MacDougall, Ian, *Voices from War and Some Labour Struggles: Personal Recollections of War in Our Century by Scottish Men and Women*, Edinburgh: Mercat Press, 1995.

Mackerras, Colin, *China in Transformation: 1900–1949*, London: Routledge, 2008.

Makepeace, Margaret, *The East India Company's London Workers: Management of the Warehouse Labourers, 1800–1858*, Suffolk: The Boydell Press, 2010.

Manlow, Veronica, *Designing Clothes: Culture and Organization of the Fashion Industry*, NJ: Transaction Publishers, 2007.

Marchant, Hilde, "The Truth about the 'Teddy Boys' and the Teddy Girls," *Picture Post*, May 29, 1954.

Martin, Richard Harrison and Koda, Harold, *Orientalism: Visions of the East in Western Dress*, NY: Metropolitan Museum of Art, 1994.

Martin, Richard and Koda, Harold, *Christian Dior*, NY: The Metropolitan Museum of Art, 1996.

Masi de Casanova, Erynn, *Buttoned Up: Clothing, Conformity, and White-Collar Masculinity*, NY: Cornell University Press, 2015.

McClafferty, Carla Killough, *The Many Faces of George Washington: Remaking a Presidential Icon*, MN: Carolrhoda Books, 2011.

McGirr, Elaine M., *Eighteenth-Century Characters: A Guide to the Literature of the Age*, Hampshire: Palgrave Macmillan, 2007.

McKay, Elaine in *Cutter's Research Journal, Volume 11*, United States Institute for Theatre Technology, 1999.

McNeil, Peter, "Macaroni Men and Eighteenth-Century Fashion Culture: 'The Vulgar Tongue,'" *The Journal of the Australian Academy of the Humanities*, 8, 2017.

Menkes, Suzy, *The Windsor Style*, London: Grafton, 1987.

Menkes, Suzy, *Forbes*, Volume 155, Issues 6–9, 1995.

Mentzer, Mike and Friedberg, Ardy, *Mike Mentzer's Spot Bodybuilding: A Revolutionary New Approach to Body Fitness and Symmetry*, London: Simon & Schuster, 1983.

Mikhaila, Ninya and Malcolm-Davies, Jane, *The Tudor Tailor: Reconstructing Sixteenth-Century Dress*, London: Batsford, 2006.

Miller, Janice, *Fashion and Music*, Oxford: Berg, 2011.

Miller, Michael B., *The Bon Marche: Bourgeois Culture and the Department Store, 1869-1920*, NJ: Princeton University Press, 1981.

Molloy, Maureen and Larner, Wendy, *Fashioning Globalisation: New Zealand Design, Working Women and the Cultural Economy*, West Sussex: Wiley Blackwell, 2013.

Mr Le Noble/Mr Boyer, *The Art of Prudent Behaviour in a Father's Advice to his Son, Arriv'd to the Years of Manhood. By way of Dialogue*, London: Tim Childe, 1701.

Nelmes, Jill, *An Introduction to Film Studies*, Oxon: Routledge, 1996.

Norberg, Kathryn, and Rosenbaum, Sandra, *Fashion Prints in the Age of Louis XIV: Interpreting the Art of Elegance*, Lubbock: Texas Tech University Press, 2014.

Nunn, Joan, *Fashion in Costume, 1200-2000*, Chicago: New Amsterdam Books, (1984) 2000.

Obregn Pagn, Eduardo, *Murder at the Sleepy Lagoon: Zoot Suits, Race, & Riot in Wartime L.A*, Chapel Hill: University of North Carolina Press, 2003.

O'Byrne, Robert, *The Perfectly Dressed Gentleman*, London: CICO, 2011.

Olsen, Kristen, *All Things Shakespeare: A Concise Encyclopedia of Shakespeare's World*, CA: Greenwood, 2002.

Ouellette, Susan, *US Textile Production in Historical Perspective: A Case Study from Massachusetts*, London: Routledge, 2007.

Palairet, Jean, *A new Royal French Grammar*, Dialogue 16, 1738.

Paoletti, Jo B., *Sex and Unisex: Fashion, Feminism, and the Sexual Revolution*, IN: Indiana University Press, 2015.

Pastoureau, Michel, *Red: The History of a Color*, NJ: Princeton University Press, 2017.

Payne, Blanche, Winakor, Geitel, and Farrell-Beck, Jane, *The History of Costume: From Ancient Mesopotamia Through the Twentieth Century*, Harper Collins, 1992.

Peiss, Kathy, *Zoot Suit: The Enigmatic Career of an Extreme Style*, Philadelphia: University of Pennsylvania Press, 2011.

Perry, Gillian and Rossington, Michael, *Femininity and Masculinity in Eighteenth-century Art and Culture*, Manchester: Manchester University Press, 1994.

Perry, Grayson, *The Descent of Man*, London: Allen Lane, 2016.

Polan, Brenda and Tredre, Roger, *The Great Fashion Designers*, Oxford: Berg, 2009.

Post, Elizabeth and Post, Emily, *Etiquette*, Toronto: Harper Collins, 1965.

Potvin, John, *Giorgio Armani: Empire of the Senses*, London: Routledge, 2013.

Reed, Paula A., *Fifty Fashion Looks that Changed the 1970s*, London: Conran Octopus, 2012.

Ribeiro, Aileen, *Fashion and Fiction: Dress in Art and Literature in Stuart England*, New Haven: Yale University Press, 2005.

Richardson, Niall, and Locks, Adam, *Body Studies: The Basics*, Oxon: Routledge, 2014.

Richmond, Vivienne, *Clothing the Poor in Nineteenth-Century England*, Cambridge: Cambridge University Press, 2013.

Robertson, Whitney A.J. in Blanco, Hunt-Hurst, Vaughan Lee and Doering, *Clothing and Fashion: American Fashion from Head to Toe, Volume One*, CA: ABC-CLIO, 2016.

Rothstein, Natalie, Ginsburg, Madeleine & Hart, Avril, *Four Hundred Years of Fashion*, London: V&A Publications, 1984.

Rudolf, R. de M, *Short Histories of the Territorial Regiments of the British Army*, London: H.M. Stationery Office, 1902.

Russell, Douglas, *Costume History and Style*, NJ: Prentice Hall, 1983.

Sadleir, Michael, *The Strange Life of Lady Blessington*, NY: Little, Brown and Company, 1947.

Scala, Mim, *Diary of a Teddy Boy: A Memoir of the Long Sixties*, Goblin Press, 2009.

Sheridan, Jayne, *Fashion, Media, Promotion: The New Black Magic*, Oxford: Wiley-Blackwell, 2010.

Sichel, Marion, *Costume Reference: Tudors and Elizabethans*, Plays, Inc., 1977.

Sichel, Marion, *Costume Reference 5: The Regency*, London: Batsford, 1978.

Sichel, Marion, *Costume Reference 8: 1918–39*, London: Batsford, 1978.

Sichel, Marion, *History of Men's Costume*, London: Batsford, 1984.

Sichel, Marion, *Costume Reference 7: The Edwardians*, London: Batsford, 1986.

Simonton, Deborah, Kaartinen, Marjo, Montenach, Anne, *Luxury and Gender in European Towns, 1700-1914*, NY: Routledge, 2014.

Sinclair, Rev John, *Memoirs of the Life and Works of John Sinclair, Bart*, London: William Blackwood & Sons, 1837.

Sparks, Jared, *The Writings of George Washington, Volume II*, Boston: Ferdinand Andrews, 1840.

Spufford, Margaret, *The Great Reclothing of Rural England: Petty Chapman and Their Wares in the Seventeenth Century*, London: Bloomsbury, 1984.

Stamper, Anita M. and Condra, Jill, *Clothing Through American History: The Civil War Through the Gilded Age, 1861 – 1899*, CA: Greenwood, 2011.

Staples, Kathleen A. and Shaw, Madelyn C., *Clothing Through American History: The British Colonial Era*, CA: Greenwood, 2013.

Steele, Valerie, *Fifty Years of Fashion: New Look to Now*, New Haven: Yale University Press, 1997.

Steele, Valerie, *Paris Fashion: A Cultural History*, London: Bloomsbury, (1998) 2001.

Steele, Valerie, *Encyclopedia of Clothing and Fashion*, NY: Charles Scribner's Sons, 2005.

Steele, Valerie and Major, John S., *China Chic: East Meets West*, Yale: Yale University Press, 1999.

Steinberg, Neil, *Hatless Jack: The President, the Fedora, and the History of an American Style*, London: Granta Books, 2005.

Sterlacci, Francesca and Arbuckle, Joanne, *Historical Dictionary of the Fashion Industry*, NY: Rowman & Littlefield, 2017.

Stinson Jarvis, Thomas, *Letters from East Longitudes: Sketches of Travel in Egypt, the Holy Land, Greece, and Cities of the Levant*, Toronto: James Campbell & Son, 1875.

Styles, John, and Vickery, Amanda, *Gender, Taste, and Material Culture in Britain and North America, 1700–1830*, Yale Center for British Art, CT: 2006.

Sweetman, John, *Raglan: From the Peninsula to the Crimea*, South Yorkshire: Pen & Sword Military, 2010.

Takeda, Sharon Sadako and Spilker, Kaye Durland, *Fashioning Fashion: European Dress in Detail 1700–1915*, NY: Delmonico, Los Angeles County Museum of Art, 2011.

Takeda, Sharon Sadako and Spilker, Kaye Durland, *Reigning Men: Fashion in Menswear, 1715–2015*, NY: Prestel/Los Angeles County Museum of Art, 2016.

Tanke, Joseph J. and McQuillan, Colin, *The Bloomsbury Anthology of Aesthetics*, London: Bloomsbury, 2012.

Tortora, Phyllis G. and Eubank, Keith, *Survey of Historic Costume*, London: Fairchild Books, 2010.

Turner Wilcox, Ruth, *Five Centuries of American Costume*, NY: Dover, (1963) 2004.

Tyrell, Anne V., *Changing trends in fashion: patterns of the twentieth century, 1900-1970*, London: Batsford, 1986.

Uglow, Jenny, *A Gambling Man: Charles II and the Restoration, 1660–1670*, London: Faber & Faber, 2009.

Veblen, Thorstein, *The Theory of the Leisure Class*, London: Penguin, (1899) 2005.

Vermorel, Fred, *Vivienne Westwood: Fashion, Perversity and the Sixties laid bare*, NY: Overlook Press, 1993.

Vincent, Susan, *Dressing the Elite: Clothes in Early Modern England*, London: Berg, 2003.

Voltaire, *Letters Concerning the English Nation*, London: Tonson, Midwinter, Cooper & Hodges, 1778.

Walker, G., *The Art of Cutting Breeches*, Fourth Edition, London: G. Walker, 1833.

Warner, Helen, *Fashion on Television: Identity and Celebrity Culture*, London: Bloomsbury, 2014.

Waugh, Evelyn, *Brideshead Revisited: The Sacred and Profane Memories of Captain Charles Ryder*, London: Penguin, (1945) 2012.

Waugh, Norah, *The Cut of Men's Clothes: 1600–1900*, London: Faber & Faber, 1964.

Williams, Susan, *The People's King: The True Story of the Abdication*, London: Penguin, 2003.

Woods, John, *A new and complete system for cutting Trousers*, London. Kent & Richards, 1847.

Yarwood, Doreen, *Illustrated Encyclopedia of World Costume*, NY: Dover, 1978.

Yuniya Kawamura, *Fashioning Japanese Subcultures*, London: Berg, 2012.

Photographic Credits

Bell, C.M., photographer. Atwater, A.J. Photograph retrieved from the Library of Congress: https://www.loc .gov/pictures/item/2016687864/

Hendrick Goltzius, *Officers in Peascod Doublets*, 1587, Rijksmuseum, Amsterdam: RP-P-OB-4639.

Costume (doublet and breeches) associated with Gustavus Adolphus of Sweden (9 December 1594–6 November 1632, O.S.)— Livrustkammaren, Stockholm: LRK 31192-31193

Frans Hals, *Portrait of a Man*, early 1650s, Oil on canvas, Marquand Collection, Gift of Henry G. Marquand, 1890, Metropolitan Museum of Art, New York: 91.26.9.

(center) Cornelis Anthonisz. (manner of), *Portret van koning Frans I van Frankrijk*, 1538–c. 1547, Rijksmuseum, Amsterdam: RP-P-1932-153.

(bottom left) Pieter Cornelisz, *The Seven Acts of Mercy: Freeing the Prisoners* (detail), digital image courtesy of the Getty's Open Content Program: 92.GA.77.

(center) Johannes Wierix, *Unknown man with carnation*, 1578, Rijksmuseum, Amsterdam, RP-P-OB-67.124.

(left) Fencing Doublet, leather, c.1580, Bashford Dean Memorial Collection, Funds from various donors, 1929, Metropolitan Museum of Art, New York: 29.158.175.

(center) Wedding outfit worn by Gustav II Adolf, c.1620, Livrustkammaren, Stockholm: LRK 31302.

(bottom left) As above: detail.

(bottom right) As above: black and white.

(center) Wenceslaus Hollar, *Standing man takes a bow*, 1627–1636, Rijksmuseum, Amsterdam: RP-P-OB-11.586.

(left) As above (detail).

(right) Anthony van Dyck, *Robert Rich, Second Earl of Warwick*, ca. 1632–35, The Jules Bache Collection, 1949, Metropolitan Museum of Art, New York: 49.7.26.

1877 cabinet card, S. M. Robinson, s & 4 Sixth St., Pittsburgh, PA, collection of Drs. K. and B. Bohleke.

Carte de visite. Backmark: Herman Buchholz, Springfield, Mass. collection of Drs. K. and B. Bohleke.

The Knoll Studio Alliance O [Ohio], c.1910s, collection of Drs. K. and B. Bohleke.

The Miriam and Ira D. Wallach Division of Art, Prints and Photographs: Print Collection, The New York Public Library. "The effiges of the most high and mighty monarch Charles the Second by the grace of God king of Great Britaine, France, and Ireland, defender of the faith etc." The New York Public Library Digital Collections. 1777-1890. http://

digitalcollections.nypl.org /items/510d47da-22bc-a3d9-e040 -e00a18064a99

Sébastien Leclerc, 1685, *Man bij muurtje, gekleed in een rhingrave kostuum en wijde mantel*, Purchased with the support of the F.G. Waller-Fonds, Rijksmuseum, Amsterdam: RP-P-2009-1071.

(center) Nicolas Bonnart, *Recueil des modes de la cour de France, 'Le Financier'*, 1678–93, Purchased with funds provided by The Eli and Edythe L. Broad Foundation, Mr. and Mrs. H. Tony Oppenheimer, Mr. and Mrs. Reed Oppenheimer, Hal Oppenheimer, Alice and Nahum Lainer, Mr. and Mrs. Gerald Oppenheimer, Ricki and Marvin Ring, Mr. and Mrs. David Sydorick, the Costume Council Fund, and member of the Costume Council (M.2002.57.38), www.lacma.org.

(bottom right) Petticoat breeches (Byxor, Karl XI), Livrustkammaren, Stockholm, LSH: 16748.

(center) Wedding Suit worn by James II, embroidered wool coat and breeches, England, 1673, Purchased with Art Fund support, and the assistance of the National Heritage Memorial Fund, the Daks Simpson group Plc and Moss Bros, Victoria & Albert Museum, London: T.711:1, 2-1995.

(bottom left) Jan van Troyen after Gerbrand van den Eeckhout, *Heer, elegant gekleed volgens de mode van ca. 1660, staand voor de stoep van een huis*, purchased with the support of

(bottom right) Breeches, 1710, Europe, Gift of Mr. Lee Simonson, 1939, Metropolitan Museum of Art, New York: C.I.39.13.165.

(center) Coat, probably German, 1720s-1730s, front view, Los Angeles County Fund (62.6.2), www.lacma.org.

(right) Coat, probably German, 1720s-1730s, back view, Los Angeles County Fund (62.6.2), www.lacma.org.

(left) Jerome Robbins Dance Division, The New York Public Library. "Das Tanzen" (detail) The New York Public Library Digital Collections. 1720–1740.

(center) Man's coat, British, c.1735, Image © National Museums Scotland: A.1978.417.

(bottom left) Jerome Robbins Dance Division, The New York Public Library. "Das Tanzen" (detail) The New York Public Library Digital Collections. 1720–1740.

(top right) Boitard, Louis Pierre, Engraver, and Bartholomew Dandridge. *Standing / B. Dandridge pinx ; L.P. Boitard, sculp.* [Published] Photograph. Retrieved from the Library of Congress, <www.loc.gov/item/93508032/>.

(center) Frans van der Mijn, *Portrait of Jan Pranger*, 1742, Rijksmuseum, Amsterdam: SK-A-2248

(left) Ensemble, c.1740, British, Purchase, Irene Lewisohn Bequest, 1977, Metropolitan Museum of Art, New York: 1977.309.1a, b.

(center) Suit, 1750–75, British, Isabel Shults Fund, 1986, Metropolitan Museum of Art, New York: 1986.30.4a–d.

(right) As above, detail.

(top left) As above, detail.

(bottom left) Anton Raphael Mengs, *Johann Joachim Winckelmann*, c.1777, Harris Brisbane Dick Fund, 1948, Metropolitan Museum of Art, New York: 48.141.

(center) Gentleman's court suit, c.1760s, Museum Purchase: Auxiliary Costume Fund and Exchange Funds from the Gift of Harry and Mary Dalton2003.123.4A-C, Mint Museum, Charlotte, NC.

(left) Woman's Dress (Robe à la française and Petticoat), France/England, 1760–65, Gift of Mrs. Aldrich Peck (M.56.6a-b), www.lacma.org.

(top right) Giovanni Battista Tiepolo, *Caricature of a Man Seen from Behind*, c.1760, Robert Lehman Collection, 1975, Metropolitan Museum of Art, New York: 1975.1.457

(bottom right) Gilbert Stuart, *Captain John Gell*, 1785, Oil on canvas, Purchase, Dorothy Schwartz Gift, Joseph Pulitzer Bequest, and 2000 Benefit Fund, 2000, Metropolitan Museum of Art, New York: 2000.450.

(center) Suit, c.1760, Purchase, Irene Lewisohn Bequest and Polaire Weissman Fund, 1996, Metropolitan Museum of Art, New York: 1996.117a–c.

(bottom right) As above, back view.

(bottom left) Waistcoat, c.1760, Purchase, Irene Lewisohn Bequest and Polaire Weissman Fund, 1996, Metropolitan Museum of Art, New York: 1996.117a–c.

(center) Wedding suit of Gustav III, 1766, Livrustkammaren, Stockholm, LRK: 31255.

(top right) As above, detail.

(left) *L'Auguste Cérémonie du Mariage de Mgr Louis Dauphin de France, né à Versailles le 4 septembre 1729 avec Marie Thérése infante d'Espagne née à Madrid le 11 juin 1726. . . . . . :* [estampe] (detail), Bibliothèque nationale de France, département Estampes et photographie, RESERVE QB-201 (98)-FOL.

(center) *Suit (habit à la française)*, c.1775, France, National Gallery of Victoria, Melbourne. Presented by the National Gallery Women's Association, 1978, D73.a-c-1978.

(bottom right) Claude Louis Desrais, *Bourgeois de Paris en habit Simple*, 1778, purchased with the support of the F.G. Waller-Fonds, Rijksmuseum, Amsterdam: RP-P-2009-1130.

(left) Probably after Samuel Hieronymus Grimm, *Well-a-day, Is this my Son Tom*, c.1773, The Elisha Whittelsey Collection, The Elisha Whittelsey Fund, 1960, Metropolitan Museum of Art, New York: 60.576.9.

(right) Man's Three-piece Suit (Coat, Vest, and Breeches), front view, Italy, probably Venice, c. 1770, Costume Council Fund (M.83.200.1a-c), www.lacma.org.

(left) As above, back view.

(right) Giovanni Battista Tiepolo, *Caricature of a Man with His Arms Folded, Standing in Profile to the Left*, c.1760, Robert Lehman Collection, 1975, Metropolitan Museum of Art, New York: 1975.1.453.

(center) Man's Three-piece Suit: Coat, Waistcoat, and Breeches, France, c. 1775–1785, Gift of Mrs. Arthur Biddle, 1935, Philadelphia Museum of Art: 1935-16-2a–c.

(left, bottom right) As above, detail (x3).

(top right) Jerome Robbins Dance Division, The New York Public Library. "The Bengall minuet" *The New York Public Library Digital Collections*. 1773-11-03 (detail). http://digitalcollections.nypl.org/items/99ca8050-f811-0132-e0ce-58d385a7bbd0.

(center) Frock Coat, c. 1784–c. 1789, Gift of Jonkheer J.F. Backer, Amsterdam, Rijksmuseum, Amsterdam: BK-NM-13158.

(top left) Frock coat (detail), c.1790, Isabel Shults Fund, 1986, Metropolitan Museum of Art, New York: 1986.181.2.

(right) Adriaen de Lelie, *Jacob Alewijn*, c.1780–90, Amsterdam Museum, bruikleen Backer Stichting, SB 5126.

(bottom left) Waistcoat, c.1780, Rogers Fund, 1926, Metropolitan Museum of Art, New York: 26.56.33.

(top left) Ribbed silk coat, c.1780s, England (front view), Shippensburg University Fashion Archives & Museum, Pennsylvania.

(top right) As above, back view.

(bottom left, bottom right) As above, details x2.

(center) Suit, 1789, Courtesy of Mount Vernon Ladies' Association, W-574/A-B.

(top right) Unknown artist, *An Unknown Man, perhaps Charles Goring of Wiston (1744–1829), out Shooting with his Servant*, c.1765, detail, Yale Center for British Art, Paul Mellon Collection, B2001.2.218.

James Gillray, *French Liberty—British Slavery* (detail), December 21, 1792, Gift of Adele S. Gollin, 1976, 1976.602.27.

(center) Sans-culotte Trousers, France, c.1790, Purchased with funds provided by Phillip Lim (M.2010.205), www.lacma.org.

(bottom right) Vest, France, c.1789–1794, Purchased with funds provided by Suzanne A. Saperstein and Michael and Ellen Michelson, with additional funding from the Costume Council, the Edgerton Foundation, Gail and Gerald Oppenheimer, Maureen H. Shapiro, Grace Tsao, and Lenore and Richard Wayne (M.2007.211.1078), www.lacma.org.

(center) Coat, 1790s, purchase, NAMSB Foundation Inc. Gift, 1999, Metropolitan Museum of Art, New York: 1999.105.2.

(top left) As above, detail.

(bottom left) As above, back view.

(bottom right) Waistcoat, c.1790, Purchase, Irene Lewisohn Bequest, 1968, Metropolitan Museum of Art, New York: C.I.68.67.2.

(left, right) Jean Louis Darcis after Carle Vernet, *Les Incroyables*, c.1796, purchased with the support of the F.G. Waller-Fonds, Rijksmuseum, Amsterdam: RP-P-2009-2825.

(far left) Coat, France, 1790s, (detail) Purchased with funds provided by Suzanne A. Saperstein and Michael and Ellen Michelson, with additional funding from the Costume Council, the Edgerton Foundation, Gail and Gerald Oppenheimer, Maureen H. Shapiro, Grace Tsao, and Lenore and Richard Wayne (M.2007.211.802), www.lacma.org.

(center) Coat, France, 1790s, Purchased with funds provided by Suzanne A. Saperstein and Michael and Ellen Michelson, with additional funding from the Costume Council, the Edgerton Foundation, Gail and Gerald Oppenheimer, Maureen H. Shapiro, Grace Tsao, and Lenore and Richard Wayne (M.2007.211.802), www.lacma.org.

(left) *Journal des Dames et des Modes*, Costume Parisien, 5 janvier 1800, An 8, (185) : Chapeau Cornette, anonymous, 1800, purchased with the support of the F.G. Waller-Fonds, Rijksmuseum, Amsterdam: RP-P-2009-2305.

(right) Friedrich Justin Bertuch, Journal des Luxus und der Moden 1786–1826, Band V, T.22, c.1787, Rijksmuseum, Amsterdam: BI-1967-1159C-22

(center) Johannes Pieter de Frey after Jacobus Johannes Lauwers, *Boer met kruik*, c.1770–1834, Rijksmuseum, Amsterdam: RP-P-OB-52.288.

(right) Johannes Pieter de Frey after Jacobus Johannes Lauwers, *Boer met mand op de rug*, c.1770–1834, Rijksmuseum, Amsterdam: RP-P-OB-52.290.

(left) Waistcoat, c.1780, purchase, Irene Lewisohn and Alice L. Crowley Bequests, 1983, Metropolitan Museum of Art, New York: 1983.157.3.

Coat and trousers, c.1830s, Shippensburg Fashion Archives and Museum, Pennsylvania.

Louis-Léopold Boilly, *Portrait of a Gentleman*, c.1800, Gift of Marilyn B. and Calvin B. Gross (M.2003.197.2), www.lacma.org.

(left) Journal des Dames et des Modes 1825, Costume Parisien (2358), anonymous, 1825, Rijksmuseum, Amsterdam: BI-1938-0115A-56.

(right) Journal des Dames et des Modes, Costume Parisien, 15 janvier

1823, (2124): *Manteau à collet de loutre,* Rijksmuseum, Amsterdam: RP-P-2009-2471.

Chesterfield overcoat, W.C. Bell, c.1860–70, collection of Drs. K. and B. Bohleke.

Caped overcoat, c.1860–90, collection of Drs. K. and B. Bohleke.

(center) Man's Coat, Waistcoat, Breeches, c. 1785–1800 (front view), purchased with funds provided by Suzanne A. Saperstein and Michael and Ellen Michelson, with additional funding from the Costume Council, the Edgerton Foundation, Gail and Gerald Oppenheimer, Maureen H. Shapiro, Grace Tsao, and Lenore and Richard Wayne (M.2007.211.51), www.lacma.org.

(left, top right) As above, detail x 2.

(bottom right) Bicorne hat, 1790–1810, USA, Gift of Dr. and Mrs. Robert Gerry, 1986, Metropolitan Museum of Art, New York: 1986.518.3.

(center) Jerome Robbins Dance Division, The New York Public Library. "Académie et salle de danse" *The New York Public Library Digital Collections.* 1800–1809. http://digitalcollections. nypl.org/items/28153940-00ba-0133-9adc-58d385a7b928.

(bottom right) Fashion plate, c. 1797-1839, *Costume Parisien* (detail), Purchased with the support of the F.G. Waller-Fonds, Rijksmseum, Amsterdam, RP-P-2009-2347 .

(left) Fashion plate, 1800, private collection.

(left) Sir Thomas Lawrence, *Lord Granville Leveson-Gower, later 1st Earl Granville* (detail), c.1804–09, Britain,

Yale Center for British Art, Paul Mellon Collection, B1981.25.736.

(right) Anthonie Willem Hendrik Nolthenius de Man, *Man met hoge hoed,* 1828, Rijksmuseum, Amsterdam: RP-P-1882-A-5286.

(center) Wool broadcloth coat and pantaloons, 1805–10, The Daughters of the American Revolution Museum, Washington DC. Gift of Mr. Tracy L. Jeffords (81); gift of Mrs. Bessie Napier Proudfit (1497) and Friends of the Museum purchase (2016.2.A-B).

(top left) Unknown artist, *Self Portrait,* c.1800–05, Dale T. Johnson Fund, 2014, Metropolitan Museum of Art, New York: 2014.512.

(bottom left) Habit à la disposition, c.1760–75, France, Brooklyn Museum Costume Collection at The Metropolitan Museum of Art, Gift of the Brooklyn Museum, 2009; Gift of Paula Fox, 1996, Metropolitan Museum of Art, New York: 2009.300.2932.

(top right) Coat, 1822, Livrustkammaren, Stockholm, LSH: 86753.

(left, right) Trousers and Jacket, (front and back views) c.1820s, The National Museum of Denmark, photographers: Roberto Fortuna and Peter Danstrøm, V.5.

(far right) Pantaloons, c.1820–30, probably Italian, Gift of The Metropolitan Museum of Art, 1940 Metropolitan Museum of Art: C.I.40.173.9.

(center) The Miriam and Ira D. Wallach Division of Art, Prints and Photographs: Art & Architecture Collection, The New York Public Library. "Scavenger." *The New York*

Public Library Digital Collections. 1820. http://digitalcollections.nypl.org/items/510d47de-1cfa-a3d9-e040-e00a18064a99.

(left) Ensemble, ca. 1820, American, Purchase, Irene Lewisohn Bequest, 1976, Metropolitan Museum of Art: 1976.235.3a–e.

(right) The Miriam and Ira D. Wallach Division of Art, Prints and Photographs: Art & Architecture Collection, The New York Public Library. "Rabbit-man." *The New York Public Library Digital Collections.* 1820. http://digitalcollections.nypl.org/items/510d47dc-998c-a3d9-e040-e00a18064a99.

(center) Man's Tailcoat, probably England, c.1825–1830, Costume Council Curatorial Discretionary Fund (AC1993.127.1), www.lacma.org.

(top right) As above, rear detail.

(top left) Fashion plate, c.1820s, private collection.

(bottom left) Anon, *Laceing [sic] a Dandy,* January 26, 1819, Rogers Fund and The Elisha Whittelsey Collection, The Elisha Whittelsey Fund, 1969, Metropolitan Museum of Art, New York: 69.524.35.

(bottom right) Linen trousers, 1830s, detail, Shippensburg University Fashion Archives & Museum, Pennsylvania.

(center) Tartan suit, c.1830, © National Museums Scotland: A.1994.102 A.

(right) Man's Hunting Jacket, Scotland, 1825–1830 (detail), Purchased with funds provided by Suzanne A. Saperstein and Michael and Ellen Michelson, with additional funding from the Costume Council, the

Edgerton Foundation, Gail and Gerald Oppenheimer, Maureen H. Shapiro, Grace Tsao, and Lenore and Richard Wayne (M.2007.211.956), www.lacma.org.

(center) Coat and 'cossack' trousers, c.1833, Catharine Breyer Van Bomel Foundation Fund, 1981, Metropolitan Museum of Art, New York: 1981.210.4.

(top left, top right) As above, detail x 2.

(bottom left) Fashion plate, c.1830s, private collection.

(bottom right) Silk dress, c.1831–35, purchase, Irene Lewisohn Bequest, 2017, Metropolitan Museum of Art, New York: 2017.70.

(left) Tail Coat, England, c.1840, purchased with funds provided by Suzanne A. Saperstein and Michael and Ellen Michelson, with additional funding from the Costume Council, the Edgerton Foundation, Gail and Gerald Oppenheimer, Maureen H. Shapiro, Grace Tsao, and Lenore and Richard Wayne (M.2007.211.807), www.lacma.org.

(right) Tail Coat, Scotland, c. 1845, purchased with funds provided by Suzanne A. Saperstein and Michael and Ellen Michelson, with additional funding from the Costume Council, the Edgerton Foundation, Gail and Gerald Oppenheimer, Maureen H. Shapiro, Grace Tsao, and Lenore and Richard Wayne (M.2007.211.958), www.lacma.org.

(far right) Man's Vest, England, c.1845, Gift of Ms. Mims Thompson (M.87.219), www.lacma.org.

(bottom) Shoes by John Golden, c.1848, Brooklyn Museum Costume Collection at The Metropolitan

Museum of Art, Gift of the Brooklyn Museum, 2009; Gift of Mrs. James McF. Baker, 1948, Metropolitan Museum of Art, New York: 2009.300.3482a–d.

(center) Men's dark blue suit c.1840, Museum of Applied Arts & Sciences, 87/1249, <https://ma.as/71577>

(left) Waistcoat, 1840s, Britain, Purchase, Friends of The Costume Institute Gifts, 1980, Metropolitan Museum of Art, New York: 1980.72.9.

(right) Fashion plate, c.1840s, private collection.

(left, right) Man's coat, 1845 and 1850, 82.33.2, ©The Museum at FIT, New York.

(far right) Man's Frock Coat, Europe, circa 1845, Purchased with funds provided by Suzanne A. Saperstein and Michael and Ellen Michelson, with additional funding from the Costume Council, the Edgerton Foundation, Gail and Gerald Oppenheimer, Maureen H. Shapiro, Grace Tsao, and Lenore and Richard Wayne (M.2007.211.61), www.lacma.org.

(bottom left) Ensemble, c.1860, USA, Brooklyn Museum Costume Collection at The Metropolitan Museum of Art, Gift of the Brooklyn Museum, 2009; Gift of Mrs. Franklin W. Hopkins, 1928, Metropolitan Museum of Art, New York: 2009.300.626.

(bottom right) Fashion plate, 'Paris Modes', Germany, c.1840s, private collection.

(center) Frock coat and trousers, Northern Ireland, c.1852, purchased with funds provided by Michael and

Ellen Michelson (M.2010.33.8a-b), www.lacma.org.

(top left) Man wearing shoe-tie. c.1850s-70s, x2, collection of Drs. K. and B. Bohleke.

(bottom left) Blackwork panel, c.1580–1620 (detail), Britain, Rogers Fund, 1935, Metropolitan Museum of Art, New York: 35.21.3.

(right) 1860–70 photograph of man in frock coat, collection of Drs. K. and B. Bohleke.

(center) Anon, L'Elégant, Journal des Tailleurs (detail), 1 October 1854, Gift of the M.A. Ghering-van Ierlant Collection, Rijksmuseum, Amsterdam: RP-P-2009-3360.

(top left) Smoking jacket, 1860s, American or European, Gift of Jessie Leonard Hill, Charles R. Leonard, Jr., and Laura Leonard Ault, 1978, Metropolitan Museum of Art, New York: 1978.477.23.

(right) Photograph, c.1860–70, collection of Drs. K. and B. Bohleke.

(bottom) As above.

Family portrait, c.1860s, collection of Drs. K. and B. Bohleke.

Photograph, late 1860s couple, collection of Drs. K. and B. Bohleke.

Photograph, J.&W Hicks, man in morning coat, collection of Drs. K. and B. Bohleke.

Napoleon Sarony, Oscar Wilde, 1882, Gilman Collection, Purchase, Ann Tenenbaum and Thomas H. Lee Gift, 2005, Metropolitan Museum of Art, New York: 2005.100.120.

(center) Sack suit, 1865–70, Britain, Purchase, Irene Lewisohn Trust Gift, 1986, Metropolitan Museum of Art, New York: 1986.114.4a–c.

(left) Summer sack suit, antique photograph, c.1860s, collection of Drs. K. and B. Bohleke.

(left, right) Anon, *Le Musée des Tailleurs illustré, 1869, Nr. 7 : Journal donnant les Modes de Paris*, 1869, On loan from the M.A. Ghering-van Ierlant Collection, Rijksmuseum, Amsterdam: RP-P-2009-3550.

(bottom left) Cabinet card, c.1860–70, Ohio, collection of Drs. K. and B. Bohleke.

(bottom right) The Miriam and Ira D. Wallach Division of Art, Prints and Photographs: Photography Collection, The New York Public Library. "Portrait of a man." *The New York Public Library Digital Collections.* 1869–1881. http://digitalcollections.nypl.org/items/510d47e1-6c50-a3d9-e040-e00a18064a99.

(center) Wedding suit of W.F. Potter, 1869, 1964.25.1.North Carolina Museum of History, photographer: Eric Blevins.

(far left) As above, waistcoat detail, photographer: Eric Blevins.

(near left) Miser's purse, 1840–60, USA, Brooklyn Museum Costume Collection at The Metropolitan Museum of Art, Gift of the Brooklyn Museum, 2009; Gift of George F. Hoag, 1959, 2009.300.2942.

(bottom right) Evening shirt, c.1860, USA, Brooklyn Museum Costume Collection at The Metropolitan Museum of Art, Gift of the Brooklyn Museum, 2009; Gift of Sarah F. Milligan and Kate Milligan Brill, 1940,

Metropolitan Museum of Art, New York: 2009.300.6450.

(center) Man's Suit (Jacket and Trousers), England, 1860–1870, purchased with funds provided by Michael and Ellen Michelson (M.2010.33.9a-b), www.lacma.org.

(bottom left) As above, rear view (detail).

(right) Cabinet photo, c.1870s, collection of Drs. K. and B Bohleke.

(center) 'University' coat, England, c.1873–75, Victoria & Albert Museum, London: T.3-1982.

(left) As above, detail.

(center) Man's Morning Coat and Vest, England, c.1880, Purchased with funds provided by Michael and Ellen Michelson (M.2010.33.15a-b), www. lacma.org.

(left) As above, detail.

(right) *Man's Wedding Suit: Cutaway Coat, Trousers, and Waistcoat*, C. Prueger & Son, Philadelphia, 1885, Gift of C. C. Whitenack, 1933, Philadelphia Museum of Art, 1933-13-1a–c.

(center) Suit worn by James Adams Woolson (1829–1904), 1880, Cotton seersucker jacket and trousers. Gift of the Estate of Mrs. Byron Satterlee Hurlbut, 58.166.20. Photography by Erik Gould, courtesy of the Museum of Art, Rhode Island School of Design, Providence.

(top right) Carte de visite, c.1880s, Pirrong & Son, Photographers. 322 North Second St. Philadelphia, collection of Drs. K. and B Bohleke.

(bottom right) Seersucker coat, 1795–99, American or European,

Gift of Mr. J. C. Hawthorne, 1946, Metropolitan Museum of Art, New York: C.I.46.82.16.

(center) Smoking Suit, England, c.1880, Gift of the Costume Council in memory of Maryon Lears (M.2012.81a-b), www.lacma.org.

(top left) Woman's dressing gown, 1880–85, America, Brooklyn Museum Costume Collection at The Metropolitan Museum of Art, Gift of the Brooklyn Museum, 2009; Gift of Lillian E. Glenn Peirce and Mabel Glenn Cooper, 1929, Metropolitan Museum of Art, New York: 2009.300.70.

(top right) Alexandre Gabriel Decamps, *Turkish Guardsmen*, France, 1841, digital image courtesy of the Getty's Open Content Program: 2016.15.

(bottom left) Slippers, Europe or USA, 1850–1900, Mrs. Alice F. Schott Bequest (M.67.8.165a-b), www.lacma.org.

(bottom right) Vest, 1860–69, America, Brooklyn Museum Costume Collection at The Metropolitan Museum of Art, Gift of the Brooklyn Museum, 2009; Gift of Sarah F. Milligan and Kate Milligan Brill, 1940, Metropolitan Museum of Art, New York: 2009.300.2729.

(left, right) *Fashionable gentlemen in suits*, 1890, Screen print, Graphic Arts/Getty Images. GraphicaArtis / Contributor.

(far right top) Cabinet card, Germany, c.1890s, collection Daniela Kästing.

(far right bottom) Portrait photograph, c.1890s, collection of Drs. K. and B. Bohleke.

(center) Man's fancy dress ensemble in eighteenth-century style: coat, breeches, and waistcoat, Artist/maker unknown, American?, Gift of the heirs of Charlotte Hope Binney Tyler Montgomery, 1996, Philadelphia Museum of Art, 1996-19-11a–c.

(right) As above, detail.

(left) Cabinet photo of man in 18th century suit, c.1890s, New York, author's collection.

(bottom right) Man's Waistcoat, Italy or France, circa 1730, Purchased with funds provided by Suzanne A. Saperstein and Michael and Ellen Michelson, with additional funding from the Costume Council, the Edgerton Foundation, Gail and Gerald Oppenheimer, Maureen H. Shapiro, Grace Tsao, and Lenore and Richard Wayne (M.2007.211.794), www.lacma.org.

Cabinet photo, c.1908, collection of Drs. K. and B. Bohleke.

The window of men's clothing store 'P&Q', USA, 1919, collection of Drs. K. and B. Bohleke.

Photograph of Hector Hogg, c.1916–17, Hogg/Edwards family collection.

Photograph of Stanley Gordon Hogg, c.1916, Hogg/Edwards family collection.

Photograph of Stanley Gordon Hogg, c.1930s, Hogg/Edwards family collection.

Advertisement for a raccoon fur coat, 1921, USA, courtesy Matt Jacobsen, oldmagazinearticles.com.

(center) Science, Industry and Business Library: General Collection, The New York Public Library. "Flannel outing suits; No. 9. The new Breakwater summer suit" (detail), *The New York Public Library Digital Collections*. 1900. http://digitalcollections.nypl.org/

items/510d47dd-fe5b-a3d9-e040-e00a18064a99

(top left) Sketch by Charles Dana Gibson, c.1901 (detail), private collection.

(bottom right) Harper, Alvan S., 1847–1911. *Man with mustache in fully buttoned suit.* Between 1885 and 1910. Black & white glass photonegative. State Archives of Florida, Florida Memory. Accessed 6 Dec. 2018.<https://www.floridamemory. com/items/show/130136>.

(left) Travel suit consisting of jacket, vest and trousers. Belonged to Walther von Hallwyl, c.1900, Hallwyl Museum, Stockholm. Photography by Jens Mohr.

(right) Suit consisting of jacket, vest and trousers. Made of patterned gray-colored camgorncheviot in stripe pattern and with light gray horn buttons. Belonged to Walther von Hallwyl, c.1900, Hallwyl Museum, Stockholm. Photography by Jens Mohr.

(far left) Photograph of the Hallwyl family featuring Walther von Hallwyl (detail), ID: 4945, Hallwyl Museum, Stockholm.

(center) Foto [sic] by Dittrich, 1107 Boardwalk, Atlantic City, N.J. [New Jersey], c.1908–10, collection of Drs. K. and B. Bohleke.

(top left) The Miriam and Ira D. Wallach Division of Art, Prints and Photographs: Art & Architecture Collection, The New York Public Library. "Arrow collars. Cluett shirts." *The New York Public Library Digital Collections*. 1895–1917. http://digitalcollections.nypl.org/ items/510d47e2-90e2-a3d9-e040-e00a18064a99.

(bottom left) Photograph of working class couple, c.1908–10, collection of Drs. K. and B. Bohleke.

(center) Full-Length Portrait of a Young Man Standing Next to a Bicycle. [Between 1890 and 1910] [Photograph] Retrieved from the Library of Congress, https://www.loc. gov/item/2006689595/.

(bottom left) The Miriam and Ira D. Wallach Division of Art, Prints and Photographs: Art & Architecture Collection, The New York Public Library. "Ride Sterling bicy[cles]" *The New York Public Library Digital Collections*. 1895–1917. http:// digitalcollections.nypl.org/ items/510d47e2-90df-a3d9-e040-e00a18064a99.

(center) Norfolk suit consisting of jacket, vest and trousers. Brown cheviot and with brown horn buttons. Belonged to Walther von Hallwyl, c.1910. Hallwyl Museum, Stockholm. Photography by Jens Mohr.

(bottom left) Photograph of Prince Philip, Duke of Edinburgh, c.1950s, GENTRY magazine (detail), courtesy Matt Jacobsen, oldmagazinearticles.com.

(center) Evening dress suit, George Dean, c.1911, gift of the Estate of A. D. Savage, © McCord Museum, Montreal: M973.49.11.1-3.

(right) The Miriam and Ira D. Wallach Division of Art, Prints and Photographs: Art & Architecture Collection, The New York Public Library. "Arrow collars, Cluett shirts. Saturday evening post, Sept 25 1909." *The New York Public Library Digital Collections*. 1895–1917. http://digitalcollections.nypl.org/ items/510d47e2-90e4-a3d9-e040-e00a18064a99.

(center) Suit and wedding dress worn by David Raymond Fogelsanger (1889–1958) and Lydia Hawbaker (1888–1935) of Shippensburg, PA, at their wedding in 1914. Suit made by tailor Abraham Lincoln "Link" Shearar, PA.

(left) Collar, c.1900–10, author's collection.

(center) Wool 'Golfing' suit, brown plaid, Shippensburg University Fashion Archives & Musuem, Pennsylvania: S1986-34-005.

(bottom left) *Harry Vardon's golf swing*, c.1910–20, courtesy Matt Jacobsen, oldmagazinearticles.com.

(bottom right) Fishbaugh, W. A.(William Arthur), 1873–1950. *Carl Byoir with another man on the golf course at the Miami Biltmore Hotel—Coral Gables, Florida*. 1925. Black & white photoprint. State Archives of Florida, Florida Memory. Accessed 7 Dec. 2018. <https://www.floridamemory.com/items/show/37236>.

(center) *Jack Buchanan wearing Oxford bags*, 1925, Getty Images, Bettmann / Contributor.

(top left) Group of friends in Egypt, c.1920s, Simmonds family collection.

(bottom right) Cambridge University rowing crew group, c.1931, courtesy Christina Bloom: https://heartheboatsing.com.

(center) *Man modeling walking suit*. Photograph. Retrieved from the Library of Congress, <www.loc.gov/item/90710715/>.

(right) Wedding portrait, South Africa, 1920s, Levy family collection.

(center) Business suit, c.1926, Gift of Mrs. Donald A. MacInnes, © McCord Museum, Montreal: M973.137.1.1-5.

(left) Sack suit, 1865–70, Britain, Purchase, Irene Lewisohn Trust Gift, 1986, Metropolitan Museum of Art, New York: 1986.114.4a–c.

(bottom right) *Edward Maxwell, architect, Montreal, QC, 1893* by Wm. Notman & Son, 1893, purchase from Associated Screen News Ltd, © McCord Museum, Montreal:II-100033.

(center) Evening suit, c.1920s, made by Mr J.R. Jamieson, Edinburgh, Image © National Museums Scotland: H.TI 23 A.

(left) Science, Industry and Business Library: General Collection, The New York Public Library. "Go formal in authentic evening wear (single-breasted tuxedo, double-breasted tuxedo, shawl collar summer tuxedo, full dress for formal evening wear, clerical frock, cutaway frock, Prince Albert frock, dress vest, clerical vest, cassock vest)", detail, *The New York Public Library Digital Collections.* 1942. http://digitalcollections.nypl.org/items/510d47dd-ff8b-a3d9-e040-e00a18064a99

(right) As above, detail.

(center) Palm Beach Suit, c.1930–39, courtesy of the FIDM Museum at the Fashion Institute of Design & Merchandising, Los Angeles, CA: 2008.5.24AB.

(bottom left) Palm Beach Suit, advertisement (detail), 1932, courtesy Matt Jacobsen, oldmagazinearticles.com.

(center) Suit, 1931, Gift of Mrs. Henry Yates © McCord Museum, Montreal: M987.182.5.1-3.

(bottom left) Wedding portrait, 1936, collection of Drs. K. and B. Bohleke.

(top right) Portrait of solider, c.1914 (detail), collection of Drs. K. and B. Bohleke.

(center) Brown pinstripe suit, c.1930s, Shippensburg University Fashion Archives & Musuem, Pennsylvania: S1983-16-004 Cory.

(bottom left) Rear view of suit, c.1930s, Shippensburg University Fashion Archives & Museum, Pennsylvania: S1983-16-004 Cory.

(center) Evening suit, 1938, Gift of Mr. John L. Russell, © McCord Museum, Montreal: M993.14.3.1-2.

(bottom left)*American actor and dancer Fred Astaire* (1899–1987), mid leap, circa 1935. (Photo via John Kobal Foundation/Hulton Archive/Getty Images).

(top) Photograph of Shell Oil employees, c.1965–6, Edwards family collection.

(bottom) Family snapshot, 1966, London, Edwards family collection.

(center) *Rayfield McGhee in a "zoot suit"—Tallahassee, Florida*. 1942 or 1943. Black & white photonegative. State Archives of Florida, Florida Memory. Accessed 7 Dec. 2018.<https://www.floridamemory.com/items/show/154912>.

(bottom left) *Yank: Army Weekly* magazine cartoon, 1945 (detail), courtesy Matt Jacobsen, oldmagazinearticles.com.

(bottom right) Avery, Joseph H., Jr. *Jimmy Reid and friends in zoot suits with jive chains—Tallahassee, Florida*. 194-. Black & white photonegative. State

Archives of Florida, Florida Memory. Accessed 7 Dec. 2018.<https:// www.floridamemory.com/items/ show/155093>.

(left) Suit worn by the Duke of Windsor, Maryland Historical Society, photograph by Dan Goodrich.

(right) Duke of Windsor's Suit: back view, Maryland Historical Society, photograph by Dan Goodrich.

(far right) NEW YORK, NY—1945: Le duc de Windsor Edward VIII et la duchesse de Windsor Wallis Simpson, a bord du navire 'Argentina' en 1945 New York City. (Photo by Keystone-France\ Gamma-Rapho via Getty Images).

(center) 'Utility' suit, c.1940s, Great Britain, Victoria & Albert Museum, London: T.242&A-1981.

(left) Wedding portrait, 1947, Hogg/ Edwards family collection.

(right) Photograph of Gordon Edwards, 1939, Edwards family collection.

(center) Demob suit, c.1940s, Great Britain, © IWM (UNI 2966).

(bottom right) Portrait of a soldier, late 1940s, Edwards family collection.

(center) Suit, 1950, Gift of Mr. A. W. Robertson, © McCord Museum, Montreal: M20470.0-2.

(right) Photograph of Gordon Edwards, c.1950, Edwards family collection.

(center) *A young Teddy Boy takes a moment out from the Mecca Dance Hall in Tottenham, London, to show off his Teddy suit.* Original Publication: Picture Post—7169—The Truth About

The Teddy Boys—pub. 1954 (Photo by Joseph McKeown/Getty Images).

(bottom right) Art and Picture Collection, The New York Public Library. "Man in Suit and Top Hat, United States, 1901s." *The New York Public Library Digital Collections.* 1908. http://digitalcollections.nypl.org/ items/510d47e0-ee92-a3d9-e040-e00a18064a99.

Suit worn by Johnny O'Keefe 1955–59 Museum of Applied Arts & Sciences, accessed 7 December 2018, <https:// ma.as/163411>

(center) Man's suit, Wash N' Wear, c.1959, Museum at FIT, New York: P88.80.1 ©The Museum at FIT.

(far left) Portrait photograph, 1959, Missouri, Wright family collection.

(near left) Portrait photograph, 1959, Greece, Tsoulis family collection.

(center) John Lennon's stage suit, 1964, National Museum, Liverpool: WAG.1996.4a

(top right) *Turquoise Nehru Jacket,* America, Gift of Louis C. Madeira, 1979, Philadelphia Museum of Art: 1979-150-9.

(bottom left) UNITED KINGDOM— APRIL 30: Young Newlyweds In London. The Groom Is Wearing A Beatles-Styled Suit. (Photo by Keystone-France/Gamma-Keystone via Getty Images).

(bottom right) Dougie Millings, tailor and confidante to the Beatles, photo by Stephen Osman/Los Angeles Times via Getty Images.

(center) Printed cotton velvet jacket and trousers by Mr Fish, London, c.1968, Given by David Mlinaric,

Victoria & Albert Museum, London: T.310&A-1979.

(left) Coat, 1790s, France (detail), Purchased with funds provided by Suzanne A. Saperstein and Michael and Ellen Michelson, with additional funding from the Costume Council, the Edgerton Foundation, Gail and Gerald Oppenheimer, Maureen H. Shapiro, Grace Tsao, and Lenore and Richard Wayne (M.2007.211.802), www.lacma.org.

(center) Dinner suit/tuxedo, 1960s, Shippensburg University Fashion Archives & Museum, Pennsylvania.

(right) Woodward, Dave (David Luther). *Young men wearing tuxedoes in front of the FSU Westcott building in Tallahassee.* 1963. Black & white photonegative. State Archives of Florida, Florida Memory. Accessed 7 Dec. 2018.<https:// www.floridamemory.com/items/ show/270385>.

Suit, 1968, Gift of M. Jacques de Montjoye, © McCord Museum, Montreal: M989.20.1.1-2.

(center) Idealized portrait of Mao Zedong towering over the Yangtze river. (Photo by Michael Nicholson/ Corbis via Getty Images).

(top left) Portrait of Stanley Gordon & Emily Mabel Hogg, c.1918, Hogg/ Edwards family collection.

(bottom right) Chinese peasant painting, c.1990 (detail), collection of Chris and Julia Edwards.

Idealized portrait of Mao Zedong towering over the Yangtze river. (Photo by Michael Nicholson/Corbis via Getty Images).

Portrait of Sue and Christopher Gordon, c.1970, Gordon family collection.

Portrait of Brett Smyth and friends, 1986–1987, Western Australia, Smyth family collection.

ITALY—JUNE 01: Boyzone in Modena, Italia on June 01st, 1999. (Photo by Eric VANDEVILLE/Gamma-Rapho via Getty Images).

(left) Man's Suit: Jacket and Trousers, designed by Bill Blass, American, 1922–2002. Made by Pincus Brothers Maxwell, Philadelphia, 1911–2004, USA, 1970, Gift of Thomas Neil Crater, 1973, Philadelphia Museum of Art: 1973-59-4a,b.

(right) Man's Suit: Jacket and Trousers, made by Thelma Finster Bradshaw, 1970s, Gift of Thelma Finster Bradshaw, 2013, © Estate of Howard Finster, Philadelphia Museum of Art: 2013-9-1a,b.

(far right) Three-piece Suit, France, c. 1765, purchased with funds provided by Suzanne A. Saperstein and Michael and Ellen Michelson, with additional funding from the Costume Council, the Edgerton Foundation, Gail and Gerald Oppenheimer, Maureen H. Shapiro, Grace Tsao, and Lenore and Richard Wayne (M.2007.211.41a-c), www.lacma.org.

(center) Suit, 1972, Gift of Morty Garelick, © McCord Museum, Montreal: M972.112.3.1-5.

(bottom left) Portrait photograph, wedding guests, 1978, Edwards family collection.

(center) HOUSE OF MERIVALE AND MR. JOHN, Sydney, Suit c.1973, National Gallery of Victoria,

Melbourne, Gift of Phil Parnell, 2004 (2004.793.a-c).

(bottom right)Palm Beach 'sand bags' illustration from 1932 advertisement, 'Suggestions for Vacation Days' (detail), courtesy Matt Jacobsen, oldmagazinearticles.com

(center) Leisure suit, 1970s, "Ludovici Milano 65% Tetoron 35% viscose polyester fiber manufactured under I.C.I patent", Shippensburg University Fashion Archives & Museum, Pennsylvania: S2008-17-003.

(right) As above, back view.

(top left) Science, Industry and Business Library: General Collection, "Model No.142: Military collar bal-raglan topcoat' (detail), New York Public Library.

(bottom left) Gabardine shorts, 'Sportsman's Choice' by Henry L. Jackson, Colliers, March 31, 1945 (detail), courtesy Matt Jacobsen, oldmagazinearticles.com.

(center) Man's suit, Giorgio Armani, 1982, Museum at FIT, New York: 85.58.7 ©The Museum at FIT.

(bottom right) Paul Smith ensemble worn by Patrick McDonald, 2007–2012, Gift of Patrick McDonald, 2012.62.1.1, Museum of Art, Rhode Island School of Design, Providence. Photography by Erik Gould, courtesy of the Museum of Art, Rhode Island School of Design, Providence.

(center) Man's Suit: Jacket, Pants and Waistcoat by Kenzo, Spring/Summer 1984, Gift of John Di Prizito, 1997, Philadelphia Museum of Art: 1997-85-2a–c.

(left) Morning vest, 1850–59, USA, Brooklyn Museum Costume

Collection at The Metropolitan Museum of Art, Gift of the Brooklyn Museum, 2009; Gift of E. McGreevey, 1948, Metropolitan Museum of Art, New York: 2009.300.2744a, b.

(center) Mitsuhiro Matsuda, Suit, c.1986, Gift of Charles Rosenberg, RISD Class of 1988, Museum of Art, Rhode Island School of Design, Providence: 2008.14.2. Photography by Erik Gould, courtesy of the Museum of Art, Rhode Island School of Design, Providence.

(far left) As above, back detail.

(near left) Detail of jacket from *Vanity Fair*, 1916, courtesy Matt Jacobsen, oldmagazinearticles.com.

(center) Suit by Paul Smith, 1988, UK, Victoria & Albert Museum, London: T.3 to E-1988 [1988].

(bottom left) Foley, Mark T., 1943–. *President Reagan with his wife Nancy Davis Reagan*. Between 1981 and 1989. Black & white digital image. State Archives of Florida, Florida Memory. Accessed 7 Dec. 2018.<https://www.floridamemory.com/items/show/134688>.

(center) Man's Bondage Suit: Jacket and Trousers with Attached Knee Strap, Vivienne Westwood, c.1990, Purchased with the Costume and Textiles Revolving Fund, 2000, Philadelphia Museum of Art: 2000-38-1a,b.

(bottom right) 'Hobble garter' image from the *Los Angeles Herald*, 24 November 1910 (detail).

WORLD, Auckland, Sanderson suit 1997, National Gallery of Victoria, Melbourne, Purchased NGV Foundation, 2009 (2009.56.a–d).

Index